H. A. Graves

Andrew Jackson Potter

The fighting Parson of the Texan Frontier

H. A. Graves

Andrew Jackson Potter
The fighting Parson of the Texan Frontier

ISBN/EAN: 9783337135294

Printed in Europe, USA, Canada, Australia, Japan

Cover: Foto ©ninafisch / pixelio.de

More available books at **www.hansebooks.com**

ANDREW JACKSON POTTER.

Andrew Jackson Potter,

THE

Fighting Parson of the Texan Frontier.

SIX YEARS OF INDIAN WARFARE IN NEW MEXICO AND ARIZONA.

Many Wonderful Events in his Ministerial Life on the Frontier Border of Western Texas, During a Long Term of Evangelical Toils and Personal Combats with Savage Indians and Daring Desperadoes, Including many Hair-breadth Escapes.

He has long been a Member of the West Texas Annual Conference of the Methodist Episcopal Church, South, and is now Presiding Elder of the Mason, or Border, District. He is generally known as the "Indian Fighting Parson."

BY THE REV. H. A. GRAVES,

Of the same Conference, formerly of the Tennessee Annual Conference.

"FOR THOU SHALT BE HIS WITNESS UNTO ALL MEN OF WHAT THOU HAST SEEN AND HEARD." (Acts xxii. 15.)

NASHVILLE, TENN.:
SOUTHERN METHODIST PUBLISHING HOUSE.
PRINTED FOR THE AUTHOR.
1881.

COPYRIGHT SECURED.

PREFACE.

FEELING a deep interest in the present and future welfare of the youth of this age, and especially of those of our own American Republic, we most respectfully dedicate this little volume to them—showing an eminence attained from the most obscure sphere of life.

No humbleness of birth, no depth of poverty, no degraded condition, no severity of hardships, no height of difficulties, and no array of living opponents, present insuperable barriers to a stable reform, and the ultimate acquisition of virtue and honor, where there is a decisive will and unfailing energy, coupled with faith in the favorable results of a just enterprise, managed agreeable to the law of right and justice. Will, inspired with the might of Faith, removes mountainous obstacles, and reaches the goal of victory. AUTHOR.

INTRODUCTION.

BIOGRAPHY is a history of the life and character of a particular individual, and is said to be of more intrinsic value to mankind than all more general narratives, as it brings to light the underlying motives which usually stimulate men to action, and connects more immediate results with their efficient causes. The faithful portrait of the life of a bad man, setting forth the baleful effects of a sinful and a vicious life, cannot fail to instruct and warn men of the hurtful results of sinful habits; while the truthful exhibit of a virtuous character, coupled with its gracious benefits to society, must of necessity be of inestimable value to society at large. The first furnishes a motive to deter from vice, the second presents an incentive to invite us to the ways of virtue. The man whose life is plainly sketched in this little volume gives us a specimen of both vicious and virtuous habits—his life having been a tripartite—*evil, good, ministerial.* His early years were passed in the haunts of vice, his after-life in the ministry of Jesus Christ. But in all the strange and crooked paths over which he traveled in boyhood and youth there was a manifest protective power about him from an occult superhuman force, sheltering and guiding unerringly to a certain ultimate, an event to be reached by intelligent design. Truly, there is a man for every place, and a place for each man, in all spheres of life; and each one needs a preparatory schooling for his respective field of action. Shakespeare said, "There's a divinity that shapes our ends, rough-hew them how we will." But the Bible phrases it better than that: "A man's heart *deviseth* his way, but the Lord *directeth* his steps." "His ways are past finding out." One thing, however, is certain, God chooses his own special agents from among mankind to carry out his gracious plans of saving men; but the initiatory training of those agents is often darkly mysterious and painfully severe, but suitable and certain in the end. How strange and wonderful the curriculum of the school of adverse fortune in which the little boy who was clad in "the coat of many colors" received his training for his eventful life! Yet Joseph piloted a nation's life through the terrible seven years of famine, and planted the germinal seeds of the world's future civilization in Judea's land. Marvelous indeed was the early life of the carol-singing boy of the sixteenth century. Little did Conrad Cotter dream that he was nursing the lion whose matured might should break the papal yoke from the neck of empires; nor did Gamaliel see in little "Saul of Tarsus" the miniature giant whose logical leverage must overturn the temples of paganism, and demolish the altars of ages, and erect Christianity on their scattered ruins. The schooling of those divinely-chosen agents was severe, but the end thereof was sure. The mother of little Andrew Jackson Potter, when in innocent glee he nestled on her maternal bosom, saw not the rough and thorny path his youthful feet should tread—the terrible *hardship-drill* 'twixt him and a day of glorious triumph; but all along the dangerous labyrinths through which his reckless young life led him a kind, unseen hand holds a protective shield over the head of her orphan child. The well-aimed arrow of the savage Indian falls harmless at his side, whizzes through the air, or pierces the heart of his comrade. What shall we call that shielding force? "Fate," "Destiny," or "Providence?" The cold-hearted skeptic replies, "Destiny," "Fate;" and scoffingly asks,

> "When the loose mountain trembles from on high,
> Shall gravitation cease if you go by?"

No; truly, it need not "cease," but a divine angel may touch your will's secret springs that you may not "go by" till the "great rock" has tumbled into the depths below.

We shall call it a Special Providence that safely guided the orphan boy through all the perilous vicissitudes narrated in the following pages—that kind and pitying Wisdom which numbers the hairs on the head of each one in the world, and sees with compassion the falling sparrow when leaden hail has crippled its wing. A man is to be qualified to plant Christianity all along the frontier-borders of Western Texas, where savage heathenism and *quasi* civilization meet and interlap. The erudite son of Gamaliel is not needed there, nor is the mild and loving John, nor a foreign-storming Apollos, among a non-reading, bookless population, but shrewd and recklessly brave. A man of themselves is wanted, gifted of nature and polished by grace, one skilled in all the tricks and arts of sin in frontier-life, and in all the modes of predatory border warfare—brave, generous, wise, pure, social, hospitable, zealous, and defiant in the face of the almost-impossible. "The All-seeing Eye" saw the rudiments of that essential character in Missouri's orphan child. Born on her early frontier, having inherited all the taste and genius for frontier-life, he continued in that school till his lesson was fully learned; and, after his regeneration, religion supplied all needed virtues for a grace-refined manhood.

CONTENTS.

CHAPTER I.
His nativity 13

CHAPTER II.
His six years' race-riding 19

CHAPTER III.
He enters the United States Army—Serves the Government six years 27

CHAPTER IV.
Indian fights and troubles on the plains of New Mexico..... 35

CHAPTER V.
Trouble with three Mexicans near Santa Fe................. 42

CHAPTER VI.
He fights Indians, and is a nurse in the hospital at Santa Fe.. 46

CHAPTER VII.
Nurses a sick man with cholera near Leavenworth.......... 56

CHAPTER VIII.
Cuts "Kentuck's" coat, and throws down an Hibernian 60

CHAPTER IX.
He goes with the "Olive Branch" Mormons................. 64

CHAPTER X.
He goes to Texas, and reaches San Antonio 72

CHAPTER XI.
He finds his brother—Has fever—His marriage............. 77

CHAPTER XII.
He and "Uncle Leed"—"Signor Blitz"—A farcical concert.. 85

CHAPTER XIII.
His conviction—Conversion—Joins the Church............ 98

CHAPTER XIV.
He is appointed class-leader—Has a revival 112

CHAPTER XV.
He visits Missouri, his native home—Has a revival—A trouble... 119

CHAPTER XVI.
He joins the Confederate States Army—His camp at Camp Verde—Hospital at San Antonio...................... 125

CHAPTER XVII.
Many incidents while at Camp Clark, etc.................. 132

CHAPTER XVIII.
He is appointed chaplain of Debray's regiment............. 145

CHAPTER XIX.
Many incidents and battles on Red River in Louisiana...... 151

CHAPTER XX.
Incidents and meetings at San Augustine................... 165

CHAPTER XXI.
His address to the troops at Houston, by Mr. Lee Rogan..... 177

CHAPTER XXII.
Meeting on Walnut Creek—Goes to Eastern Texas—Returns. 186

CHAPTER XXIII.
He knocks down a man in church—*Status* of "Freedmen"... 196

CHAPTER XXIV.
He is sent to the mountains—First year on Kerrville Circuit. 204

CHAPTER XXV.
Incidents of two years on Kerrville Circuit—Many good meetings 217

CHAPTER XXVI.
Incidents on Somerset Circuit............................. 224

CHAPTER XXVII.
On Uvalde Circuit—Letters from J. S. Gillett and Bishop Marvin—French Smith................................ 228

Contents.

CHAPTER XXVIII.
Second year on Uvalde Circuit—Trip with the Rev. Wesley Smith, Superintendent American Bible Society......... 235

CHAPTER XXIX.
A fight with four Indians—The Bible and the sword........ 240

CHAPTER XXX.
Visit to San Felipe—Burial of young Pulliam and Evans.... 249

CHAPTER XXXI.
His temperance speech in Frio Cañon, etc.................. 255

CHAPTER XXXII.
He is Bible-distributer—Dr. West's letter, etc............... 263

CHAPTER XXXIII.
Preaches at a military outpost—A man put in jail—Cruelty to prisoners... 272

CHAPTER XXXIV.
A make-believe Indian—Shot at twice from a thicket—He is unhurt.. 278

CHAPTER XXXV.
A dangerous difficulty with a desperate young man.......... 282

CHAPTER XXXVI.
A trip with Dr. Walker—He preaches at an outpost—Singular proclamation 289

CHAPTER XXXVII.
A terrible fight with a desperado at Boerne, Texas—He is not hurt... 296

CHAPTER XXXVIII.
His visit to Mexico with his sick son—His son dies—Great sorrow.. 304

CHAPTER XXXIX.
Incidents on Bandera Mission—His charity, and its repay.... 310

CHAPTER XL.
On Kerrville Circuit—Goes with Dr. Walker, presiding elder—Good meetings....................................... 318

CHAPTER XLI.

Incidents on Uvalde Mission—A Baptist minister, the Rev. Mr. Harris—Travels with the Rev. W. T. Thornberry, presiding elder.. 322

CHAPTER XLII.

His and Mr. Thornberry's travels, etc....................... 328

CHAPTER XLIII.

Mr. Harris's letter, etc.. 338

CHAPTER XLIV.

Mr. Gillett's chapter... 351

CHAPTER XLV.

Dr. West's second letter, etc................................. 362

CHAPTER XLVI.

A gambler's burial at night.................................. 368

CHAPTER XLVII.

A sermon from Mr. Potter................................... 375

CHAPTER XLVIII.

His reply to atheist "Bruno"................................. 395

CHAPTER XLIX.

His cheerfulness, etc.. 400

CHAPTER L.

His letter from old Camp San Saba......................... 408

CHAPTER LI.

His letter on the wing, etc.—A little grave................ 415

CHAPTER LII.

Mr. Miller—Ben Ficklin—Old Family Bible, etc............ 427

CHAPTER LIII.

His presiding-eldership—Closing treatise.................. 431

CHAPTER LIV.

A chapter devoted to his wife................................ 438

CHAPTER LV.

Ministers' wives, etc... 443

CHAPTER LVI.

An address to young men and young ministers............ 448

ANDREW JACKSON POTTER.

CHAPTER I.

Andrew Jackson Potter was born in Chariton County, Missouri, April 3, 1830. He was the son of Joshua and Martha Potter, natives of Kentucky. Andrew's mother was his father's second wife, by whom he had seven children—four boys and three girls—Andrew being the third son. His father was in the British war of 1812, and he greatly admired the victorious hero of the battle at New Orleans (having been in that battle); hence the name of his hopeful son, "Andrew Jackson Potter."

In the course of events Mr. Potter moved to Carroll County, and then to Clinton (now Gentry), on North Grand River, where Andrew spent most of his early boyhood. Clinton was then a border county, and the facilities for an education were quite meager; indeed, there were rarely any school privileges; and besides, his parents were too poor to afford even the rudiments of an education to their children. About three months was the whole term of little Andrew's tuition at school. He, however, continued to spell at private spare time, after leaving school, till he could read a little in an easy reading-book, but did not learn to write.

His father died about 1840, when Andrew was in his tenth year. At that age he was turned out upon the cold charities of the world, an inexperienced boy, without any help, to earn his own living in the battles of life, his father's estate not leaving a sheltering home for those he left in the world. Being entirely without any resources, he was employed by a sportsman to ride horse-races. That employer learned his little employee three branches of his early education: the spelling-book, card-playing, and horse-racing. The most humiliating forms of vice generally hold dominion along the border of all frontier countries contiguous to the regions of uncivilized and savage life. The three grand agencies of civilization—the school, the press, and pulpit—do not plant their combined influences far out on the border, where settlements are sparse, and life is not safe from the arrow and the tomahawk of the untutored savage. The reckless adventurer and the soldier must drive back the savage, and fix the central nucleus of communities, before the arts of peace and refinement go forward and erect their standards in the new fields "beyond." Usually, we believe, the preacher leads the van; then follow the school and the press. All along their pathway, as a golden zone, the virtues of Christian civilization shine. "Beyond" the dark clouds of vice spread their shadowy gloom. The avenues of sin are wide, ever open and easily found by the unsuspecting young, especially in border-life, where evil is not under the restraints which handicap it in the older states of society. Besides, the fascinating charms of romance are draped about a frontier-life to the young mind; and where a mother's advice is not heeded, in the absence of a father's restraint, the young heart will naturally incline to identify itself with a roaming, unstable mode of society.

The father of little Andrew was a frontierman, and transmitted his border proclivities to his son. No law of our being is truer, surer than that we inherit the ruling elements of our ancestry. Children bred and born in the time of great wars inherit the worst factors in humanity, and those born on the spheres contiguous to savage life, where life itself is ever in a state of contest to maintain itself, early develop a pugnacious and aggressive disposition.

Born with these predispositions, and early environed by all the influences of semi-savage life, Andrew Potter easily ran into the mazes of sin in the outset of his career. Man, in his intellectual and moral make-up, is fashioned by his surroundings. All his ideas, all his emotions, are awaked and stimulated to action by the outer world around him. On the *will's attitude* to *motives* turns his *accountability*, and the consciousness of guilt for evil-doing, and the self-approbation for acts of virtue. Society everywhere is responsible for the moral and intellectual character of its young people. The means, the temptations, and the aids to a thriftless, ignorant, and vicious course, are furnished them on their entering upon the stage of life. The dance-house, the theatric-hall, the race-turf, the bar-room, the gaming-saloon, and all other helps to worthless and dissolute habits, society stations on the way to entrap and ruin the rising generation. If the enlightening and refining agencies are supplied to the youth, society must provide them: schools of high and low grade, churches, and all the learned books, and clean periodicals of the modern press—these, with all other novel aids of science and art, society must afford its youth, to insure the greatest harvest of a high-typed humanity—that of intelligence and virtue.

Andrew's first decade on the earth having been passed amid the rude scenes of border-life, where men were daily armed with the deadly implements of predatory warfare, where and when schools and churches were little thought of, and having a natural inclination to combativeness toward an enemy, the disposition to fight early displayed itself in his youthful activities; yet there were other opposite, neutralizing elements in his germinal character, which ever held a balancing and a compromising force in his conduct in all his later manhood. A deep sense of the right, a gentle sympathy for the wronged and the oppressed, unfaltering truthfulness, an undying regard for order, and honor, and true generosity—these several traits constitute the foundation of his remarkable character, which is so clearly elucidated by his strange and eventful future. These early inborn principles, hallowed and made predominant by our divine Christianity, make up the marvels of his wonderful later career.

His mother was a communicant of the old Calvinist Baptist Church, and early impressed his young mind with a kind of general sentiment that there was such a thing as religion and the Church; but he formed no definite conceptions as to its nature and doctrines: so soon was he entirely inclosed by irreligious associations that he seldom heard it spoken of, and rarely ever thought of it himself; but when it intruded upon his reflections, it was soon dismissed as an inconceivable mystery, of which he could have no insight; yet he always felt that he was a sinner, having some undefinable interest in its unrealized facts. He formed no religious creed, nor indulged in any methods of skepticism. Up to the day of his conversion he was simply a bold, zealous man of sin, yielding to the strongest current of influences about him, and his heart's natural inclination; while the cry of reason was unheeded, and the voice of the underlying better elements of his nature was hushed amid the tumult and onward rush of the events of the day. Revenge, a fearful monster, seemed delightful to him, where he thought an enemy had designed, or had truly inflicted, a serious injury on his person or character, or that of his unfeigned friend. *Cowardice* and *cruelty* he literally *despised* from childhood, and woe to the boy or man who displayed either in his presence along his march through the world. If he was fortunate to escape the pounding of his club, or mallet-like fist, he was sure to fall a victim to his keen-edged wit, or feel the smart of his poisoned satire. Fear had no place in his composition. Energy of force characterizes his entire life in sin and in religion. What he did, he did with energy; he was in *earnest* in the business activities of youth. He seemed to put new life into all things about him. When he ran a horse-race, it was a common saying, "That it did not matter about the speed of the horses: the one that little Potter rides is sure to win."

There were two other prominent principles running all through his whole career, both in his highest reach in sin, and in his later religious life—that of sincere devotedness to a friend, and kind attentions to the suffering, either friends or foes. He was never known to desert a friend, even in the face of the extreme of peril, nor to turn away from a sufferer when his attentions were needful. In the palmy days of wickedness, his heart was moved at sight of human misery.

CHAPTER II.

ABOUT six years of the young life of our juvenile hero were passed in the demoralizing practice of race-riding, gambling, and drinking: those periods in the life of a boy include the most vital of his formative state — from ten to his sixteenth year. Most young men have molded the shape of their manhood before they have passed their teens. If the main course of their life of evil habits is changed thereafter, it must be the result of some reformatory or regenerative force. The process of molding character must be commenced when all of its elemental parts are in a soft and pliable condition, as when the potter shapes the fashion of the vessel out of the yielding, miry clay. Instruction, restraint, and active training, are imperious to form the model of a good character. Instruction imparts ideas, restraint holds back from evil acts, and training is the practice of right deeds—all are needful in the education of the young, and must be undertaken from the cradle—no time is to be lost 'twixt the cradle and a matured manhood. Whoever may dare to risk the chances here, must do so at the serious peril of their dear child, and the hazard of their own sorrow.

> A pebble in the streamlet scant
>   Has changed the course of many a river;
> A dew-drop on the baby-plant
>   Has warped the giant oak forever.

A multitude of little evil passions, tempers, thoughts, and acts of childhood and youth, mark out the channel of manhood, or give bent to all after-life. Alas, for little Andrew! he had not the restraint of a father's discipline after he reached his tenth year, for then his father died. Just at the moment he most needed a father's counsel and control, he was left fatherless, to drift out into the sinful world, a homeless and friendless stranger-boy, on a half-savage frontier, where little more than the most hurtful forms of vice were daily seen. What else could have been expected of an undisciplined boy of ten years, in such a state of things, but to see him plunge headlong into the open vortex? Any other course would have been unnatural.

O how terribly awful is the responsibility of wicked men, who, by their example, and sometimes by their invitations, entice and lead the orphan-boy, or giddy youth, into the foul haunts of dissipation!

We hope the reader will pardon us for making a digression just here, and pardon the immodesty of a personal reference to the writer of this narrative, as it is done to do good, by calling the attention of men of evil habits, who may chance to read these pages, to the danger, and their accountability, of leading the orphan-boy and the silly youth into the paths of ruin. Long years ago, in the city of Nashville, Tennessee, the writer of this book was an inexperienced boy, and boarded at a house where several men often met at night to take a game of cards. They were unmarried men, about forty years of age. The house was the bachelor's retreat. The premises generally constituted a modern Sodom. South Nashville now covers the domain, and the parties are now all gone from among the living save the corrugated-featured old man who penned this story. We had been to a Methodist Camp-meeting, and professed religion, and joined the Church, and began to read the Bible near the light on the small table on which they played their cards at night. Sometimes some of them would venture to ridicule religion — at one time they concluded their games with a mock prayer, one of them leading audibly. In the close of their sacrilegious devotions, the leader prayed for the little Methodist whose occupation placed him in their midst, saying that their evil example might lead him astray. One of their number, who was a man of learning, saw that they had ventured too far. Meeting me in private, he said that as I was away from parental counsel, and among bad men, he was constrained to advise me. Said he: "I see that you are reading the Bible. I am known in the city as an infidel; but I say to you, my little son, stick to your Bible. I see men who read and follow the Scriptures make a mark in the world. I am a bad man—formed evil habits in early life. Read your Bible, and try to follow its precepts." That honest gambler's counsel has followed us through the vicissitudes of nearly a half-century.

Such advice might have been a godsend to young Potter at the threshold of his outset in life, on the border-plains of Missouri, when he first left the abode of his widowed and penniless mother. But instead of being persuaded not to follow the evil habits of sinful men, a sportsman employs him to ride races, and allows him to deal in cards, and to drink the dangerous beverage. Six years of his maturing youth, spent in such habits, among vicious society, at the grog-shops and race-courses, must have greatly weakened his good principles, and powerfully strengthened the bad tendencies of a depraved nature. It is not a matter of wonder that a boy of such training was inclined to stray deeper into a semi-savage life, when an opportunity opened up the way for him to leave his mother and kindred, and the scenes of his childhood, for the perils and hardships of war, and the privations and hazards of a thousand-miles trip across the desert-plains, infested by warlike Indian bands. The tenderest and the strongest attachments of childhood's heart cling to home—the natal-place, or the scenes of its earliest recollections—as those of the entwining vine grasp the twigs and branches of the tree about which it clambers. To detach them, is to sever and rend the most delicate, the purest sympathies of humanity. To become an orphan, is to have torn asunder all those tender endearments—it is to loose the magnet of central gravitation. To be fatherless and motherless, truly is to be homeless. Earth's vocabulary contains no words of sadder import than "orphan," "fatherless," "motherless." "The lone bird, forsaken of its mother," in its woodland home, is not so sad a thing as an orphan-child. Deep in the shady woods, made of little sticks and fibers, fastened among the waving leaflets, is the birdling's nest. In that leaf-bound house day and night sits the scanty-fledged baby-bird, chirping, chirping the long, long summer-day, till night spreads its dismal shades over the timbered solitudes, when despair, like the dark of forest-night, crushes the birdling's heart. Death, in pity, soon ends the forest-infant's grief. But, ah! the long years of the homeless orphan's sorrows! man has no art the grief-filled tale to tell.

But at the time indicated in our story little Andrew's mother still lived, and there are some untold facts associated with his earlier years which will throw some explanatory light on the apparent mystery of his seeming to readily forget all home and family affinities for the companionship of wicked strangers. Those facts too may set forth the folly of parents showing partiality among their children: such discriminations never end in good. Much evil happened to good old Jacob for partial regards to the son of his old age.

For several years Andrew was the youngest, and became the pet of his mother, which, as in the case of Joseph of olden fame, stimulated the other children to jealousy, and even to envy. So poor "Andy" was soon the scape-goat for bearing all the bad things of the rest of the children, and soon it was declared that he was the worst boy in all the neighborhood; and whether he was guilty or innocent of the charge, all the evil that was done was credited to "Andy." Once a minister visited his mother, when the usual amount of depravity was alleged against him. The minister, listening at the grave charges made upon the little miniature man, put his hand on his head, and said: "You all may say what you please about Andy; he'll make a man some day; he'll make a mark in the world yet." That greatly elevated the spirit of the abused little man. Whether that minister was a guesser or a prophet, he guessed right that time. In Texas "Andy" has made a mark not to be erased. A lady once said to his mother: "Mrs. Potter, Andy is the handsomest child you have." That again stirred his manly little pride and self-respect to be something in the career of life. Meeds of praise are soothing to the spirit of childhood as well as of manhood, and often stimulate a laudable ambition to deserve and attain positions of usefulness in after-life. As the small dust on the balance determines its preponderance either up or down, so little words of censure or praise often determine man's eventful life. Encouraging applause for little meritorious deeds, fraught with an earnest prediction of future usefulness, are laid up in the memories of a boy, and often come as a giant to his help in the battles of life in long after-years—coming as a well-armed recruit: his failing energies take on new vigor, and, freshened with hope of success, he enters anew into the strife. But, on the other hand, frequent censures, accompanied with ill omens of prophesied evils as the sure events of a boy's future in this world, often discourage his hopes, and unnerve his energies in the hour of the greatest peril. But true merit and real demerit should be cautiously praised and wisely blamed in the life of a boy. But he careful lest you bestow too little on the one, and an undue share on the other. Amid all his wanderings in after-life Andrew did not forget these early accusations and evil predictions, on the one side, and those gentle epithets of approval and hopeful anticipations of his ultimate position in useful spheres, and in the darkest days of adverse fortune their memory shed a beam of hopeful light on the gloom which hovered about the heart. Sad recollections crowding memory's page, after the death of his father, weakened and detached his fraternal affections from those who, through home-like jealousies and child-like envies, had piled on his name such an amount of deserved and undeserved criminations; and he looked to the domain of non-kindred for those little heart-communions which flourish not but in the rich garden of home-life. Thus the attractive forces which usually hold youth within the domain of home-influences were mainly broken loose, and "gravitation turned the other way." Those dissolving and disruptive germinal agencies in the boy-heart must have well-nigh neutralized the natural feeling of fraternal affection in the long years of his youthful, reckless career. In all the great catalogue of names which the fame of the ages has handed down to us, we read of but one Joseph who seemed to forget the cruelty of his brethren, save that "Man of Sorrows," who "never reviled again."

Having made the foregoing deflection and retrospect in the order and line of our consecutive narrative, to let in light upon the occult causes of developed character, we now return to our point of departure, to revel in the mazes of another six years' term in the life-daring events of our young hero. Here we find him just entering his sixteenth year, and becoming a soldier. Most of those six years are passed in great peril, while crossing and recrossing the great thousand-miles plains between Missouri and New Mexico and Arizona. In the six years he traversed these dreary, uncivilized regions, quite a number of times in the face of the untutored, unfriendly savage, making hair-breadth escapes from the air-piercing arrow and the hurled lance of the cruel warrior. The arrow shall not hurt thee, nor the pestilence harm thee, if God be with thee in the dangerous day.

CHAPTER III.

In the year 1846 a state of war existed between the United States and Mexico, and General Sterling Price was to march from Missouri to Mexico, operating in New Mexico and Santa Fe *en route*. Andrew, being now in his sixteenth year, volunteered to go on that perilous expedition. He entered Captain Slack's company, and moved forward to Fort Leavenworth, where the troops were inspected, and none but able-bodied men were received into service. Andrew, being so young, and too small a pattern of physical manhood to be admitted into ranks as a knapsacked soldier, was taken into the Quartermaster's Department as a teamster. About the first of September, 1846, a train of wagons, drawn by ox-teams, and laden with army supplies, left Fort Leavenworth for Santa Fe, Andrew driving a team. For meritorious conduct he was tendered an easier position, which he declined. Soon after entering the unpeopled plains, where the wild Indian roamed unrestrained by civilization's laws, they were unwise in not posting pickets to guard their camps from savage cruelty by night, and the wily foe approached their camp under cover of night, and fired upon them: one bullet, passing through the lapel of Andrew's coat, killed a man standing by his side; but picket-guards ever after prevented another night alarm. Winter threatening to set in upon them before they could reach Santa Fe, it was decided that they should travel the Bent Fort route instead of the Cimerone. The Bent Fort road passed through the Rattene Mountains, and was much the longest road, but afforded better timber, water, and grass—the Cimerone route leading over a vast arid desert. Their chosen way led them up the Arkansas River, and before reaching Bent's Fort they were surrounded and overpowered by the Cheyenne Indians. It was a feat of Indian chicanery and duplicity. Pretending friendship, two of them came into the camp at early morn and took breakfast with the teamsters, and remained as friendly visitors. Teams were yoked and hitched to the wagons, and the train moved forward. Presently, two other Indians who were seated by the road-side, journeyed with the train; again, larger squads joined them, and then other larger bands, in friendly attitude, till a seeming friendly host was about them; then suddenly three hundred tattooed warriors rushed on the train. Their bows strung, they gave the doleful, diabolical war-whoop, and demanded a halt. There were only about forty teamsters, and they had about twenty old-time flint-lock muskets, and they were in the wagons; so there was no chance for a defense. One tall Indian drew a bow at a venture, and cried, "Wo! wo! Cheyenne shoot, by dam!" The front teamster, dropping his whip, ran back along the train, and each teamster in succession retreated till reaching the rear, where they all huddled together awaiting their destiny. For three hours of awful suspense they were held by the savage men of the plains, looking each moment for the work of slaughter to begin. Many of them dismounted and let their ponies loose to graze. From the manner in which they eyed Andrew, he thought it their intention to capture him and bear him off into the deep solitudes of the mountains, or the vast prairie-wilds, as he was a ruddy-looking lad. But Andrew did not exactly fancy that kind of a home, and keeping his eye on the best-looking pony, he intended to mount him and give them a race, if the work of massacre should begin. Young, and robust, and active, he could spring upon a pony as if he walked on India-rubber feet. Soon, however, it was ascertained that the intention of the savages was not to kill the men, but to lighten the wagons of their cargo. The chief made his men hold the train at a stand-still, and, by signs and words, gave the wagon-master to understand that it was provisions he wanted, and not the men. The master tried to make a covenant-contract with the chief to give him a certain amount of meal and flour if he would leave, and never again infest his road. But the chief required more. At length a great cloud of dust was seen rising up in the rear, and the pent-up teamsters raised the distressing cry—to the wily Indian—"Soldiers! Soldiers! Soldiers!" The Indians soon accepted the master's terms, and, laden with their captured plunder, hastened away and were soon lost in the blue depths of their wilderness home. It was not the dust bestirred by the hurried tramp of advancing troops, but that of another wagon-train, of which the retreating Indians had no knowledge.

The man whom God has chosen for a special work in the world shall not fall a victim to natural or artificial agencies till that work is fulfilled, whether he be preacher or soldier. A thousand may perish by his side, and ten thousand fall by his right-hand; neither the flying arrow, nor fiery, whizzing ball, nor wasting pestilence, shall slay him till his divinely assigned mission has been finished. Who can doubt a special providence? Every *force* and *agency* in the universe is at the Divine disposal, to carry out his wise designs, and all his own unlimited, unoriginated energies. Sacred history gives us an analogous scene. Benhadad, King of Syria, had besieged Samaria, till the devastations of famine were about to force her to a surrender to Syria's victorious thousands; but as the victor king stretched out his hand to take the victor's prize, Victory turned her banners to the other side. Listen to the historic voice of ages: "For the Lord had made the host of the Syrians to hear a noise of chariots, and a noise of horses, even the noise of a great host; and they said one to another, Lo, the King of Israel hath hired against us the kings of the Hittites and the kings of the Egyptians to come upon us." Here it is said that the Lord had made the Syrian hosts to hear that noise: the tumultuous roar of hundreds of war-chariots and rushing steeds, hurrying to battle. Here the rushing, roaring winds must have made that battle-tumult, which put to flight the affrighted Syrian bands; but the distant, dusty clouds intimidate the brave Indian hosts, and send them on speedy retreat to the far-off mountains' sheltering shades. In the first instance, the angels of the winds, under divine control, cause the Syrian hosts to hear a storm-like roaring, by stirring the air into sudden commotions, or by special electric touches on the drum of the ear of each soldier in the great army, so that his bravery is instantly turned into cowardly fear and bewildering panic—driving each into half-crazed alarms, and causing them to leave all their tents, munitions, and commissaries, in their wild, precipitous flight, in the hands of their almost vanquished foes; and all that to fulfill God's predicted word by the mouth of his prophets, and to save the head of his faithful servant. But in the Indian defeat, the sight of a cloud of dust in the distance disarms them of their savage fury, and they haste away from imagined dangers. One single flight of arrows, and defenseless Andrew and all his helpless comrades would have fallen bleeding victims to their barbarous rage, and all that vast train would have fallen into their hands, to have been driven into the far-off desert solitudes. But no; a special protecting providence says, "Not so; do not hurt my chosen;" and instantly "the chariots of Israel," and ten thousand "horsemen thereof," are round about the object of divine protection.

Gentle reader, do you doubt a special providence? Then go to the rich bituminous plains on Sodom's ill-fated morn. Read the record. A special angel is sent to warn one man, God's servant, to flee the pending danger. He tells Lot to get out, for the day of doom had come. Look on the face of the distant horizon, as twilight's morning curtain fades into light. See that rising dark-blue cloud, spreading out its wings over the widened plains. Look at the fierce flashes of lightning along its advancing front. Hear the fearful roar of hail and thunder, and the dread rush of warring storm-winds. Look, see its hurried sweep along the skies. It draws nigh the doomed cities. The affrighted mortals run to and fro in the streets; others, in tremulous fear, gaze at the terrible scene. But O look at each end of the storm-wing! see at each tip thereof a fiery-robed angel, holding in his hand an electric chain, curbing back the ranting storm-cloud, till something is done below. See, the lower angel takes hold on Lot, and says, "Haste, get away; I can do nothing till you are gone." Look, Lot hurries along; now he enters into Zoar, and the fiery-clad angels unloose their hold on the sulphuric tempest's wings. O see its rushing fury! hear the roar of its maddened winds. See the spiral dashes of streaming lightnings along the face of the rolling clouds. Look at the blazing, fiery hail pouring upon the cities, and the intervening plains, till all is in a world of flame. Soon the ruin is complete and the burning earth sinks down and entombs their ashes and cinders in a bitter liquid grave. So it is written, "The Lord rained upon Sodom and Gomorrah *brimstone and fire*." Surely, a special interposition of a gracious providence shielded Lot from that wholesale catastrophe which ruined Sodom.

Some of our earnest readers may not question a special guiding providence over the good, while in the path of obedience, yet many honestly question a shielding agency over those whom God, in his purpose, may have chosen to useful stations, while they may still live in sin. That postulate brings the question in hand to a direct issue. We claim that young Andrew Potter was God's called agent to plant Christian civilization along the frontiers of Western Texas in the period of his mature manhood; and though his being exposed to the hazards of savage warfare was of his own choosing, and did lead him into much sin, suffering, and danger, yet the good and great Being did not see fit to do violence to the decisions of his own free-will; he kindly preserved him from destruction in the hours of peril, with a view of his future obedience to the divine behest—though now in the path of disobedience; and, furthermore, the all-wise Being saw that he could and would cause his sad schooling in sin's rough and thorny road to result in fitting him the better for the sphere of his future operations as the agent of the gospel of peace. Therefore, Andrew Potter did not fall a bleeding victim to Indian cruelty in the day of danger. Jonah was the chosen of God; and though for disobedience the terrible monster ingulfed him, yet a special providence spared his life, and brought him to do the bidding of the Lord in warning Nineveh of her impending danger. The ancient King of Egypt was raised up from the deaths sent on his kingdom, while very sinful and wicked, that he might be the medium of transmitting the name of Jehovah to after ages. Although Andrew Potter, in his young days of sin and exposure to such imminent peril, may not have been conscious of any design in himself, or even thought of any divine intentions in regard to him, yet the sequel shows that the all-seeing Eye was upon him, as his chosen minister.

CHAPTER IV.

During the short stay of the train at Bent's Fort, Andrew was attacked by that dangerous disease, "camp-fever," and when the train moved on it was first decided to leave him there; but the assistant wagon-master had formed a great attachment to the young man, and agreed to yoke and hitch up his team each morning, and loose them at evening, and let the sick youth sit in the front of the wagon, and command his team, which would follow the train. In that way he set out with the train from Bent's Fort toward Santa Fe, a distance of three hundred miles. He soon began to mend. Winter set in on them severely in the ravines of the Rattene Mountains, and having frequently to lie by, it gave young Potter a good time to recruit his lost strength. The Indians having got part of their supplies, and on account of detentions in the mountains by ice and snow-storms, they had to be put on short rations. The cook was required to bake each one's cake separately, and as near the same size as possible, that there might be no grounds for complaining. But sometimes one might seem a little larger than the others, when those who were more selfish than generous would desire the cakes that seemed to be larger. Among the teamsters there was a certain large bony man, noted for his cross-grained selfishness, who formed a dislike to young Potter, who was a favorite with the most of the crowd. This ill-natured man always contended for the largest cake of bread. One evening Andrew came in from herding the oxen, tired and hungry, and told the cook to give him his rations, and he would eat his supper. The cook handed him the one the stingy man had fixed his eye on for himself, and just as Andrew took hold of it, the cruel, selfish man knocked it from his hand, and it fell into small pieces in the sand. This brought on an encounter between them, and the stout man abused and bruised the boy's person. Andrew possessed a strong appetite for that bitter thing called *revenge*. That was the most objectionable trait early manifested in his character. It, being combined with his native combativeness, rendered him fearfully dangerous, when fully aroused to a sense of having been seriously wronged. He went off and whetted his butcher-knife sharp and keen, and when night came on he procured a seasoned oak wagon-standard. Being fully intent on revenge, he approached the camp-fire where his antagonist stood with his back toward him, and struck him with the standard, from the force of both hands, on the back of his head, when the large man fell into the fire. At the same time he drew his knife to finish him; but other parties staid the hand of the angry youth, and pulled the fallen man from the fire. He, however, soon became conscious, but was seriously hurt.

This affray caused quite a division and stir in the camp, and the little offender was imprisoned in a covered wagon near by, where he could hear all that was said about the row. He could hear himself called a "mean, low-bred boy," and that he ought to be made to know a boy's place, etc. That abuse only sharpened the boy's craving for revenge; so he found an old flint-lock musket in the wagon, raised the wagon-sheet, pointed it at the squad, and pulled trigger; but the powder flashed in the pan, only making a noise sufficient to scatter the crowd. That raised such an excitement in camp that it seemed that a general *mêlée* would ensue; but the wagon-master quelled it till the return of morn, when a consultation was held, and it was agreed that the master should rebuke the trespassing youth, and there it should end. Accordingly, the master said to him: "Andy, what did you strike that fellow so hard for? his head is nearly split open. You are a boy, and should keep in a boy's place." Andrew replied: "If it is my misfortune to be a boy, that is no reason why I should be imposed on. A man should keep in a man's place." Here the trouble ended, and the train rolled on its tortuous way amid the wild Indian domain.

That rash act of our little hero—going behind his enemy to take his life—is the only seeming cowardly deed we find in the entire history of his life, from early boyhood to his latest manhood. As we have already stated, cowardice and cruelty he really despised from childhood; but in this single instance, the peculiar nature of the difficulty, and his strong love of revenge, got the better of his bravery. Being physically unable to measure strength with a giant-like man, he saw no way to get the better of him but to hit him a stealthy blow. There are surely palliating considerations connected with the affair: the ill-natured, selfish man and his cruel abuse of the boy were greatly to be censured; but the boy's conduct was rash and reckless, and cannot be approved by the strict rules of morals, and is at the same time a true development of that pugilistic character he ever displayed in after-life, till the day of his regeneration; and even then, when he deemed it needful, he did not hesitate to chastise men for injuries to others more than for self-defense.

The winter being severe, the train did not reach Santa Fe till some time in January, 1847. The army had already taken Santa Fe, but General Price enlisted the teamsters, and advanced on the Mexicans. Young Potter enlisted among the rest of his comrades, and at the close of that campaign he remained in the service of the United States Government till 1852. That part of the army to which he belonged operated in Arizona and New Mexico, and its duty obliged it to traverse the vast plains lying between Missouri and New Mexico, where thousands of savage Indian warriors roamed in quest of the scalp of the civilized pale-faced intruder. For five years he crossed and recrossed that dangerous Indian-peopled domain, having many bloody skirmishes with those cruel and vengeful tribes. He became skilled in all the modes and arts of Indian warfare. Having entirely recovered from the debility caused by that severe attack of camp-fever, he had matured into a robust and active young man. Indeed, truly was he an *athlete* in the raids on Indian bands. Really, such a thing as fear seemed never to have had any place in his mental or moral make-up. The wild yell of the Indians' terrible war-whoop, sounding over the open plains, or echoing along the dismal mountain glens, struck no terror to his dauntless heart. In the face of their darting arrows, or amid their up-lifted lances, gleaming in the light, he faltered not, nor grew pale with fear while his comrades-in-arms fell in blood and anguish beside him. Yea, in the rage of battle, in the hail-storm of lances, arrows, and leaden balls, in the midst of the dying wails of his partners, he fearlessly defied the heartless savages till the voice of Victory calmed the rage, or called the contestants to a safe retreat. A braver, truer-hearted soldier seldom ever enlisted in the defense and protection of his country than young Andrew Jackson Potter; yet he was endowed by nature with a feeling of sympathy and pity for the injured and suffering as deep as his bravery was firm. When the war-strife ended, he laid aside its bloody robe, put on the garments of commiseration, and sought to aid the dying, or relieve the wounded. Never was he known to forsake a fallen comrade, even in the presence of the most alarming dangers. Though just passing into the full age of young manhood, he was a model soldier, and a fair specimen of pitying kindness to the distressed. When all tender attentions failed to relieve, and only death could quiet the agonies of the slain, young Potter was ever ready to perform the last acts of human kindness to the cold, pale corpse—to gently close the sightless eyes, tenderly fold the rigid arms across the unheaving bosom, and commit "dust to dust" in the solitudes of the expansive wilderness, where no kindred's eye shall ever see the little head-board marking the lonely spot where rests the fallen soldier's painless head.

At one time the vengeful savages caught a straggler from the camp, and abused him with nameless cruelties: made him move on "all-fours;" having put a bridle in his mouth, they rode him as a pony, inserted their rough spurs into his side, and mercilessly beat him, and finally, taking off his scalp, they left him alone, unpitied by human eye, till death ended all his misery. No tongue can tell, no pen can adequately depict, the bitterness of Indian hate, and the cruelty of their revenge.

Many an unknown fallen stranger sleeps beneath the American frontier sods, who, in the day of his doom, was wept for and mourned over by living loved ones, who also have now passed away. Almost all the soils now tilled by Civilization's arts, and tramped by the enlightened millions of great cities, tenanted by the predatory roaming tribes of barbarous humanity in the days gone by, have been stained by the life-blood of the soldier and the hardy pioneer. Every vale and mountain-side of Western Texas has drunk up the warm, red blood of the adventurous, enterprising men of the border who have been slain by the stealthy Indian. Their graves are sheltered by the leaf-roofed mat, the shade of the great live-oak, or the slanting mountain dell; while civilized arts have driven the untutored red man nearer the unbroken solitudes of the Rocky

Mountains. Onward still Progress drives her aggressive car to the hidden plateaus toward the Great West. Railroads are penetrating the old homes of Nature's thriftless children, driving off their game, and breaking up their wigwam villages, till hope seems to leave them naught but submission to Christian refinement or a dip in the Pacific wave—extinction. Away back in the old ages the changeless decree was revealed to mortals from the councils of heaven, "The gods which have not made this earth, nor fashioned these overhanging heavens, shall pass away from the earth, and from beneath these heavens; and the nations and peoples who will not submit to the evangelizing reign of God's divine Son shall surely perish from the face of the earth." The wisdom and generosity of the civil government, and the pious zeal of the Church, may yet enlighten and elevate many of the remaining predatory tribes. Surely the human impulses of a grace-refined manhood prompt to such a benevolent enterprise.

CHAPTER V.

In the winter of 1847, Mr. Potter was detailed to cook for a squad of men who had been sent eight miles from Santa Fe into the pine-woods, to cut wood. While there, one of the men died of measles, and young Potter was sent into town post-haste to get a conveyance to carry the dead man to his burial. He started on foot. On the way, he fell in company with a Mexican and two boys who had wood packed on their jacks. They had their axes with them, and they undertook to alarm the young man with menaces, or make-believe efforts to kill him. The man would make the boys raise their axes and pretend to aim a lick at his head, but would strike the ground near him; and the man would draw his butcher-knife and motion as if to stick it in him, then take a large stone and draw it over his head, just missing it; and then the boys would try their axes again in the same manner—torturing and tormenting him for several miles. He was without any means of defense. On arriving at Santa Fe he secured a gun, and spent two days in searching for those tormentors, but could never come up with them. In such cases of cruelty the young man's thirst for revenge was deep and bitter, and had he overhauled those impertinent Mexicans, they no doubt would have fallen at his hands. A Mexican's great weapon of defense and attack is his butcher-knife, and he does mortal work with it. He is generally respectful to Americans, and does his work of carnage in the shades of night. But in this instance, that Mexican must have held some national prejudice against the Americans occupying that country, and no doubt would have slain the young man had not fear of detection prevented his doing so; but he sought to satisfy his hate in torturing and alarming the unprotected youth. His moral instincts and sentiments raised that low-down Mexican only a grade above a savage. Hate which seeks relief in the torment of helpless youth is as cruel as the grave, and renders its subject a monster, or a demon in human shape. Mexico contains many noble specimens of a refined manhood, mingled with her myriads of greaser-tribes of low and vile instincts. Most of that class are spawns of a crossed or hybrid race. But even among these there are some humane and worthy outgrowths; but the worst grades are bad samples of the *genus homo*. Much of their want of the lineaments of refinement may be justly awarded to the depressing tendencies of a corrupt form of a national religion which strives to enslave its subjects in ignorance and vassalage.

The grand gospel lights of a divinely illumined Protestantism are casting their radiant beams all over the great domains of Montezuma's land, and the dark shadows of ages are fading into the day-dawn. Soon the great railroad magnates of modern times shall with iron bands tie the two late republics into one unified brotherhood, constituting an empired republic, ocean-bound. An age of great locomotion is to fill the earth with knowledge. "Many shall run to and fro, and knowledge shall increase." Happy the day when the nations shall have learned the right, and attained unto the disposition to obey its wise dictates! Look up, reader, and see, the morning cometh!

In the youthful prime of an unrenewed heart, Mr. Potter felt that it was his birthright, due himself, to follow his insulting assailant to the bitter death—to gratify the craving of revenge even in the destruction of the life of his escaped enemy. In his youth he must have been a noble type of physical manhood. He was now near, or quite, seventeen years old; but when fully matured, in all the perfection of life's prime, he was no doubt a man of great muscular powers—no surplus flesh, but symmetric in manly mold, and well-knit in body and limb; there was life in his motions, and fire in his eye.

He is now in the fifty-first year of his age, and is about five feet eight or nine inches high; weighs about one hundred and fifty pounds; well clothed with muscles and sinews, and just enough of sound flesh to make up a stout, healthy body. Time and toils have made no wrinkles on his features; not a gray hair in his raven-tired head; his cheek still glows with the rose-tints of the morning—ruddy like young David in his early days, but now adorned in the unfaded hues of a firmer manliness; his forehead indicative of nerve and brain, his nose slightly aquiline, and his mouth, like Henry Clay's, of immortal fame, from ear to ear. A fine model for Grecian artist to enchisel the orator from the marble shaft. He never shaves—he wears a moderate crop of dark beard. No man of woman born ever looked out on the world through a pair of keener eyes; see them once and you can never forget them—of a light bright-blue, as transparent as the unsullied morning ether, resembling at times the crystal-like glass marbles or the transparent prism.

CHAPTER VI.

We now give the reader Mr. Potter's own account of incidents connected with his first trip to Santa Fe, when a soldier boy:

"We made slow but pleasant progress while passing over the Cimerone Desert, till reaching the crossing of the Arkansas River. At twilight we pitched camp on the opposite side of the river, and arranged our wagons as a barricade. The moon shone dimly through a thin cloudy veil. While eating our evening meal, suddenly the alarm-cry rang out upon the night-air, 'To arms, to arms! the Indians are upon us!' Their wild war-whoop broke the stillness of the night-shades all along the resounding river vales. They were only armed with bows and lances; we were armed with long flint-lock muskets. The wagon-master quickly formed us on the outside of our barricade. We had about sixty men; the Indians were in large force. One-half of us only were ordered to fire on the first charge. I was of that number. The chief addressed us; but, not understanding his speech, we supposed that they designed some pretended friendship to gain an advantage. We remained silent, and they rushed at us. One-half of our men fired, repulsing them. My heavily-charged old musket kicked me back so rudely that, staggering, it was with great difficulty I could keep my feet. My nearest comrade, seeing me careening, thought me wounded, and asked if I were hurt. I replied, 'Not much;' though I thought I had unwittingly taken hold of the wrong end of my gun. I soon recovered. While reloading, the Indians made a charge on the other end of our line; but a quick fire repulsed them once more; and our end of the line again poured such a heavy volley upon them that they fled in dismay. Leaping over the bank, they plunged into the river, splash and dash, for nearly an hour, as a stampeded herd of wild buffaloes. Quite a number of their ponies lay dead on the field of contest next morning. How many of the red warriors we slew, we could not tell, as they usually carry off their slain. Next morning we saw their tattooed bands moving slowly away into the distant wilds."

"As the train moved slowly on, I got into the careless habit of going on in advance, and grazing my mule a half or quite a mile ahead of the wagons. One day I was grazing my mule, and on looking around I saw a party of Indians coming at breakneck speed to cut me off from the train. I mounted my mule without doing up my long dragging rope —no time for that. I tell you, I got the speed out of my hybrid that time. My rope trailed the earth like the stream of a shadow along the plains. Though my animal could ordinarily overtake the affrighted buffalo, at this time it seemed inspired with the speed of Job's wild ass of the wilderness. Not treading on the trailing rope, he bore me whizzing through the air; yet to me it seemed too slow a business, when darting arrows fell about me, and gleaming lances were uplifted to be hurled at me in a few moments more. Several mounted men, with the advancing train, seeing my fearful danger, sped to my rescue, and made the connection just in time to save my youthful scalp. The band of savages wheeled and retreated into the deep gloom of the wilderness."

"In the latter part of 1847, I was employed as a nurse in the hospital at Santa Fe. On entering that place, I saw an affecting scene: a large number of helpless men, sick of scurvy, measles, and pneumonia, were lying on narrow bunks crowded so closely together that there was just room to pass between them. My time of nursing came on the first part of the night, and it was an awful half night to me. Many of the sufferers, in their fevered delirium, would rise up and gather their blankets, saying that they were going home. By the time I would get them quieted, others would be crying out, 'Goodby! I am going home!' at the same time making efforts to get up. Never shall I forget those dreary half nights spent there with the dead and dying. O the sweet thoughts of home, 'sweet home!' They came as a dream-charm over the fevered brain when visions of wife, babes, and loved ones at home, entered the mind. But O me! I was an orphan-boy— a homeless stranger—and the world as seen through that soldier pest-house was dark and forlorn.

"At length a train set out for Fort Leavenworth to carry home all the sick who were able to stand the long trip across the plains. I was one of the attendants. As our ox-teams slowly moved up the hill, I took my last lingering look at the old adobe town of Santa Fe, with eyes dimmed by unshed tears, as I gazed for the last time on the graves of so many brave soldiers, who lay side by side on the tomb-covered hill beyond, not to arise till Death's long reign is past. Many of our sick died in the great wilderness, and we rolled them up in their blankets, and hid them in earth's cold clay, at intervals in our long journey from Santa Fe to Fort Leavenworth. Their unmarked graves are in the unsettled wilds of Nature's solitudes. Friends and dear ones at home know not of the place of their rest. When we wrapped their cold, dead bodies in their soldier-blanket shrouds, and shaped the grave-mound over them, the hardy soldier would perchance moisten the earthen monument with a pitying tear. To me it was a terribly gloomy thought to leave them alone in savage lands, to be trodden under foot by the wild, roving bands of Nature's untamed children, in their merry dances over the dust of their vanquished foes, or gored down by the wild buffalo when jubilant over the defeat of his fellow. Then, too, no slab shall point out the little spot where the soldier sleeps, and no kindred eye shall ever see the melancholy place, nor come there at solemn eventide to shed a tear, and lament his fall in a strange land. O is Death's heart breaking to continue his reign over man forever? Is there no peaceful clime where long-parted loved ones may meet to part no more? Is the grave an eternal victor over ruined man? Shall the bright stars of night, from their far-off spheres, ever look sadly down upon the tombs of earth's fallen dead? The voice of Hope cries out, in strains as sweet as angels sing, 'Thy dead men shall live again.'"

"At Ash Creek we killed a buffalo, and one man crippled another so that it ran off and lay down, and on nearing it, it would get up and run a short distance and lie down again, till it got a mile or more from the train, the train still moving onward. Two footmen followed the wounded buffalo and butchered it. In the meantime I proposed to a Mexican and Joe McGuire that we go and assist in capturing the buffalo. Joe was a boy about my age. They readily agreed to go; and we wheeled our nags around and started off. But in a short time I had a presentiment not to go. Halting, I said to the other two, 'Let us not go.' They insisted on my going, saying, 'Don't back out." I never liked the words "back out," but the impression not to go was so strong that I returned to the train. Joe and the Mexican went on, and aided in the slaughter of the wild cow. They packed the meat on their horses, and started toward the train, now some four miles away. Soon a squad of Indians dashed upon them, killed Joe, hurled lances into the Mexican, scalped them both, took their horses, meat, and all, and fled into the depths of the wilderness. Some of the party pursued the two footmen, but when they presented their guns the Indians retreated. Then the footmen fired off their guns to stop the train. Presently they were seen coming at their utmost speed. They reached us nearly exhausted, panting for breath, and told us of the sad fate of Joe and the Mexican. A call was then made for volunteers to go in quest of the dead, and only eight were willing to go. I was one of that number. We hitched two yoke of oxen to a wagon, armed ourselves as best we could, and set out on the dangerous undertaking. Indian smoke-columns, which they used for signals, rose high in the air in many directions; and the terrified buffaloes were running and making the trampled earth tremble and roar as mighty thunders, running over their calves, and crippling and crushing them. But we moved on in the general confusion. When we found the place of carnage, the Mexican was sitting up in untold agonies. He had several shallow lance-wounds on his body, and a gory, scalpless head, the sight of which was as frightful as his pains were torturing. But alas! poor Joe was dead! He had received seventeen wounds, an arrow was fastened in his heart, and his bloody, skinless head was as raw as a butchered beef. Most of their clothing was taken with their crowns. We carried them safely to the train, and buried poor Joe on the margin of Walnut Creek, leaving him to rest painless in his unknown grave till the last trump shall awake him from his lonely sleep; but we carried the Mexican to Fort Leavenworth. His scalp all healed over except the mold, but his sufferings were indescribable, and in about three months he died."

These several extracts from Mr. Potter's manuscripts, in memory of the sad events of his young life, set forth the prominent early traits of his developing manhood. His native, unassumed valor, his self-possession in moments of peril, his obliging tenderness for the sick, and his respect for the dead, made a good foundation for his later life of piety. When their cook was taken with Asiatic cholera, and all others fled, young Potter never left him, but remained with and nursed him during a long and toilsome night. When Joe McGuire and the Mexican fell into the cruel hands of the blood-thirsty savages, he was among the first to seek to recover their remains from barbarous cruelty—risking his own life to secure the gory bodies of his dead comrades to entomb them. The sufferings of the sick soldiers at the hospital in Santa Fe, made an ineffaceable impression on his tender sympathies, while listening to their illusive dreams of home; and the last heart-melting adieu of the cemetery, where so many soldier dead lie in silence to-day, should command the inspiration of the poet's muse in strains as sadly sweet as those of the "Maid of Monterey." His attachments to friends and associates in life were strong, and, unsevered by the pale chill of death, they united his boy affections to the dead in the tomb, at sight of which he shed the farewell tear, though no kindred tie allied their memories to him. Reading the touching story, we thought of the "Soldier's Dream," and of Burns's "Soldier's Return;" and we cannot resist the inclination to transcribe a few stanzas of the latter, to rekindle in the heart of the reader the tender emotions which have nestled in bosoms once like unto our own, though now long since unfeeling and dead—emotions which long, long ago stirred up the fevered hopes of Santa

Fe's dying soldiers when thoughts of returning home touched the heart-ligaments which bound them to its sweet memories:

> When wild war's deadly blast was blown,
>   And gentle peace returning,
> With many a sweet babe fatherless,
>   And many a widow mourning,
>
> I left the lines and tented fields,
>   Where long I'd been a lodger,
> My humble knapsack on my back,
>   A poor but honest soldier.
>
> With a clean, light heart within my breast,
>   My hands unstained with plunder,
> And for fair Scotia's home again
>   I cheery on did wander.
>
> The humble soldier ne'er despise,
>   Nor treat him as a stranger,
> For he is all his country's stay
>   In the hour and day of danger.

The valorous soldier puts his life between his country and its foes. His breast is the barricade to resist the assaults of its enemies. For her weal he gives up all the endearments of life, and when the banner of peace is unfurled, all home affections reenkindle in his heart, and in his wild flights of fancy, when disease excites the brain, he longs to be at home. In the cheerful buoyancy of health and hope, he arms himself against the valiant foe; but there is a deadly enemy against whose subtle wiles the soldier thinks not to equip his mortal body—insidious disease. Contagion and deadly pestilence haunt the warrior's camp, and paralyze the manly arm. Death's gaunt angels breathe their mildew-blight on the sleeping soldier's tent, and disease pales him for the warrior's grave.

We also see in these brief sketches marked proofs of a special providence over God's intended agent, who is to act a prominent part in warring against a mightier enemy in coming days amid other scenes. In all the strange events of peril, a guardian angel turns away the death-missile. Mr. Potter says, when he had started to go with Joe McGuire and the unfortunate Mexican on that fatal day, that a sudden impression was made on his mind not to go, and so powerful was its influence on his will that it overruled his former decision; and that too under the buoyant youthful tendencies to yield to the persuasion of his young friend, who urged him not to "back out." He calls it a "presentiment." History testifies to the occurrence of presentiments of strange and wonderful events, in different ages, to many persons in high rank in life. No sane man can doubt the facts. Much has been written to assign to them efficient and natural, or intelligent, causes. A presentiment is a special impression made on the sensibilities, or on the mind, and by acting on the will of a person, by some intelligent agent, to caution or warn that one of some pending danger, in order to so control the conduct of that person as to avoid that peril, or to inform that person of some happening event or coming transaction which may affect such a one either for good or evil. These cautionary impressions do not only happen now and then, as the mere result of blind accident, but they come before the mind just at the time their warnings are needed to profit their subject, and must be kind interpositions of an intelligent and affectionate agent, or cause. We call it, in a general way, a providence, but to be more theologically and logically definite, we state, the real efficient agent must be the divine Spirit himself, or some angelic agent, or both, or sometimes one and at other times the other. The Bible teaches both. The Holy Spirit is to lead us into all truth. David prays to be guided by the divine Spirit. Angels shielded the head of young Israel when resting on a stone, and wet with the night-dews of the great wilderness. Could not an angel, though unseen, touch the electric meshes about the will of young Potter so as to turn him around into a path of safety as surely as the manipulating fingers send a thrill along the lengthened wires to distant realms? The unseen angel charioteers guided the "chariots of Israel and the horsemen thereof" along the hill-sides about the prophet and his servant, in the moment of peril. When the immaculate Son of God fell on Gethsemane's cold bosom, under the pressing weight of a world's guilt, till the blood of death dripped from every pore, an angel's soft finger touched his breaking heart with a new life-thrill, which enabled him to endure unto the bitter end. The angel which stood in the way to turn Balaam from an evil path also reversed the purpose of his will, and made him bless, instead of curse, the chosen of God. So the angel of God turned young Potter from the evil hour.

CHAPTER VII.

In the year 1851, Mr. Potter made his last trip across the plains to New Mexico from the State of Missouri. He was employed to drive an ox-team for the United States Government, starting out from Fort Leavenworth in the spring of that year. Here we transcribe the incidents of that expedition from his manuscript:

"A government train was fitted out with farming implements and other appliances, to cross the plains to go to New Mexico, to open a government farm at Fort Union. I was employed at twenty dollars a month to drive an ox-team. We had an escort of soldiers, and the whole outfit was under the command of Major Rucker. Captain Bowin and family were in the train. Just before the train started, the cholera broke out in the post, and our camp being near, our men were greatly alarmed and ready to stampede. A stranger came to our camp and feigned sickness. He lay down and rolled up in his blanket, and when asked what ailed him he would curse, and say it was nobody's business. He created quite an excitement in our camp, the men fearing that he might have cholera. He no doubt wanted to create that impression, hoping to frighten the men so as to run them off, and thereby make hands scarce, and raise wages. At last, the wagon-master said to me, 'Potter, can't you rouse that man up from there?' I answered, 'I can try.' I asked him if he was really sick, and he told me to 'go to h–ll.' Some old, seasoned oaken clapboards lay near by, and I gathered one and lit in on him. He arose and ran, and my clapboard followed him about fifty yards, hitting him at each jump, pop! pop! Then the cholera excitement cooled down in our camp. But at last the dreaded moment came. Our cook was stricken down with that frightful plague late one evening, and every man ran off and left me alone with the sufferer. One man would come near and I would go out to him and get the remedies to treat the poor suffering man with, which he could obtain at the post, such as fourth-proof brandy and pepper and vinegar. It was an awful battle for life the whole night. My great aim was to keep the cramp out of his body by rubbing his legs and applying the stimulants externally and internally. The night being warm, I stripped him of his clothing and rubbed him with all the power that was in me, till I would fall over from pure fatigue; but when the cramping pains would make the poor fellow scream out, it would arouse me again to my tiresome task. Several times he would say that he would die, but I would encourage him to hope. Memory can never conceal that terrible night. As day began to dawn the change came: he passed into a state of ease. When the sun's rays fell upon his pale and death-like features, he could barely use hand or foot; only life was left him. He got well and went home, and onward moved our train toward the plains."

We do not remember to have heard or read of a more remarkable instance of disinterested kindness on the part of a young man than the one we have just recorded. Chivalrous youth has rushed into the face of extreme peril when hope has presented before it its chaplet of honor; young men have elevated their country's fallen standard in the presence of the vanquishing foe, in the midst of a storm of leaden hail; but the honor of their country's name was to be lifted from the dust of defeat, and a meed of glorious renown stood glistening in the eye of their hope. We have read of the angel-like deed of that generous little maid who volunteered to deal out the commissaries to the poor, the sick, and the dying, from that house of death in the city of New Orleans, on those dark days when the angel of death had breathed his blasting chill in the fatal room; we have sung too of the seraph-spirit of the "Maid of Monterey," when that black-eyed señorita administered to the wounded and dying of her defeated country's foes, when thickly strewn along the battle-plain. These were females—true patterns of woman's native heart. Woman! a body of pitying love; woman! when pain and death pale the brow, a pitying angel! yea, woman, model of celestial seraphs, and image of gentle angels in Eden spheres, where pain cometh not. But here we register a toilsome, night-long deed of a young man just entering his twenty-first year—when youth is timorous in the perils of disease of mortal name, and life to it is dear; when all its life-tide of feeling shrinks at sight of suffering and the agonies of death. Here there were no motives to hold him in the tent of the plague's suffering victim but those of benevolent duty—a true morality. All men have fled in dismay, panic-stricken under the mingled power of the love of life and the fear of death. He was not bound to the plague-smitten man by any kindred tie save that of a common humanity, which imposed no stronger obligations on him than on those who deserted in the critical hour. He had not been taught that fame-deserving act by precept or example, and no hope of reward but that of danger and death could have been before him. That awful night-vigil and toil sprung spontaneously from an inborn benevolent feeling which melts at sight of human woe, of friend or foe. Loss of sleep, fatigue from toilsome rubbing of the death-panged sufferer, and the exhausting force of night-long, intense excitement—he would topple over from sheer debility; yet the cry of the death-like agony from his patient would renerve him for duty. The disinterested deed of that fearful night should be printed in the records of fame's glory-adorned temple; it should awake some poet's tuneless lyre which may immortalize it in song. How strangely do the extremes of two opposites meet in that marvelous young man! *Loving pity and revengeful hate!* At one time he is in pursuit of an antagonist with a death-dealing weapon in his hand, inflamed with all the dire intentions of murderous slaughter; at another time he labors to mitigate mortal anguish at the fearful risk of his own life, as if imbued with the spirit of Him who wept at sight of human woe.

We do not remember to have heard or read of a more remarkable instance of disinterested kindness on the part of a young man than the one we have just recorded. Chivalrous youth has rushed into the face of extreme peril when hope has presented before it its chaplet of honor; young men have elevated their country's fallen standard in the presence of the vanquishing foe, in the midst of a storm of leaden hail; but the honor of their country's name was to be lifted from the dust of defeat, and a meed of glorious renown stood glistening in the eye of their hope. We have read of the angel-like deed of that generous little maid who volunteered to deal out the commissaries to the poor, the sick, and the dying, from that house of death in the city of New Orleans, on those dark days when the angel of death had breathed his blasting chill in the fatal room; we have sung too of the seraph-spirit of the "Maid of Monterey," when that black-eyed señorita administered to the wounded and dying of her defeated country's foes, when thickly strewn along the battle-plain. These were females—true patterns of woman's native heart. Woman! a body of pitying love; woman! when pain and death pale the brow, a pitying angel! yea, woman, model of celestial seraphs, and image of gentle angels in Eden spheres, where pain cometh not. But here we register a toilsome, night-long deed of a young man just entering his twenty-first year—when youth is timorous in the perils of disease of mortal name, and life to it is dear; when all its life-tide of feeling shrinks at sight of suffering and the agonies of death. Here there were no motives to hold him in the tent of the plague's suffering victim but those of benevolent duty—a true morality. All men have fled in dismay, panic-stricken under the mingled power of the love of life and the fear of death. He was not bound to the plague-smitten man by any kindred tie save that of a common humanity, which imposed no stronger obligations on him than on those who deserted in the critical hour. He had not been taught that fame-deserving act by precept or example, and no hope of reward but that of danger and death could have been before him. That awful night-vigil and toil sprung spontaneously from an inborn benevolent feeling which melts at sight of human woe, of friend or foe. Loss of sleep, fatigue from toilsome rubbing of the death-panged sufferer, and the exhausting force of night-long, intense excitement—he would topple over from sheer debility; yet the cry of the death-like agony from his patient would renerve him for duty. The disinterested deed of that fearful night should be printed in the records of fame's glory-adorned temple; it should awake some poet's tuneless lyre which may immortalize it in song. How strangely do the extremes of two opposites meet in that marvelous young man! *Loving pity and revengeful hate!* At one time he is in pursuit of an antagonist with a death-dealing weapon in his hand, inflamed with all the dire intentions of murderous slaughter; at another time he labors to mitigate mortal anguish at the fearful risk of his own life, as if imbued with the spirit of Him who wept at sight of human woe.

CHAPTER VIII.

Among the teamsters was a large man from the State of Kentucky. He was called "Kentuck." He was rather a cruel man and, easily irritated. One morning he became incensed against a little lad who was with the train, and taking hold of the boy he raised him from the ground and began to knock his head against the tire of a wagon-wheel. Potter, seeing the cruel act, stepped up, saying, "Don't do that, 'Kentuck'—don't do that! You will ruin the boy." The huge, giant-like Kentuckian let go the lad and began to curse and abuse Potter, saying, "Do you take it up?" in that instant feeling for his pistol. Potter, understanding his intention, being armed with a "jack-knife," snatched it from its scabbard and made a stroke at "Kentuck's" back, inserting the point of the huge knife into his coat-collar, making a split to the tail of his frock, without damage to the flesh. "Kentuck's" lower extremities were taking his body out of danger at the time that gleaming knife entered the collar of his coat. His quick and long strides saved his epidermis that run. Before "Kentuck" could get his pistol or turn to use his "Arkansas tooth-pick," they were arrested and put under guard. The train could not move till that quarrel was settled. The wagon-master inquired into the affray, and finally told

"Kentuck" that if he did not agree to a settlement, one or the other must be discharged, and in that case he would be the man, as Potter was one of the best hands he had, and besides was not to be blamed; that he did not insult him, but kindly asked him to desist from his abuse of the person of a helpless boy; and furthermore said to him that when he had cooled off his anger he would look at it in that light himself. He then agreed to drop it, and a friendly hand-shaking ensued with the parties; teams were then hitched up, and the wheels rolled on their long prairie-road. "Kentuck" was ever after a fast friend to Potter.

When daring men have encountered each other's rage, and felt or narrowly escaped the smart of each other's steel and then become reconciled, they usually maintain their friendly *status* to the end of life. In their dread contests they exhaust their magazine of bitterness, or else their friendship is mingled with a deep sense of fear and a kind of respect for each other's valor, which leads them to a delicate carefulness not to give just cause of irritation. Enemies in great wars, after the terrible bloody strife is past and peace restored, and associations of friendships are formed among those who bravely stood before each other's steel in the death-dealing hour, learn to love with endearing ties, till called to that land where swords and enemies cannot go. Certain species of vegetation eaten out or trodden down in the soils are succeeded by other kinds. So of the heart—hate being eradicated or quelled, kindness and love spring up therein. Even in early youth, Mr. Potter was a sure enemy of cruelty, and must interpose to prevent or suppress it at the cost of his own peace and safety. His traits of youthful character enlisted the admiration of strangers.

At another time two uncouth Irishmen fell upon a Dutchman, and got him down and were pelting him severely, when Potter interfered and pulled one of them off, and the short, stubby Irishman pitched into him like a mad-cat, and scratched his face. Mr. Potter felled him to the earth, when the Hibernian cried out, "Do n't hurt me, Mr. Potter; do n't hurt me!" That was a timely prayer; he let him up, and hit him not. Potter was not in favor with Captain Bowin, and he notified him that he should report him to Major Rucker, who was on a bear-hunt. Accordingly, when the major came into camp, the captain went to his tent to report the youth, and Potter accompanied him to hear the issue. The captain laid before the major quite a mass of accusations against the young man. Major Rucker said, "Mr. Potter, I have heard the captain's charges against you; now I want to hear what you have to say about them." The young man rehearsed all the facts in the case, whereupon the major sharply remarked, "Mr. Potter, it is eating bear-meat that has caused all this fussing in the camp; and now I say unto you, Mr. Potter, you shall not eat any more bear-meat unless that thing is stopped." The captain felt the keen edge of that humorous retort, and silently retired, not altogether in fellowship with the major's views. The major had a high regard for the elements of character the young man had displayed in the affair: his sense of just and equal rights in not permitting two men to mercilessly beat and mangle one man; his sympathy for the sufferer, the vanquished; his indisposition to punish a fallen enemy. When the truculent Irishman pleaded for mercy, his plea was instantly granted, though he had tried his utmost to disfigure the face of his victor—as soon as the piteous cry reached Potter's ear, he staid his hand and let his defeated victim arise and go unharmed. These early rudiments of meritorious character were not learned, acquired—they were native, inborn; no school of ethics had taught them to him, no associations had imparted them to his young, immature mind. He was not yet fully developed in physical or mental manhood. He was just merging from a boy into the young man, but he was endowed with more than ordinary native powers of each. He could dash upon the ground the thick, rough Irishman as if he had been a boy; and a knowledge of his great strength and dauntless prowess made him feared and honored in the camps and esteemed by his unenvious superiors. He was quick and shrewd in judging of men and things, and with proper training would have made a military man of great renown. The elements of character just pointed out enter into the composition of great soldiers who have inscribed their names on fame's bloody scroll.

CHAPTER IX.

"In 1851 we began our work at Fort Union. It was situated near a large spring which burst out of the earth. We called it 'the hole in the ground.' It was about ninety miles east of old Santa Fe. The depth of the spring had never been fathomed. It ran boldly off into a creek large enough to irrigate thousands of acres of land in the vale. There were no houses there—only tents. But when our train arrived, with all the implements for farming and building, the work went on with great haste. A saw-mill, run by horse-power, was erected; pine timber, from an adjacent forest, was cut and sawed into lumber for buildings; a number of plows were started to turn up the soil to receive the good seed, while others were engaged in cutting irrigating-ditches; and rapidly the great government farm was being opened up.

"About that time a train of some twenty small wagons, drawn by oxen and milch-cows, came along and camped near the post. I went down to find out where they were from and whither they were going. I was very much surprised to find women and children in their camp—a strange sight in that distant wilderness. On inquiry, I learned that they were Mormons of the 'Olive-branch Division'—opposed to Brigham Young—and were enemies to polygamy.

They were going to the mouth of Colorado River, in Lower California, where they had agreed to concentrate and build a large city—the nucleus of an independent kingdom. Mr. Bruster, their prophet, had gone with a party one year in advance to that chosen location. They had a book containing the revelations of God to their prophet about their journey across the plains. It did not allow them to resist the attacks of the Indians. The Lord was to shelter them from harm in all that perilous road, and no enemy should molest them. They believed that the great Rio Bravo del Norte, or Rio Grande River, was the silvery line that was to separate the righteous from the wicked; that all east of it was the land of Bethsullie—the land of the wicked, which is now Texas. They predicted the downfall of the United States. But still she is erect. They taught that all west of that grand old stream was the home of the righteous, which the wicked shall never inherit, as God had set it apart for the saints of the latter days. May be so. Mexico and California may yet be sainted. They had songs composed to accord with their faith, which they sung with great animation, as,

> Low down on the banks of Sedonia,
> Where love crowns the meek and the lowly.

"I soon made up my mind to go with them to their celestial city at the outlet of the famed Colorado. They had goods to sell to the Mexicans *en route;* but they could not speak Spanish. They agreed to take me through free of charge, if I would trade their goods to the Mexicans. This I consented to do. I settled up with the quartermaster, and set out with that strangely deluded people in the long journey to the Pacific shore. We crossed the Pecos River at a little town called Anton Chico, on the west side of the Pecos. We encamped on the east bank, opposite the town. That night I did not stake my mule, but turned it loose with the other stock, with a drag-rope. Next morning my mule was missing. I was satisfied that the Mexicans had stolen him. I borrowed a horse and rode over into the town to inquire about my mule. After getting into the town, I looked back across the river and saw several Mexicans on foot, trying to rope my mule, which was coming out of a mountain-gorge above the town. It was trying to come to camp, but the four Mexicans were striving to head it off. The mule would dodge their ropes and run around them. I spurred my horse, running through gardens and fields which were not fenced, and plunged into the river. I soon dashed in among them with a 'pepper-box revolver.' The Mexicans drew their butcher-knives, or 'billdookies,' as they called them. As one of them ran at me, I shot him in the breast, and he fell to the ground. The others cut at me, but my horse would jump out of their reach. Just as I was pulling trigger at another of the thieves, all three ran off, and I pursued, wounding two of them. But soon they reached the Pecos River, and took shelter under its bank. The fight was seen from camp, and some of the party ran to my aid; but the retreat came off before recruits reached me. My mule came safely into camp. We expected trouble from the Mexicans, but they did not molest us. A knife is their weapon in bloody strife, and they use it dexterously, but they fear fire-arms.

"We soon reached the division-line, the noble old Rio Grande River, and traveled down it and crossed over into 'Sedonia,' the sun-bright clime of these saints, at the town of Socono. Here they found a number of their brethren who had preceded them the year before. At this place they erected an arbor, convened a conference, and arraigned their prophet, a Mr. Bruster, for false predictions about their new empire. The trial lasted several days, and resulted in his expulsion as a false prophet and an impostor. There was great confusion and division among them. A number desired to go on, and some decided to remain at Socono. Our party moved on its way down the west bank of the Rio Grande River until we reached the little town of Santa Barbara, where we were to take Cook's road to California. Here another division occurred among them, and only seven families decided to continue their journey. Winter was approaching, and I declined to go on with so small a number. I then made up a company of twenty-six men to explore the mines in Arizona. The Mormons who refused to go to California went with us. We reached the mining regions at Santa Rito del Cavera, near the old copper-mines. We soon erected a rock fort to protect ourselves from the attacks of the Apache Indians. These mines had been worked years before that period. Great tunnels had been cut into the mountain-sides, and deep shafts let into them. We did not have the needful machinery to work the mines; we could only wash the dirt in the beds of the ravines. We found some gold, but not enough to pay for the labor.

"A Mexican and myself went out one day, to look after our stock, and came up with two Indians. We exchanged shots with them, but neither was hurt. The Indians hoisted a white flag, and called the Mexican to come to them. I objected to his going, but he said there was no danger. On his reaching the Indians, who were only about one hundred yards from me, one of them put his gun against the Mexican's breast and shot him through the heart, and he fell dead from his horse. I had a German 'yorger,' the longest range gun in use at that day; I took deliberate aim and fired, bringing one of the cowardly poor wretches to the ground, and seeing a crowd of Indians coming over the hill, I had to retreat to the fort. We sent out a party of our men in the afternoon and brought in the unfortunate Mexican, and buried him near our little rock fort. After remaining there about five weeks, I found I could accomplish nothing by a longer stay, so I got five or six men and went back to the Rio Grande, and spent the winter at the little town of Santa Barbara. Here we bought corn and beans and such things as we could get to live on until spring. As spring approached, we went down to Fort Fillmore, about sixty miles above El Paso. At this place I armed and equipped seven men to escort me to San Antonio, which took all the means I had. On the 17th of March, 1852, we set out on our perilous journey."

In all Mr. Potter's dauntless valor, we are deeply impressed with his cool and deliberate caution in the midst of danger, his accurate knowledge of human nature in general, and his deep insight into Indian and Mexican treachery. When those deceptive Indians raised the flag of peace, Mr. Potter was not deceived thereby, though the poor Mexican was led by it into instant death. In all his battles with either Mexicans or Indians, he was never decoyed into danger unawares. Once when in the service of the United States Government, a Mexican spy came into camp as a citizen-friend, and, though but a boy, Mr. Potter clearly read his intentions, and when he went to depart, Mr. Potter took him prisoner and marched him to head-quarters. When the older troops suspected no harm, the boy-soldier's suspicions were rightly founded, and his judgment and valor saved their camp.

It is no matter of wonder that young Potter should go with that olive-branch of Mormons under the circumstances. He was then about twenty-one years of age, a homeless orphan-stranger, an adventurous young man looking out to see what was in the world, and in search of its El Dorado. He had no ties of kindred attachments to bind him to any associations. The presence of cheerful females and merry children, which is a novel sight to a hardy soldier in a savage land; the air of romance woven around their story of that semi-celestial Sidonian land, their New Jerusalem on the distant Pacific shore; the future renown of their new empire, stretching from the banks of the Rio Grande to the Pacific wave; the personal honors of the humble subjects of the new kingdom, bestowed on them by a superhuman hand, of which they sung hopefully around their night-fires while encamped in the wilderness, *en route* to their new Eden home:

<small>Away down in Sidonia's land, where *love* crowns the lowly;</small>

that they had a holy book telling of the uprising of the glory-adorned empire; that all the land east of that Heaven-favored clime should come to desolation; that they would carry him through free of charge if he would do their trading with the Mexicans on the way—in view of the confiding nature of his young mind, and the sad fact that he had no knowledge of the Bible, no religious creed, the marvel is that he did not adopt their faith and join the band of "Latter-day Saints." He did not adopt their fanatical, romantic faith. The fact of his natural gifts, and a gracious providential care, can alone account for his strange escape from that wild, fascinating delusion. Nature had given him strong reasoning forces, which greatly aided him in throwing aside the insidious charms of air-castled imaginings of a deluded fanaticism. His native perceptions were clear-eyed, and he looked beneath the veil of surface-beauties to view bottom facts, and the light of an ever-present beneficent Spirit enabled him to see the vanity of that gossamer creed. Here the innocent child sees the thorn when its dimpled hand is outstretched to grasp the blooming rose; it begins to taste the bitter lying under the sugar-coating of the whited pill ere it has swallowed it down, and with disgust and dread turns away from bush and pill unhurt, but wiser as to the deceptive glare of this world's outward glories.

Our hero is filled with an inexhaustible store of energy of purpose. Defeated at one thing, he is ready to try another. He tries the inspiring gold project. Failing there, another scheme is in his mind to engage the activities of his restless, untamed, unsettled nature. What future experiment illumined the horizon of his hopes along Texan skies is not apparent, but some unrealized better future must have loomed up along the heaven of his plans to lead him there—an invisible, secret agency, inspiring thoughts and creating glowing hopes in the mind as a luminous mirage on life's arid sands, leading and guiding to a wonderful future in a strange, and by him an untrodden, land. In his long, hazardous route to Texas, he passes through the wilderness-world where, in the roll of years, he is to lay deep the foundation-stones of an empire for Him whose kingdom is to last to the end of the ages.

CHAPTER X.

Having spent six years of his maturing youth as a soldier, and having become tired of the perils and hardships of a frontier camp-life, Potter armed and equipped seven men besides himself, at his own expense, to escort and guard him to West Texas, the then nearest point of civilized life. After a dangerous journey through a trackless wilderness, they reached San Antonio in the year 1852. On arriving at San Antonio, our hero was a model of iron-sinewed young manhood. Having just passed six years in camp-life on the high and healthy plateaus of New Mexico and Arizona, he was the impersonation of good health, but, to use his own phrase, "a moral wreck." He said himself that he found he was not fit for civilized society. He could read a little, but could not write his name. Having practiced nothing in all his past life but sporting, fighting, gambling, and drinking, and having heard nothing but the rough and blasphemous language of soldier-circles, he clearly saw the wide space between intelligent society and the rude state of barbarism. He said that the intellectual refinement of San Antonio was much in advance of his anticipations, and its manifest superiority and his semi-barbarous habits quite dispirited his ambition, and weakened his hopes of attaining an equality with the American element of that polite city of the West. He consequently returned to his habits of gambling and drinking, and soon grew worse instead of better under the shadow of great cathedrals and the domes of mammoth churches—for the bar-room and the gaming-saloon were in close contiguity to those proud temples of a pageant-robed gospel. Satan ever plants his altars of ruin where God's saving temples are erected, as sure as the thorn is near to the rose. It is an easy matter for sinful men to resist the good impulses given them by gracious influences. The Divine Spirit no doubt awakened the long stagnated better elements of young Potter's nature. Tired and sickened out with *quasi* savage life, the hunger and craving for better food was readily stimulated into being, and the oppressed factors of a higher nature moved the will to choose a purer life, and those divinely awakened impulsions resulted in his determination to migrate to Texas, the scene of his future strifes and triumphs. No doubt his arrival at San Antonio would have been the dawn of a reformatory day with him—the beginning of a new era in his history—had he but yielded to the desires enkindled by the Spirit of God for associations of a higher, a purer grade. Just there was the pivot on which turned several more years of sin and deeper degradation. Great door-shutters turn round on the bolts of small hinges; so on the fine pivot of the WILL turns the *character*, the *destiny*. Right here Andrew Potter snapped the tender ligaments of divine guidance and restraint, and yielded himself to the baser propensities of a depraved heart and the tempting allurements of an outside evil world. With all the aids to a virtuous life in this refined age, society furnishes the temptations and provides the means to lead astray and ruin her unsuspecting children. When our young hero entered the thronged streets of San Antonio as a pilgrim, seeking a city of peace and delight, had there been naught but schools and churches—no well-trod paths or smooth-paved ways to the haunts of vice, no bar-rooms, no gaming-houses, no temptations on her sidewalks—then he had begun to rise on the upward instead of descending on the downward grade. Finding all these paths to a sinful life open and firmly paved, and daily thronged by gay, silly thousands, he readily fell into the tide of their influence and drifted rapidly into the dark vortex, where the garbage and slum of polluted men meet and mingle in hellish glee in the gloomy-screened dens of whisky and rum. Jonah ran off to the uninhabited seas when God called him to go to Nineveh and preach its doom, but young Potter declined into the seas of iniquity. How long a period of time may have elapsed between Jonah's flight to a sea-faring life and his obedient return to the discharge of his divine call is not stated, but our young man remained four dismal years in the deepening sinks of vice. The plain of sin leads into ever-increasing gloom, as inclined grades reach into lower and still lower vales. He had just escaped the perils of wild beasts in the mountain forests, the perils of robbers on the lonely plains, the dangers of roving Indian bands;

but now he is captured by the deadly foes mingled with the grades of civilized life, when in a dark moment despair of reform seemed to spread its sable veil over his hopes. How strong the attractions of sin! It is the spirit of the power in the air that now worketh in the children of disobedience, or in disobedient children.

If the Federal, the State, and the municipal governments would remove temptations from the youthful path—close all bar-rooms, demolish gambling-saloons, obliterate all race-courses, and establish orphan and stranger's homes, schools and asylums, in their stead, then would the car of progress mount a higher plane. Many thousands of promising young men, nobly gifted by nature, and even learned and polished by art and grace—the proudest hopes of paternal love—are attracted by the fascinating glare of those palatial dens of moral demons just when their life's destiny is on the pivot on which it closes or opens to the incentives of virtue; they turn from the door of virtue and enter that of sin, to come out no more. Whether young Potter had any clear ideas of a higher sphere of associations for himself than this world's, or even confused notions of such a thing, when he first reached the city of San Antonio, is not clear to our mind; but it is evident to us that a benign Providence steadily followed him, as it did Jonah, in all his self-chosen retreats into sin, managing and guiding wisely to the gate of reformation without violently forcing the free action of his will.

The noble gifts with which nature had endowed

him were not to be lost forever to virtue's fame, as the luster of the gems which the dark unfathomed caves of ocean bear, or the sweet perfumes of flowers born to blush unseen, and waste their sweetness on the desert-air. Grace will yet unveil the sparkles of the one, and fill the Church with the odors of the other. His uncultivated intellect, strong in native capacities; his undaunted bravery; his unfeigned heart-tenderness for the helpless; his strong dislike to cowardice and cruelty, all make a good foundation, on which grace has erected a noble character. True Christian courage and a heart to melt at sight of human woe are two grand elements in the character of a soldier of the cross.

CHAPTER XI.

Leaving San Antonio in the year 1852, Mr. Potter visited a brother who lived near the head of York's Creek, in Hays county. Here he had a long and severe spell of typhoid fever. At one juncture of the disease he thought he might die, and called for a Testament, that he might try to read something about the future state of man to which he thought he might soon have to go. Helpless man, how doth he seek light when nearing the gloom of the grave! On his recovery his medical bill amounted to sixty dollars, which rendered him insolvent, having spent about all his gains in equipping and paying his guard from Arizona to San Antonio. He told his doctors that they had guessed well at the value of his horse, but that they could not get him; he could not part with his last tried friend, but he would try to make the money and pay them. He went to driving an ox-team at fifteen dollars per month, hauling lumber from Bastrop county to San Marcos. He soon earned a good mule, which he gave to liquidate that claim, and then he was free. While staying at York's Creek, he went to hear a little Methodist preacher preach in that vicinity— Rev. I. G. John, now editor of the Texas *Christian Advocate*. The appearance of the little, youthful preacher, with his keen, penetrating black eyes, deeply impressed him for good, and the text was printed in capitals on his memory's page. It is legible there to-day: "Who is the wise man?" That day opened the door of religion to him. He never forgot it. It planted deep among the rubbish of his soul an undying regard for the young man ordained of God to call sinners to repentance, and a slight faith in that mercy which might be extended to him some time in the days to come. Ever after he would go to hear *his preacher* when an opportunity offered. In going to Bastrop after lumber, he made the acquaintance of, and on the twenty-fifth day of August, 1853, was married to, Miss Emily C. Guin, a native of Missouri. For awhile he labored to earn a living, but the clouds of adverse fortune hovered about his way. He gave way to desponding views, and began to fall back into his old horse-swapping, gambling, racing, and drinking. A foppish braggart of a land agent came riding up to the grocery, one evening, and proposed a horse-swap. He was dressed in style, with a large golden chain pending from his watch-pocket, and was riding a good horse. Mr. Potter had a splendid-looking horse, though it was permanently lame. The fine gentleman inquired, "Is there no chance for a trade?" There stood the crowd. Mr. Potter was dressed in cottonade trousers and hickory shirt. A man remarked, "That man there," pointing to Mr. Potter, "may trade with you." The land agent looked at Mr. Potter, and said, "I can cheat him out of his boots." Mr. Potter told him his horse was in no trading plight; that in running him over rocks after cattle, the day before, he lamed him a little, though he would be all right in a few days. The men standing by indorsed the story, and the trade was made. The man being a little doubtful, said to Mr. Potter, "Now, if there should be any thing wrong about this horse, where shall I find you?" Mr. Potter replied, "You will find me at this grocery; I office in there." Sure enough, the braggart found out the fraud, and returned for a rue. But no; he had ensnared himself that time by his own folly. Mr. Potter refused to exchange. The stranger tried to frighten him into terms; in that he had found the wrong man—Mr. Potter was incapable of fear. He calmly said to the rich stranger (for he was a rich man), "I have kept that horse hitched up here day after day for just such a case as yourself, and you came along, and unsolicited bit at the bait, and now you are caught." He began to grow furious, when Mr. Potter said, "Hold on! don't say any more; you have said enough." Those quiet words, full of meaning, calmed the rising storm. The defeated man went off, but returned next day. Entering the grocery, he did not speak to Mr. Potter (who was in the room) until after looking around awhile, when he said: "Mr. Potter, come up and drink. You have traded me out of my horse, but it was my fault, and I am able to stand it, and there is no use to fuss about it. Come up and drink with me." So there they buried their rising difficulty in the fumes of the destroying poison.

Not long after settling in Bastrop county, Potter

found out that his favorite little preacher lived within four miles of him, and was going to preach not far from his home. He went to hear him, and ever after, when Mr. John was to fill the pulpit, he would deny himself a Sunday horse-race to hear him preach. He seemed to have no regard for the pulpit ministrations of any other man; the germ of that first sermon he heard on York's Creek remained in his heart, ever vegetating and threatening to crack the surface-soil; but he continued to overlay it with new sinful deeds, until that great revival at Croft's Prairie, where he was converted.

When his strongest partner in vice (Smithwick) joined the Church, his mighty, sinful fabric felt the shock, as some great building is shaken when its principal girders give way. He went to the meeting, some ten miles, though with no good intentions. There the archers hit him, and he got Smithwick to walk away in solitude with him to tell him all about religion. One was happy, the other was grief-smitten. He had undoubted confidence in his deserted, happy friend, and when they were alone, where none but God and angel-bands could see or hear, he said to him: "If you will say to me upon the honor of your soul that there is a reality in this religion, I will seek for it." Smithwick said to him it was true, and urged him to begin at once to seek as others had done who were then happy. He resolved to do that, but said he must first return home after his wife. Smithwick feared if he went home he would not return; but no, the arrow was in his soul. While at home he had a trial: the horse which his wife was to ride could not be readily found. She asked him if he was ready. He replied no, adding that he could not find the d——d horses. "There now!" she said, "you have lost all your religion." Deeply mortified, he replied, "It shall be the last." Sure enough, it was the last word in his profane vocabulary. His wife returned with him to the meeting, and joined the Church with him, as will be seen in another chapter.

While he was standing under the conscience-storming appeals of Mr. John's sermon, as seen elsewhere, a Baptist gentleman by the name of Lieu Holbert approached him and invited him to the altar, and just then Smithwick came up and insisted on his going, but the poor sinner was chained to the earth; he could not move. He said to his friends, "I cannot go." He was then assisted to the altar—a wounded, crippled soldier of sin. But now he forever deserts his old master. Mr. Holbert was much delighted and greatly rejoiced to see the chief, the captain-general of vice in the community won over to the Church. After Mr. Potter embraced religion and joined the church, Mr. Holbert said to him: "Now I can invite you to my house; the latch-string is now always outside for you. Come, and you are welcome. Heretofore, such were your habits and your associations, I could not invite you to my house. Now you are more than welcome." Mr. Holbert was a politician, and Mr. Potter had been his advocate and supporter among his grocery associates. Mr. Holbert used to say to him in his campaign: "Mr. Potter, I cannot treat, but here is some money; buy melons for my friends"—which he did. Years after, Mr. Holbert moved to Washington county, and when Mr. Potter had become a traveling preacher he called to pass the night with his old Baptist friend and brother in Christ. It occurred on this wise: he had made a hard day's ride to reach the house of a Methodist preacher, and got there at evening twilight, intending to remain all night. After the usual greetings, the good brother said: " Brother Potter, I reckon you will have to stay all night; but the old woman is not well, and I suppose you and I can do the cooking," etc. That was enough for Mr. Potter. He said: " I will *not have* to stay; it is about four miles to Brother Holbert's, and though fatigued, I shall go there." The brother saw that he had made out a clear unwelcome to the itinerant's mind, and said, "Brother Potter, don't leave my house that way." It was too late; his decree was not to be repealed. He found a cheering welcome at the plentiful home of Mr. Holbert, and next morning, when the parting greetings were said, he laid in the good-by hand some material aid to the messenger of Christ.

In the case of that Baptist brother there is a Christian example worthy of imitation by the communicants of all Churches. He rejoiced to see sinners won to Christ, even though they were not immersed as taught in the ritual of his own denomination, and ever made good men feel a hearty welcome to his private hospitalities.

There is one circumstance in the foregoing narrative of Mr. Potter's horse-trade with that boastful stranger that wears a shade of wrong, which, as a Christian moralist, we cannot pass by with silent approval, lest we might lead our young readers astray in the line of *morals—duty*. The great custom of exchange in commerce is morally legitimate within certain limits. The exchange of a horse is as proper as that of any commodity within the sphere of trade. A horse in the common market may be valued at one hundred dollars, but another valued at seventy-five dollars may suit my special circumstances better than the first one. In that case, a fair change of property is proper if both parties are agreed, and there is no art of deception employed in the transaction. But to resort to any efforts of deception is fraudulent and criminal. Trading for gain is quite alluring to the young mind, but let not our youthful readers be led away into the mazes of deceptive arts, to make a gainful trade in any thing. A life unspotted from the cradle to the grave is a gem which the roll of eternal ages can never dim. An illumined path, along which no cloud spreads a shadow, leads to endless day. That which unregenerate Potter did with sinful glee is now spurned by Christian Potter with pure disdain, and, though the blood of the atoning Lamb has washed all its guilty stains away, yet if he could, Mr. Potter would gladly undo the evils of his life, and remove their shadows from memory's retrospective path. Young reader, how sweet the thought to memory's taste that you have done no harm in the world, injured no one, caused the falling of no tear, made no heart feel a pang! But if you sin you can never taste that nectar-drop. Sin imbitters the sweets of life, and hangs a dismal gloom between the cradle and the grave. Set out in the career of life, dear young reader, with this motto upon your banner: "I shall aim cautiously to do no harm to my race." Determine that the world shall not be worse because you have lived in it, but strive to make it better. Be positive; do good; then shall your conscience approve, and God and angels will love and bless you.

CHAPTER XII.

The community of which Mr. Potter has spoken in another chapter as being so wicked was on Alum Creek, in Bastrop county, and the place of preaching was in Croft's Prairie. There was scarcely a religious organization there; the old Hard-shell Baptists preached there once a month, and had some members there, and the Methodists claimed a few. Old Brother Leed Rector was class-leader and steward, but was a leader almost without a class. He and old Aunt Cilla (an ancient colored sister) would meet, sing and pray, and rejoice. Brother Rector was a man of stern integrity, a precious good man, and Mr. Potter had a great regard for him, and always greeted him politely when they met, but when he was intoxicated would hide behind the grocery door-shutters when Mr. Rector was passing by. Having sold some pine-timber to a man who owned a saw-mill, reserving the small trees in the bargain, Mr. Rector learned that the man was violating the contract by cutting the exempted timbers, and sent him word not to trespass on the reserved timber. The man said if old man Rector came up there fooling with him he would horse-whip him. That ugly reply very much upset good old class-leader Rector's better nature; he was in a muddle—a quandary. What now could he do? He was being imposed on; the reckless man was slaying his young pine-trees in violation of a plain stipulation, and was going to chastise his old frame if he went up there to talk about it—enough, indeed, to stir up the old Adam in him, if he had any left to be raised up; and besides, he was class-leader, and must not fight; and it was too much to be "cow-hided" in one's old age, on one's own premises, and about one's own rights. Truly, it must have been a puzzle to the veteran churchman. But he ferreted it out at last, and laid his plans for help. He knew Mr. Potter; so he mounts his old Conestoga and rides down to the grocery, where Mr. Potter spent most of his time. To the grocery? Yes, he rode to the *grocery* for help. He hails; Mr. Potter, as usual, steps behind the screen to hide from the old man. He inquires, "Is Mr. Potter here?" "He is," was answered. Yea, he is here; no chance to dodge now. Mr. Potter steps out—"Here I am, Mr. Rector." Then the white-headed sire made known the object of his visit to the grog-shop, saying, "Mr. Potter, I do not want to get you into a difficulty, but I want to ask a favor of you. There is a man trespassing on my rights, and he threatens to horse-whip me if I go up there to contend for them. I am an old man to take such a drubbing, and I thought I would ask you to ride up there with me, and see it well done." Mr. Potter politely replied, "Certainly, Mr. Rector, I will go with you." Accordingly they rode up there, and found the man literally slaying the forbidden timber. Mr. Rector told him he was violating his contract, and that he had come up to take that horse-whipping, and had brought Mr. Potter with him to see it well done. Mr. Potter then said to the trespasser that as to the timber he and Mr. Rector could settle that, but as to the drubbing the old gentleman was to take, he had come to take that, and Mr. Rector might stand aside; he should manage that part of the settlement himself. The gentleman, knowing Mr. Potter, knew that meant "business." That was enough—he came to terms at once, saying he would pay for what he had cut, and would cut no more. That saved the old man's epidermis. Returning, by way of remuneration the old gentleman gave Mr. Potter a good moral lecture. It was not the intention of Mr. Rector, as he truly said, to get Mr. Potter into a fight, or to get him to chastise the trespasser on his rights; but knowing Mr. Potter himself, and knowing that the offender knew him too, he took that course to prevent a conflict; for, indeed, he well understood the power of Potter's name to quell all such ripening strife—all beasts of the forest slink away in fear at the approach of the lion. Among the many redeeming traits in the character of Mr. Potter, in his worst days, is that he never made an attack on an innocent man—never was aggressive on the unoffending. His conflicts have ever been with the trespassing, the hurtful. The terror of his name has been a prophylactic against evil deeds.

As time rolled on, bearing its busy millions along in the crowded marts of trade, lowering one here and elevating another there, our dissipated hero grew no better, but under the sure law of retrogression he passed from bad to worse down sin's widening road, and there seemed little hope of a future reformation from his long course of evil habits. The grocery, the gaming-table, and the turf, consumed nearly all of his waking hours. Day after day he was there, mingling with the slum of grog-shop life. The blasphemous squad, the drunken sots, and the gaming sharpers, were his constant whisky-house associates. Among them he was as king, and with that medley of humanity he was in frequent rows and fights, which often brought him before the mayor's court in the town of Bastrop, where frequent fines and costs ate up his trading and gambling gains. These are the petty courts referred to in the Rev. Mr. Harris's letter, in another chapter of this book. The low state of his finances led him to devise the vocal concert, as narrated below, to replenish his wasted funds. Here we extract from Mr. Potter's papers, and let him tell the reader his own story of that farcical affair:

"The circumstances giving rise to the concert in Bastrop, under the name of 'Signor Blitz,' were as follows: Almost every time I went to town I was invited over to the mayor's office, charged with violating some corporation law. The mayor, Judge O'Connor, was a good-hearted man, and generally let me off with a moderate fine. On a certain occasion the city marshal got a writ for me, in which I was charged with riding on the sidewalks, and creating a noise on the streets. I told him he had better deputize some gentlemen to arrest me—that if he undertook it, I should hurt him; but he persisted, and I struck him down, knocking out two of his teeth. I then told them all 'to hands off;' that if they would let me alone I would go to the mayor's office and pay my fines, which I did, being followed by quite a large crowd. I walked in, and told the mayor I supposed I was in his debt some, and was ready to settle. He said I was charged with two offenses, and that he would fix the fines at five dollars and costs in each case, and I paid off the bill. It was Saturday evening, and I managed to dodge out of town before they could arrest me for striking the marshal. I went back to town the next morning, knowing they would not disturb me on Sunday. I saw the mayor, and told him I would come in, plead guilty, and submit the case to him. So I went, according to promise. I tried to slip in along a backway, to prevent attracting attention and gathering a crowd about the mayor's office, but I was discovered, and quite a number rushed into the room. I addressed the mayor, saying I had come for another settlement, and telling him I had been a good customer, and thought he should let me off as lightly as possible, when he said: 'Andy, I have sent on for your land-warrant for your services in the Mexican war; I think it will be on in a few days.' I said: 'Contrive the Mexican war! it is this miserable corporation war that is bothering me now; I want to know what I owe you.' He replied: 'Andy, you know that it is a very serious matter to strike an officer when in the discharge of his duty.' 'If your Honor please, I do n't know any thing about that; I only want to know what I am going to have to pay.' 'Well, Andy, I have considered this case in the light of all the facts, and I have come to the conclusion to impose a fine on you to the amount—' (and here he paused). 'To the amount of what? if your Honor please,' said I; 'I am getting very anxious to get through with this settlement.' 'Well, Andy,' he then replied, 'there are a combination of circumstances connected with this anomalous affair; and, as mayor of this city, it is my duty to see that the laws are duly executed in the name of God and liberty and municipal authority.' Here he assumed an unusual amount of gravity, and said, 'I fine you five dollars, and no costs.' I instantly drew out the money, and said, 'Sir, we can trade; here it is.' That decision brought down the house, and the farce ended with a hearty laugh.

"These oft-repeated fines began to weaken my finances, and I had to put my wits to work to get my money back. It occurred to me that I might humbug the town with a concert. Knowing that I would have to assume some big name, I selected that of 'Signor Blitz.' I learned afterward that Blitz was not a vocalist, but a necromancer, or sleight-of-hand performer; but the citizens seemed not to know any better than myself. I made out the following programme: 'Signor Blitz, from the London and New York theaters, respectfully informs the citizens of this place that he will give one of his celebrated entertainments at the court-house, at early candle-lighting, on next Saturday night, to which the public are respectfully invited. The extraordinary vocal powers of Signor Blitz has been the theme of universal commendation throughout the North, and in Havana, as well as in Europe, where his concerts have been honored with the presence of royalty and nobility. He bears about his person a medal, presented to him by Her Britannic Majesty, Queen Victoria, at a private concert which he gave at Windsor Palace. The whole is to conclude with a laughable and stirring piece. Admittance fees: for grown persons, one dollar; for man and wife, one dollar and fifty cents; for children and servants, half price. Front seats reserved for the ladies.'

"I went to the printer with my programme, and let him into the secret, engaging him to print all the hand-bills I wanted, including a long list of songs, for seven dollars. I got every thing ready by Friday night, Saturday night being the time set for the great concert, as there was to be a horse-race in town on that day, and I knew I would catch a large crowd. So on Friday night, after every thing was quiet, I slipped stealthily around and tacked up my hand-bills all over town, on the doors, and posts, and fences. I then rode out, and scattered them along the roads leading into town. Next morning the first thing that attracted attention was the bills announcing the grand vocal concert at night. I was much amused during the day at hearing the discussions about the grand things they were to witness that night. I had to employ a door-keeper, and divulge my plans to him. Near sunset I began to prepare for the splendid farce. My door keeper procured me an old-fashioned 'claw-hammer' coat, a pair of tight-fitting trousers, and an old cap, and then blacked my face. In this garb I entered an office in the court-house. My porter lighted up, and the anxious crowd began to assemble, and soon filled the house, and began to stamp the floor for me to come out. I thought I had better have the thing over, so I walked out and began to sing a negro-minstrel song. I did not know but that I might have to fight out of the scrape, so I had armed myself with a revolver and a bowie-knife. No one recognized me, but a certain doctor advanced with his pistol, and said, 'I want to know who you are.' I put my hand on my revolver, and told him to take his seat, and I would tell him who I was at a proper time. He obeyed me. I thought then that I had carried the joke far enough, and proceeded to say: 'Ladies and gentlemen, inasmuch as Signor Blitz has failed to attend, I thought I would give you the best entertainment I could. I am simply A. J. Potter. I think I am now about even with this corporation.' Then they laughed, roared, and stamped, as if they would tear down the house. They took me off to the bar-room, and made me sing until one o'clock; then they took soap and water and washed the blacking from my face, and reclothed me. So the thing ended.

"Several years ago, at the session of our Annual Conference at Gonzales, I had the pleasure of meeting my old mayor, Judge O'Connor, who now resides near that city. I was in the post-office, and a gentleman stepped in and, looking me in the face, said, 'Mr. Potter, you have gone back on me; you do not seem to know me.' 'Sir, if I am not mistaken, I was brought before your Honor often enough when you was mayor of Bastrop to remember you now. This is Judge O'Connor, is it not?' The usual greetings then passed between us. The judge is a noble man, and one of my life-long friends. He carried me in his buggy to supper at his neat home some two miles from the pretty little city of Gonzales."

That remarkable "take-off" of a farcical concert was truly a bold and hazardous enterprise with the citizens of a corporate city, but it only marks out the fearless daring and large stock of native humor of the man, and of his strange, natural power over men. It also gives us a little insight into the condition of early Texan society, and its extreme fondness for sport, fun, and almost any kind of amusement. A merry, jolly life is characteristic of native Texans. Feasting, dancing, shows, and all kinds of theatrical exhibitions, will attract a crowd even now in almost all the dense settlements, and at that early day no doubt such things were more popular. Mr. Potter struck the right vibrating chord when he devised the plan of his great concert to draw a crowd. The race-turf, too, held a prominent place among the sports of that day; and it is even so yet in many places where a higher moral element has not grass-sodded the old beaten race-paths. Their exquisite taste for joke and fun led them to cheerfully give up their dollar door-fee, to be repaid in a number of funny songs at the bar-room, all of which were richly spiced, no doubt, with a good supply of the cheerful stimulants of the bar.

There must have been too a mingled fear and a sort of respect for the man, in the minds of all men who knew him. Anybody but the wonderful Potter would have been arrested or miserably abused by the crowd of citizens that Saturday night. There were brave men there, but he was known to be the bravest of the brave, king of valor. He never sought to evade the penalties of law by precipitous flight. He ever tried to cheapen his fines to as low a rate as possible, to lengthen out his finances as far as might be done, and he generally succeeded in his efforts.

Mr. Potter must have entertained some unkind feelings for the city marshal, which caused him to refuse to submit to an arrest by him, and led him to strike him to the earth when he persisted in the forbidden job. The marshal must have been an unpopular officer, or the fine for striking him would have exceeded the little sum of five dollars and "no costs." It never entered Mr. Potter's plans to commit any crime of a high grade against law, and yet his manner of life and the class of his daily associates endangered his life almost every day, or might have imposed upon him the necessity of taking some one's to save his own; but in all his drunken or sober affrays, nothing more serious than painful knock-downs occurred. But let not the young reader in the least think his example in these things worthy of imitation; neither the shrewd plan nor the humorous playfulness of the scene comports with pure morals. There is a rebound to ocean's wild wave, and Mr. Potter was nearing the end of a long, sinful career—a rebound into a new and better life.

"I once lived neighbor to an old German who was in the habit of whipping his wife. He would beat her with a club, as one would an ox. One cold afternoon, my wife told me that she had seen old Mrs. P. going in the direction of a neighbor's house, all bruised and bleeding, and said that her old man had been beating her with a club. There was a fearful norther blowing, and it was very cold. I said to my wife that I would go over and see if I could settle the difficulty. It was getting dark when I reached the place. I found the old woman sitting by a fodder-stack, crying and sobbing most piteously, and shivering with cold; the cruel old man had the door barred, and would not allow her to enter. She could speak but very little English. I approached her and asked, 'Won't the old man let you in?' She answered, 'No, no; nein.' I said to her, 'Come on, I'll see that you get in.' On reaching the door, I knocked, and said, 'Let us in.' He muttered out something which I understood to be a refusal, so the door being made of clapboards and hung on wooden hinges, I soon burst it open. The old cruel wretch was sitting near the fire, and having a rock in my hand which I had picked up in the yard, I threw it at him, striking him in the back of his head and knocking him into the fire. I instantly sprang, and jerked him out of the fire, laid him on the floor, straddled him, and said, 'Whip vrow, no good.' He screamed manfully, and the old lady began to pull me away from him, and I left them to finish their troubles alone. The old lady said that her man was not conscious until about midnight; that she poured water and vinegar on his head all night. When he got able to walk, he went to a justice of the peace and made complaint against me. He said: 'Dot Botter beesh von bat man; he kums on mine house, und sthrike me on der cope mit a sthone, und I'll ish bleed. Me no vash tink of mine goon ober der door, or Ish moken shoot mit him.' The magistrate, knowing that he had abused his wife, led him out to a pile of clapboards near the door, and said: 'Now, sir, if you do n't go home and behave yourself, I will take one of these boards, and wear it out on you; and if ever I hear of your whipping your wife again, I will get Potter, and come over and hang you to a limb.' I never heard of his mistreating her any more while I remained in the community."

The pill was a bitter one, but it was effectual in breaking up the disease; but inveterate evils require severe remedies. Mr. Potter, as a semi-official, usually conquered a peace. The last discharge from his battery silenced all opposing ones, and peacefulness was enthroned again. His serious chastising methods resulted in such memorable victories that they ended all future strifes. Their final benefits to society in a sense deprived them of guilt, and elicited tacit public approval. By the infliction of private pains and penalties on evil-doers, he became a sort of public benefactor, to whom society sometimes felt itself no little indebted for his encountering and subduing the cruel and the lawless; for in many instances no legal means were used to prevent or suppress misdemeanors, or higher grades of crime.

CHAPTER XIII.

It will be seen in this chapter that Mr. Potter was enlisted in the grand cause of Christianity in the year 1856, at the great camp-meeting in Bastrop county, which lasted nearly if not quite a month, mainly by the united labors of the Rev. Charles Thomas, who was in charge, and the Rev. I. G. John, now editor of the Texas *Christian Advocate*. Here we shall take our seat, and let Mr. Potter hold a love-feast or a class-meeting with the reader, by telling his own striking experience:

"We are commanded to give a reason for the hope that is within us; and when the great Apostle of the Gentiles told his experience, Felix trembled, and King Agrippa said, 'Almost thou persuadest me to be a Christian.' As my conversion to Christianity is a marvel to some who knew my former life of wickedness, and almost a wonder to myself, I shall briefly state my own view of the matter, and some of the connecting circumstances my arrest in the path of great wickedness. In-1, I was a moral wreck, and my case seemed ›st hopeless. But as I had never had any mortraints thrown around me from early boyhood, aving had even the benefits of good society; · heard but little preaching; having never read ᷄ chapter in the Bible—in fact, could scarcely read at all, and could not write my own name; having never seen a Sunday-school; I had imbibed no religious theory, had formed no creed; neither had I entertained any infidel notions, nor was I gospel-hardened. I only knew that I was a wicked sinner, and that it was nobody's business but my own, thinking that no one had any right to interfere or meddle with my affairs. So it is seen that I had much to learn, and a long way to travel to get into the Church. I was converted, or born again, at the great camp-meeting in Bastrop county, in the year 1856. The community was one of the worst I ever saw. For many years the gospel had struggled to reform the people with but little success. Perhaps I was the ringleader in sin. On the Sabbath-day, large crowds under my leading would assemble at the grocery, and drink, get drunk, blaspheme, fight, gamble, and horse-race. A young man by the name of Smithwick and I seemed to have an affinity for each other, and went, as it were, arm in arm in the deepest iniquity, and never forsook each other in the most trying perils with desperate men. Having just escaped a bloody affray with a dozen or more of them against us two alone, Smithwick said to me: 'Potter, you and I have well-nigh run our race; it is time to stop; I am going to reform.' These words struck with great power on my hard heart. He was the best friend I had. He went to the camp-meeting, was converted, and united with the Church. Here I had lost a strong brace in sin. The camp-meeting went on, and finally I went, with no good purpose. I learned, to my great indig-

nation, that quite a number of my old comrades in
vice had been what they called 'converted,' and
others were at the altar as seekers. I drew near
the scene of action to try to put an end to such
foolishness, and rescue some of my deserted associates.
Although I could curse and swear on an
equality with the worst of men on ordinary occasions,
I did not feel at that time that I had a sufficient
magazine of blasphemy on hand to do justice
to the subject. I was truly outraged. Like
Goliath of Gath, I had gone there full of heaven-defying
wickedness in my poor heart, to defy the
hosts of God's conquering Israel, but I soon suffered
a similar defeat. Although I knew little of preachers,
and cared less, yet I had formed a favorable
opinion of Mr. John, and felt great respect for him,
as he was ever polite and kind to me. I had frequently
denied myself of a Sunday spree to hear
him preach, but on this occasion he seemed to
preach with greater power than ever before; and
when I reached the arbor, he was in the stand,
preaching with great pathos. I stood at the outskirts
of a large assembly, and he seemed to fix his
keen, black, penetrating eyes on me, and his shrill
voice fell like thunder-peals of warning on my ears,
such as I had never heard before. Peal after peal,
as the roaring surf telling of distant storms, startled
my guilty soul, while bitter remembrances and tormenting
fears came over me. I had been in many
a close place of alarming dangers, meeting in deadly
contest overpowering numbers of daring savages,
their arrows flying, their uplifted lances gleam-

ing in the sunlight a moment, then piercing the heart of a comrade by my side; I had seen them fall, bleeding, dying, and dead; I had heard their groans and piteous wails in the dying strife, while my heart was nerved with bitter hate and cruel revenge; but now I was standing in the thickest range of JEHOVAH's divinely-hurled arrows. My heart was pierced by the cold iron of sacred truth. About me Israel's valiant hosts, all clad in the panoply of heaven, stood in bright array. As one deserted of his friends, I seemed alone, disarmed and helpless, like unto the solitary oak in the old field, barkless and limbless, peeled by the scathing lightning constantly streaming from the wrathful heavens, while the earnest preacher poured on my naked heart the divinely-fired truth. He showed that the wise man should look well to the foundation on which he builded. I felt my foundation giving way. He pointed out the wise ship-master, who would not venture upon storm-troubled seas, where mad waves rolled high in the path of tempest-winds, without first inspecting every part of his vessel—see if the hull were sound, if the machinery were in order, if the sails were in place, and all the crew were at their posts. I felt that the bottom of my craft was rotten, and no soundness in any part; that there was no safety in such a voyage. Eternity's boundless ocean was near, and on its dangerous bosom I must venture, but my vessel would go under. Dives in his tormenting flames could not have suffered much greater agonies of soul than rent my troubled mind. The guilt of a miserable life lay all its ponderous weight upon my writhing conscience. There I stood, as if chained to the earth, a mass of spiritual ignorance and guilt. But soon I felt the iron fetters of my heart begin to loosen their clasp upon me. My old hardness of heart began to relent, and unbidden tears flowed down, as if a mountain of snow had dissolved within me. There I stood still, a weeping prisoner of a thousand tears. The sermon ended, and mourners were invited to the altar; and while a lively song was being sung, the altar was thronged with pleading penitents; and now and then one would arise and praise God for his redeeming grace, which sounded to my soul as a death-knell on a starless night. Some of my old associates in crime were singing, others were shouting, and some talking to mourners. Truly did I feel forsaken in a dreary world. My soul seemed pierced with the grief of ages in a single moment. I tried to throw off my convictions. My old pride came upon me, and made a brave struggle to disentangle my feelings. I strove to conceal my convictions, but my efforts were fruitless. I then determined to leave the meeting, but I could not get away. My wounds were too deep to heal. Next morning an experience-meeting was held, and all the young converts were requested to speak. As one after another arose and told how the love of God had been shed abroad in their hearts, their experience made a powerful impression on me. A simple statement of babes in Christ greatly impresses the mind.

Some of my most intimate friends ventured to

speak to me about my soul's salvation. I treated their advice with respect. I lingered about the meeting three days, and my condition increased in intense sorrow. In the afternoon Mr. John made another fearful attack on the sinful, which compelled me to a full surrender, and by the aid of two good men I was enabled to reach the altar, all melted into penitent tears. I truly 'cried' unto the Lord for mercy till the close of the hour's service, when an invitation was given to join the Church. I was asked to unite with the Church, which I refused to do, on the grounds of my ignorance of Church matters, and of my former abandoned course of wickedness, lest I might relapse into sin and disgrace myself and the Church. But I was told that it was a means of grace, and in the act of joining the Church I might be enabled to make a full surrender of myself to Christ, and receive the blessing of pardoning grace. I revolved the subject in my mind, and resolved to join the Church, and reform my life, and do all and whatever God might require of me; and I arose and gave the preacher my trembling hand, and just then heaven seemed to open and pour its treasures of bliss into my willing heart. 'My joys were immortal.' An angel's tongue might tell love's wondrous story, but mine could not. As a love-inspired poet said:

> Tongue cannot express the sweet comfort and peace,
>   Of a soul in its earliest love.
> That comfort was mine when the favor divine
>   I first felt in the blood of the Lamb.
> He hath loved me, I cried, he hath suffered and died
>   To redeem a poor rebel like me.

"It seemed to me that every faculty of my soul had a voice, and each shouted, 'Glory to God!' Heavenly inspirations fell upon me, and enkindled divine thoughts and fancies, and sweet hopes and thrilling joys, in my new-born heart. My whole being was pervaded with heavenly power, so that I had no control of myself. O, I shouted and praised God, in the full volume of a strong and love-imbued voice! Blessed old arbor! 'Thou dear, honored spot; the fame of thy wonder shall ne'er be forgot.' O while I write, my heart burns under the warm enkindlings of 'sweet memories of thee.' The joys of by-gone years rise up and enter the citadel of the soul, and I must sing the befitting old song:

>Amazing grace! (how sweet the sound!)
> That saved a wretch like me!
>I once was lost, but now I'm found,
> Was blind, but now I see.

"That good old song has lifted up my soul many a time when depressed by trials, and sufferings, and dangers, along this rugged world. I have made these wild mountain solitudes ring with its pathetic strains, when none but God and angels could hear its mellow cadences. So also have we in the mountain's lone, deep shades at night, far away from the home of man, sung the faith-inspiring hymn:

>Though like a wanderer,
> The sun gone down,
>Darkness be over me,
> My rest a stone;
>Yet in my dreams I'd be
>Nearer, my God, to thee,
> Nearer to thee!

And then:

> I love in solitude to shed
> The penitential tear;
> And all his promises to plead,
> When none but God can hear.

"Yes, in the lonely hours of night, with my head pillowed on a mountain stone, looking deep into the homes of the distant stars, I have sung those sweet notes of love when gentle angels seemed to smile upon me from every twinkling, glowing star in the great firmament.

"When I joined the Church I had all to learn. I could not write, and had never read but a few chapters in the Bible; but I felt that God loved all men as he loved me; as I was the chief of sinners, I could testify that much for Jesus. I put all on his altar, and was willing to do any thing, or go anywhere. I was appointed class-leader after having been in one class-meeting.

"When entering the itinerant ministry, I felt impressed with a sense of duty to offer myself for the frontier mission-field of West Texas, as my experience in border life and Indian warfare clearly pointed me out for that sphere; and for thirteen toilsome years I have borne witness for Jesus in all the towns and rural settlements from the Colorado to the Rio Grande rivers."

We have copied this long narration of Mr. Potter's religious experience from his own manuscript, with some verbal alterations to suit this volume, because of its great value to the Church, and also to men earnestly seeking reformation from a career of sin. And now we wish to offer some natural deductions therefrom. By it we are reminded of the incalculable value of the old camp-meeting battle-ground to the cause of Christ. Many of the ablest veterans in the Church were converted at the old camp-meeting altars. They used to call out a large class of men that never enter city steepled churches, or those in rural places—men who never hear the gospel anywhere else. When, like Israel in olden days, the Church leaves Egypt and camps in the wilderness, God spreads out his cloud of glory about it, and sinners coming there realize that it is holy ground, and saints are made strong like David in the might of God. Better for the Church, better for sinners in reach of gospel mercy, that in some form the old camp-altar be rebuilt. We are also taught the encouraging lesson to the earnest, faithful preacher, never to despair, as he cannot tell the result of his efforts to win sinners to the Divine Master, who has called him to the pulpit. He cannot tell when that Spirit, which is to be with the devoted preacher "to the end of the world," shall bear his message to listening sinners with power and convincing light. Truly our zealous reverend friends, Thomas and John, both of whom still live as faithful ministers of Christ, who held that month-long camp-meeting, when more than eighty sinners were enlisted in the cause of Christ—some, too, of the most fearful characters—have great cause of grateful joy at the great harvest of good being now gathered from their sowing of the good seed on that wonderful occasion. A

Potter and a Smithwick are sheaves from that sowing.

Smithwick we never knew, but know his character, his fame, as Potter's companion in sin; but when he was converted he soon began to preach, and was as zealous for his new Master as for his old one. "He led in the van of the host;" soon, however, "he fell as a soldier, but died at his post." We have often stood over his tomb among strangers, at Sandies Chapel, on Rancho Circuit of the West Texas Conference. We have stood by his silent grave, and thought of his zealous, brief ministerial career, and felt the warm emotions of that loving hope whispering so softly, We shall meet thee "over there, over there." But O what of more than eighty others who joined the living hosts on that day? Preacher, thank God and take courage for the coming battle-days. We may likewise say to the reader of these religious stories, if he still is a stranger to their blessed realities, if he is a sinner, and even a great one, even a chief among those unsaved, The remarkable experience of Mr. Potter lays down broad and firm grounds for hope. All manner of sin and blasphemy shall be forgiven men who properly seek it, save that one lone sin against the Holy Ghost. Gamaliel's literary son said that God showed mercy to him, the CHIEF of sinners, as a pattern of mercy to all great sinners, in all after-ages. Read Potter's life, and do as he did at that consecrated camp-ground; turn unto the Lord with full purpose of heart, consecrate all to him, and he will receive you.

Still another fact we are taught by his conversion and speedy call to the ministry: that God chooses his ministers from all spheres and stations in life. He chooses men suited to the fields they are to cultivate. The learned and the illiterate, the rich and the poor, the most degraded and the most highly elevated, are all to be preached to, and God selects the preacher. In ages gone by not a majority of the learned or great have been called. The majority of mankind are still of low and moderate grades, and God calls many from their ranks to fill the pulpit. He often chooses weak things to subdue the strong, and the illiterate to conquer the wise, that the vital, efficient cause of success may appear to be of God and not of men. But men thus chosen of God do not remain in a state of ignorance. As the roughest ashler taken from the native quarry is polished smoothly by the hand of the artist, so the Divine Artist instructs, refines, and elevates his ministers, to be equal to the duties in their allotted spheres. There is a divine qualification for each preacher, without which his ministry is a mere tinkling cymbal. That spiritual baptism, "that tongue of fire," that inward call, that holy anointing, that being "endued with power from on high," is of God, and is the key to success; it is the *indispensable*. When by it talent and learning are hallowed, it truly is the endowment of power from above; it moves the dry bones, and stirs up the dead sinner to consciousness, and imparts spiritual life to the Church. Anciently it gave the apostles power to speak languages they had never learned,

and with Mr. Potter it seemed almost refulfilled.
He could not write, and could barely read a little.
Soon he began to preach to sinful men the simple
story of the love of Jesus, who had so signally
saved him from the deepest pits of sin. He tells
us that his mind was divinely illumined; that a
holy unction, a divine power, was upon him; that
it gave him courage and zeal. It no doubt opened
the faculties of his understanding, stimulated his
thirst for learning, and excited zealous effort to
acquire that knowledge so essential to qualify him
for his future triumphs. Onward he steadily moved,
till honored by his brethren with the responsible
place of presiding elder in the Church of his choice.
Lastly, we are made to think of the *likeness* and the
contrast between this modern border preacher of
West Texas and the great Apostle of the Gentiles.
Saul of Tarsus was a learned, proud Pharisee—a
Jewish moralist; Mr. Potter was an unlearned,
wicked sinner, denizened with the slum and garbage of the world. Saul was a bigoted zealot, persecuting the Church of God—in Scripture phrase,
"he breathed out threatenings and slaughter, and
made havoc" of its members; Mr. Potter had no
religious creed, but drank, gambled, blasphemed,
and fought any one who might enrage his ire,
whether good or bad. Saul was arrested with great
spiritual power; so also was Mr. Potter. Saul was
converted in a little room on the street which is
called Straight, in the historic city of Damascus.
Mr. Potter was converted at a camp-meeting. Saul
joined the Church in that little room, and was bap-

tized by a lay Jewish convert, named Ananias; Mr. Potter was baptized by a Methodist preacher at a camp-meeting. Saul prayed and fasted three days and nights, in great trouble, before he was converted. Mr. Potter was several days in untold anguish of mind. Paul began to preach Jesus soon after his call; so did Mr. Potter. Paul planted Christianity in the domains of the pagan world; Mr. Potter planted it on the empired frontier of West Texas. Dear reader, are you a young minister, from a humble sphere? Care not for that; think of the heights others have attained from the depths below you. Consecrate your soul and body to Him who has called you to such distinguished honors. "Ask the Saviour to help you—he will carry you through; he will carry you through!" Inscribe on your banner Mr. Potter's motto: "I can, and, by the grace of Christ Jesus, I will be superior to my circumstances." Let not circumstances subdue your efforts, or in the least discourage your zeal for Christ. Learn how to abound, and how to be in want; how to be abased, and how to be exalted. No vale is so low that the heights above it cannot be reached by omnipotent faith—it is "the victory that overcometh the world." Aim high, and strive to reach the mark of your high calling of God, as a minister of his dear Son Jesus Christ.

Once when Mr. Potter was asked a reason for his great zeal for Christ, he answered: "Those who have much forgiven love much; as the poor cured maniac of Gadara, who had lived among the tombs, but being in his right mind by the side of Jesus, did not leave him, but wanted ever to be with him; in love for what Jesus had done for him in rescuing him from the dominion of Satan, and fearing if he got away from his Lord's presence his old enemy might overcome him again. Near to Jesus, the enemy must not harm you; at a distance, as Peter, he shall attack you. Near the cross, *divine light and power center and radiate;* beneath it, take your stand against all opposing forces, and ever sing in your heart, 'Closer and closer let me cleave to my Redeemer's side;' and *here* yours shall be the victor's song, but *there* it shall be the victor's *crown.*"

CHAPTER XIV.

"In the year 1857, the Rev. I. G. John was appointed to the Bastrop Circuit, and organized a small society on Pin-oak Creek, in a neighborhood about ten miles east of the Colorado River. He appointed me class-leader when my six months' probation had not expired, and I had never attended but one class-meeting. There had never been any preaching in that community until Brother John took it into the circuit that year. It was a heavy cross, but I took it up, and began by holding a prayer-meeting at a private house one night in each week. That was not only a new thing there because it was the first held in the community, but the newly converted Potter was going to hold it, and some of the people said, 'May be he is going to hold out, after all.' I never shall forget my feeling when I held that first prayer-meeting. I thought the people never would stop coming—men, women, and children—house full and yard full. I thought that a great many had come through mere curiosity. Only one man besides myself would lead in audible prayer. I began the service by reading a chapter and singing a hymn, and then tried to pray. After prayer I talked till I ran out of something to say; then I called on the other brother to pray, and then we sung again, and by the time we had prayed two or three times by turns things got into such a fix that I was at a loss to know what to do, and I began to think that the whole thing was a failure, and dismissed with a downcast heart. But I appointed class-meeting for the following Sunday, and on that day the gathering was large. I kept up prayer-meetings on Saturday nights, and class-meetings on Sundays. We had a glorious revival in that community that year, and many of the converts dated their conviction to that first prayer-meeting, which I thought to be such a great failure. Our members increased until that place became one of the best appointments on the circuit. Brother John did a noble work that year. He was succeeded by the Rev. J. W. B. Allen, who traveled the Bastrop Circuit in 1858 and 1859. I served as class-leader under him part of 1859. He often put me up to preach or exhort. He was a good and true man. He once appointed a protracted-meeting at Alum Creek, but when the time came he was sick, and could not attend; but we all met at the arbor on the appointed day, and consulted together, and concluded to carry on the meeting ourselves the best we could. Old Brother Rector, a class-leader, and old Moses Gage, a Primitive Baptist, who often spoke in public, and Lieu Holbert, a Missionary Baptist, a zealous man and able in prayer, and myself, a class-leader—these constituted all our available working-forces. It was agreed that I should take charge of the meeting, and fill the place of a preacher by exhorting, they agreeing to follow me in turns, and then we would have several prayers. So our meeting went on increasing in interest until Sunday night, when we had a general move—fifteen mourners at the altar. But some of the learned 'scribes' of the community concluded that it would never do for the Lord to carry on a meeting and bless people without a preacher, and they sent to Bastrop after Professor Connor to come and preach on Sunday. I said to Brother Rector, 'I am glad we are going to have a preacher;' but he said that he was sorry, adding that we had carried on the meeting, and the Lord had blessed us, and that he was afraid that a change would ruin the meeting; and so it really turned out. The preacher came and preached two fine sermons, and the meeting closed without a single penitent at the altar. I often attended revival-meetings, and was used to exhorting, and inviting the seekers to the altar. I frequently rejoiced with a full soul all aglow with love and peace. O the peaceful hours I then enjoyed! how sweet their memory still!"

How dear to us are the tender memories of gentle childhood, when we first begin to exercise our physical powers without the aid of others! So also are our fond recollections of our infancy in grace, when we begin to use our little stock of grace and strength in a public manner; when we begin to exercise our gifts in the sacred pulpit as an advocate of the religion of Jesus! As the unpracticed little man-boy sometimes topples and falls, so the juvenile preacher often staggers and tumbles into the valley of humiliation in his early years. Precious years! full of the deepest earnestness and a simple, overpowering zeal. No wonder the Holy Spirit does not refuse to be associated with such a child-like sincerity and honest concern for the souls of men. Childhood in grace is as innocent as the infant constituting a part of the kingdom of heaven. The apostolic Christians were simple, zealous people, and the preaching in that day, for the most part, was a plain, unpolished statement of gospel facts, imbued with the love and tears of a humble heart. God was in all; Jesus and the resurrection was the theme; art, science, and literature, were left to the world; but thoughts of Jesus and salvation burned in their minds and shone in their lives as the radiance of beauty; and more than eighteen hundred years thereafter we see the same earnest spirit in the hearts of a few good men, away in Texas, at a revival-meeting, without the aid of ministerial talent, carrying on the Master's work as Philip did at Samaria in the long-ago. Great, learned sermons are not the strongest and most efficient batteries of grace. The mind enlightened, and the heart unmoved, does not move sinners to penitence; it is that truth that passes through the mind into the inner heart that enlists the will in the interest of Jesus. More men are *impressed* with a sense of the truth of vital religion by its fruits as seen in the lives of their fellow-men than by the arts of logic or the charms of oratory. A new heart is the fountain of all genuine religion, and when we see the heart of our fellow moved into tears by its soul-stirring fires, the electric current passes into the secret resources of the soul, and we own its power to save. We think it not strange that God should own and make strong Mr. Potter and his simple-hearted band of humble men at that religious revival, for he "exalts the humble, but resists the proud." The two able sermons of the practiced preacher seemed not to have the companionship of the all-powerful Spirit—hence it moved no one, as zephyrs moving among the highest tips of the forest-trees never touch nor shake their roots. The young, uninformed minister sets out with fear and trembling with a single eye to tell of his dear Saviour's love. He is humble; he is in earnest; he puts his humility, his burning zeal, into all his poor efforts to win men to Christ; and God makes his feebleness strong, and he "waxes valiant in fight." As he advances in the labyrinth of knowledge, he grows more self-reliant, and begins to feel that he has a pulpit character to maintain by preaching great sermons; and the holy influences forsake him, and failure paints itself on the front of his pulpit.

"In the year 1859, I sold out in Bastrop county and purchased a place in Caldwell county, nine miles east of Lockhart, to which I moved the latter part of that year. Here I was licensed to preach, and began my ministry with great success. There was a fearful drought that year—the severest known in the history of Texas—and it was extremely difficult to get breadstuff, and horse-feed could not be had. One of my neighbors had some corn to spare, but he would not sell it for money. He said he was compelled to have some rails split, and it was doubtful about getting them made for money, but he knew he could get it done for corn, for people were obliged to have bread. That was my only chance; so I threw aside my coat, and took my ax, maul, and wedge, and went to work, and truly by the 'sweat of my face,' and the whole man, I got the pabulum of life for my family. Years have rolled away, and the old stumps are there, standing with their heads above ground, monuments of what the woodman's ax has done. Whenever I pass along that way, they recall to mind the many hard-aimed blows I dealt on their fallen forest-giants to get bread for self and dear ones. My poor horse failed for want of food, for the drought burned up the weeds and grass of woodland and prairie. After cutting and mauling through the week, I walked from seven to twelve miles on Sunday to fill my appointments; and God greatly blessed me, and I would rejoice in my work. I lived near neighbor to the Rev. J. G. Mabry, of the Methodist Protestant Church. He was a holy, good man. He has gone to his reward, and no doubt is in 'the better-land,' with many who have gone 'over there' through his ministerial labors. He and I worked together in 1861, and the Lord greatly blessed our work with gracious revivals. That year was not crowned with a rich harvest, but I made corn enough for bread and some horse-feed, and recuperated my dilapidated horse, so that I could once more ride to my appointments."

The great drought of 1859 will never be forgotten by the settlers in Texas, as they merely got through it by the "skin of their teeth." Mr. Potter's resorting to the ax, maul, and wedge, is another evidence of the energy of the man in proportion to the demand of circumstances. His motto is, "I will be superior to circumstances." Cut, maul, walk, and preach—there was zeal. Such events try the materials of which man is made, as terrible sea-storms test the strength of the timbers of which ships are built.

The zeal of a faithful minister of Jesus is stronger than the love of life or the fear of death. "What mean ye to weep, and to break mine heart? for I am ready not to be bound only, but also to die at Jerusalem for the name of the Lord Jesus," said the devoted, the zealous Paul. Mr. Potter's earliest ministry was greatly blessed with immediate sealing results. Many were brought from darkness to light by the Spirit's influences accompanying the word uttered in the simple earnestness of a mind imbued with the love of Jesus, yearning for the salvation of souls. He had little knowledge of books, but his lesson was a short, concise one; it was this: "This is a faithful saying, and worthy of all acceptation, that Christ Jesus came into the world to save sinners, of whom I am chief." Of that one thing he was confident, and he told it with heart-felt zeal, and God owned and blessed his word.

CHAPTER XV.

"DURING the winter of 1861, I felt powerfully impressed to go back to Missouri, my native State, to the old home where I was born, and bear witness for Jesus to my relatives and near kindred, who were still living and lingering in the same old scenes of my earlier years. My means being quite limited, Mr. Miller, of Lockhart, was going to take a herd of cattle through to Kansas, and prevailed on me to go through with the herd. It was a slow and irksome trip to me. My patience gave out, and I regretted a thousand times having started; but a hard bargain needs the more nerve to carry out its stipulations. We made the trip in forty-seven days, but I was then about one hundred miles from my old home, from which I had been absent ten long, eventful years. Mr. Miller fitted me out with a suit of clothing, and I took a farewell parting with 'the cow-boys,' whose hardships I had shared along the weary 'trail,' and set out for my long-desired destination. As I approached nearer and nearer, my anxieties doubled upon me, and my feelings were irrepressible; and when I reached the scenes of my early boyhood, I was a captive to tears, and a submissive slave to the alternate emotions of regret and joy. My father had located on the border, where there were no neighbors near to us; but now there were houses and farms, and where I used to play on the banks of old Grand River there was a grist-mill and a little town. Here I met a few old acquaintances, but I was still four miles from the home of my dear sister, wife of Mr. Jesse Jennings. I hurried on, and gave them a great surprise. O the great rejoicing! News of my arrival soon spread all over the community, and the people flocked in till there was truly a crowd; and none of us slept that night of kindred joys. An appointment was made for me to preach on the coming Sabbath, and when the day arrived there was a general rush to the church to get seats. This saying was in the mouths of all: 'Andy Potter has come back, and is a preacher, and he is going to preach here to-day.' How strange events in life excite us! The gathering was large indeed. The country was no longer frontier. Some old people walked several miles to hear the new-born Texas preacher. On that day it was as the return of the prodigal; there was crying, shouting, and praising God. 'O the lost boy, the wild, reckless, wandering Andy, who used to ride races, has come back, and now he is a preacher!' Could it be possible? Indeed, it was true. Praise God, and let the angels say Amen! How mysterious and wonderful are the ways of God! What incredible changes come up in the lives of men!

"A revival began that day which lasted some three months. All denominations, far and near, invited me to preach in their churches, and I also preached in private houses and under bush arbors. On a week-day in a private house we had fourteen conversions, one after another, in the same hour. My brother-in-law, who had been a seeker twenty-five years, was one of the happy converts. I preached nearly every day, and sometimes two or three times the same day and night."

Dear reader, think of the gushing tides of joy and nameless emotions that bestir the heart when a long-lost wanderer returns to loved ones at childhood's home. A kind of central affinity attracts the heart to the scenes of our early associations, as the needle is drawn to the pole of the earth. Man, in all his journeyings, on land or sea, feels a heart-tenderness when thoughts of home glide through his brain. These sweet home-thoughts make him a child again, and all the tearful sympathies of boyhood awake in his heart; and when, after strange wanderings, in hardened manhood he returns to those remembered paths of childhood, and time and art have wrought their changes there, and death has taken loved ones away, language hath not a name for the mingled emotions which rend the heart and ripple the pool of feeling. Almost all animals feel some endearment to the scenes of their nativity—beasts of the field and forest, birds of the grove, and even the tiny minnow in the little pool—but childhood is allied to home with almost indissoluble heart-ties, stronger than the tendrils binding the vine to the massive oak. Kindred ligaments entwine with those of home associations to render domestic pleasures like those in the heaven above. Surely there must be somewhere in the illimitable universe a place where man may find a permanent home, where all the family may meet, and where long-severed ties may be mended by a reunion of hearts, to be parted no more! Hail, all hail, happy place!

Mr. Potter's visit to Missouri was rich in a revival-harvest to the Church to many denominations. A minister bearing evidence of God's efficient grace crowning his labors instantly gains the confidence of man. The man whom God honors men will accredit. If he be learned or illiterate, no matter; if God owns and makes effectual his labors, all is right; let not man reject him. But when men see the presence of divine power with the most unlearned minister, it is enough to inspire faith; hence Jesus said, "Lo, I am with you alway, even to the end of the world." "Tarry ye at Jerusalem till endued with power from on high." On that spiritual presence, that power from above, depends pulpit triumph in the world. What but that could have made Mr. Potter a power in the sacred desk, even in the first years of his ministry? God's Spirit gives liberty.

But in the man's nature there seems to be the unification of opposites, and in his life a strange coincidence of paradoxes. With all his great revivals in Missouri, he had an unpleasant encounter with a man connected with his family by marriage; but it was of a nature that did not attach blame to Mr. Potter, as the sequel will show. He had a niece who had married a young man who was sick at his father's house; and the old gentleman seems to have been a rough, cruel sort of a man, and being displeased with his daughter-in-law, he abused and chastised her while her husband was bed-ridden. Having a knowledge of Mr. Potter's former pugilistic character, he said that he would now have her Texas uncle to kill, as he knew that he would "take it up" and defend her. He accordingly borrowed a gun, and belted a dangerous knife to his side, and passed about, thus armed, for that ostensible object. Mr. Potter chanced to meet him, when the cruel man said to him, " Do n't you come here," pointing the gun toward him; but Mr. Potter walked on, the man saying the while, " Do n't you come here," till Mr. Potter approached, seized the gun, wrenched it from him, and then said, " Hand over that knife; " but he refused, when Mr. Potter jobbed him a little with the muzzle of the gun, and he handed it over. " Now," said Mr. Potter, " you must ask pardon of that young lady you have treated so cruelly." That was a hard thing for the old sinner to do, and he hesitated, saying, "You have the advantage of me; you have my gun and knife." Mr. Potter replied, "You had them, and I took them from you—here, now, take them, and I will take them from you again;" but he refused to take them. " Well, now, out with that petition for pardon;" and he said the hard thing to be uttered, and Mr. Potter handed him his arms, telling him to go home and behave himself.

After spending about three months with friends and kindred, he bade adieu to his native State, and returned to his Texas home in Caldwell county, and spent the remainder of that year in local life, preaching with the Rev. Mr. Mabry, of the Methodist

Protestant Church, with great results of good to the Church and country, as will be seen on another page.

Often the humanly weak, divinely strong, confounds the worldly strong. "When I am weak, then am I strong," said a great missionary evangelist; "most gladly, therefore, will I glory in my infirmities." He preached not Christ with wisdom of words, lest the cross should be made of none effect by men's faith rooting in the wisdom of man, not in the power of God. "I will give you a mouth and wisdom that all your enemies shall not gainsay." "God hath not given us the spirit of fear, but of love, and of power, and of a sound mind." *God giveth it.* But Mr. Potter has advanced in the knowledge of men and books till he leads in "the van of the host." Do not grow strong in worldly wisdom and become ignorant of divine things.

CHAPTER XVI.

Mr. Potter at this time was a local preacher, and not being in the regular itinerant ministerial ranks, was subject to the Confederate conscript law. Conscription not being agreeable to his patriotic taste, he volunteered as a private soldier in Captain Stoke Homes's company, Woods's regiment, Thirty-second Texas Cavalry. Captain Homes's company was then encamped on the Salado, near San Antonio.

"The company was organized at Prairie Lee, in February, 1862. My younger brother, and nephew, and brother-in-law, and a large number of my most intimate friends, had already joined the company. About that time Dr. P. C. Woods, of San Marcos, began to make up a regiment, to which our company was attached, and we were ordered to Camp Verde, in Kerr county, to take charge of the prisoners taken at San Antonio, at the surrender of General Twiggs. Soon after reaching Camp Verde, the measles broke out among the soldiers, and raged fearfully; there were hardly enough well ones to nurse the sick. Two of our men died, and we buried them near the post, close to the beautiful Verde, all walled in by the near mountains. All traces of their hidden graves may now be obliterated, but God has noted the spot, and will know where to find them at the last day. Dr. Ship and myself would feel our way through darkness in the dismal nights, from place to place, to give those poor sick ones their remedies. I often preached to 'the boys' on the gallery of Mr. Bonnel's dwelling. I also preached to the prisoners, who ever gave good attention. I frequently got permission from the clever captain to go out into the country and preach, and the young men would avail themselves of the opportunity of getting permission to go with me to my appointments. One time I went to Bandera, and several of them proposed to go with me, saying if I would select my hymns and loan them my hymn-book, they would practice during the week. I loaned it to them, telling them to be ready at eight o'clock Sunday morning. They appeared at the appointed time, all neatly dressed, and we started for Bandera, about fifteen miles. They ran several horse-races on the road before reaching the place. Before time for preaching, I told them they might walk about town until the hour, but be sure and be there in good time. At eleven o'clock I walked into the preaching-place, and found a large congregation, and my soldiers sitting together on one bench. I gave out my hymn and started the tune, the soldiers joining in to the admiration of all. I introduced them to the people of Bandera, who gave them an invitation to dinner. We returned to Camp Verde that afternoon, and the men gave a full detail of our trip. I also preached several times in Kerrville, to large and deeply-impressed congregations. After remaining about three months at Camp Verde, we were ordered to

San Antonio with the prisoners, and camped for some time on the Salado, at the Austin crossing. While so many of our men were sick, the captain prevailed on me to act as a non-commissioned officer. There was a certain man in the company by the name of F.; he weighed about one hundred and eighty pounds, and was well formed. He was very quarrelsome and overbearing, and a make-believe bully. Most of the men really dreaded him. He was a bitter enemy to religion, and availed himself of every opportunity for hurling his sarcasms at me, taking a kind of infernal pleasure in wounding my feelings. I tried to shun him all I could. When we were at San Antonio we camped one night on the San Padre, and it was my night for duty. Mr. F. was on guard, and I had to relieve him when his two hours were up, and knowing that he would likely complain if he was not relieved at the minute, I was careful to relieve him just at the time; but when passing the next morning I heard him say to a group of men, with bitter oaths, that the parson put him on guard and kept him three hours. That was more than I could bear, and I asked, 'Who put you on guard and retained you three hours?' He answered, 'You did.' I said: 'Sir, you are a liar; and if you take that you are a coward. You have been trying to bring this thing on for some time, and now if there is any fight in you let us have it.' He walked up to me, and I put my hand on his breast and pushed him back, and said: 'You won't fight; now I will talk to you a little. You have made a mistake; you have made the impression in this company that you are a first-class bully, a real man-eater, but you have waked up the wrong man. I have now demonstrated the fact, right here before all these men, that you are a coward, and that there is no fight in you. There is not a boy in this company but may insult you when he sees fit to do so, from this time on.' So the foam all passed away, and Mr. F. never was an object of terror any more in that company, but was ever a fast friend of mine."

There are no assumed traits of character with Mr. Potter. He is what he is. He tells men plainly what he desires them to know, without putting on any varnish, or seeking to mitigate his phrases. If a man prevaricates, he hesitates not to tell him of it. A more conservative mode might result as well in some cases.

"While we were camped on the Salado some of our men were attacked with typhoid fever, and taken to the hospital at San Antonio. They sent word to Captain Homes that they were not receiving good attention, and requested that I should be ordered into the hospital to nurse them; and I was detailed to attend the sick. I spent many long and sleepless nights in watching over my sick and dying comrades. The first that died was a young man by the name of Marion Ralls. I sent for his parents, and they reached the place before their darling boy passed away. His parents were Baptists. His mother would kneel down by his couch, and pour out the full tide of her lacerated soul in prayer for her dying son. At last the sad hour of his departure came, and Marion was no more. It was a hard trial to those fond and doting parents. I had then sat up three nights, without closing my eyes in sleep. The next one to go was a youth named Doc Persons. I saw that he was nearing his end, and sent for his parents, and they got there in time to see their son breathe his last. He had been entirely delirious for twenty-four hours, talking incoherently. His father was a very wicked man, but his mother was a noble Christian lady. One morning, just as the sun began to throw his rays through the windows upon his pale and death-like features, we were standing near to see the last struggles of the sufferer, when he suddenly roused up out of his stupor, and seemed entirely rational, and thanked me for my attentions to him, saying also that he hoped to meet me in heaven. He then gave an affecting farewell talk to his mother and sister, and addressed his wicked father, saying, 'Pa, will you meet me in heaven?' He sobbed out, 'I will try.' The dying son said, 'I am afraid you will not; give me your hand;' and the cold hand reached out, taking hold of his father's, and the plighted hands sealed the solemn engagement to meet in that land where friends never part. Dropping into a stupor, his unfettered spirit went home to God, leaving his soulless body still in death. I had only slept one night after the death of young Ralls, and had now spent three sleepless nights in nursing this one, and was so nearly exhausted that the captain sent me home to rest; and there I preached the funeral of young Ralls, at a Baptist meeting, at the request of his devoted parents, the ministerial brethren yielding me their pulpit."

What strange contrarieties meet in the brief history of our remarkable hero! Thus is nature; and some men's lives strictly pattern after natural forms. Old ocean's liquid world is rent and tossed to the skies by tempest-winds to-day, but to-morrow its vast bosom is as quiet and smooth as the face of a great mirror, while golden light glistens on the wide domain. Wintry winds howl along the hills and vales in the dismal night, but the calm is on the forest-world at the opening morn. Men are in health to-day, and rejoice with a merry heart, but at evening-tide they are sick, and wail in dying agonies. Lovely flowers regale our eyes with their modest hues in the sparkling, dewy morn, but at high-noon their beauties have wilted, and they hang drooping on their stems. Man is happy to-day, to-morrow he is in sorrow. Now he is in a good humor, and is as gentle as the face of the windless Pacific, but soon all his elements of passion are stirred into a tempest-rage. Such are life's changing scenes, and such are man's fitful tempers—nature's own child. But Mr. Potter seemed never roused into a rage by the most exciting scenes. Ever cool but resolute—not enraged like a tempest, but determined and dauntless in purpose—he moves on in an even manner, as a Nemesis to chastise men for their errors, and as an angel to comfort the distressed. You see him going to flagellate Mr. F. for falsehood, and disturbance of others; then you see him in the hospital with the sick, toiling through successive nights and days, without rest or sleep, to alleviate the pain of the sufferers, though no blood kindred of his. The cry of suffering and the voice of want ever touch his heart, and no sacrifice of ease, no hardships too severe to deter him from efforts to relieve the distressed. Waiting around the couch of the dying to administer to both soul and body, then preaching their funerals when dead —a man ready for all things relating to time, and those bearing on eternity; a man respected by the bad and beloved by the good. To know Potter and not like him, is not to be man, but akin to demons; even those whom he has chastised, finding him out, have become his friends. There is a principle in the human mind that leads men involuntarily to do homage to the factors of truth and candor in character.

In Mr. Potter's religious character there is a conservative vein which runs through all his ministerial career, rendering him acceptable to all good people of all denominations. That liberal Christian element in the man, and his tender, devoted kindness to their departed son, influence the parents of young Ralls to have him preach the funeral-sermon of their dear lost child. Disease haunts the soldier's camp—it is a foe that the brave soldier is not prepared to combat; man is often called to yield up his life under the most trying circumstances, away from home and loved ones, and in youth's hopeful morn; but religion illumines the most dismal gloom, as when young Persons passed away under the radiance of its glory.

CHAPTER XVII.

"When Col. Woods's regiment was camped on the San Marcos River, at Camp Clark, below the town of San Marcos, at which place our company, which had been on detached service for several months, was ordered to join it, it had an arbor, and had regular preaching. In the regiment were J. H. Cummings (Chaplain), Preston Phillips, W. R. D. Stockton, Columbus Sawyers, and myself, Methodist ministers; the Rev. Mr. Powell, Missionary Baptist, and the Rev. James Baker, Primitive Baptist. Mr. Baker said that it was against the rules of his Church to worship with other denominations, and asked that the fourth Sabbath be left to him alone, and it was granted to him. He said that when he was through preaching he was done for that time, and if any friend had any thing to say he might speak, and I frequently closed up the services by prayer, etc. When the regiment was organized, Col. Woods tendered the chaplaincy to the Rev. Preston Phillips, but he generously waived his claim in favor of the Rev. J. H. Cummings, who was in poor health, being afflicted with that fearful disease, consumption. Mr. Cummings was a very popular man, and was held in high esteem by all the regiment, but he soon became too feeble to stay in camp and preach. He then proposed to resign, but being a poor man, the other preachers agreed among themselves to do the preaching, and let him remain at home and draw the pay of the chaplaincy. But he declined rapidly, and some time in 1862 he closed his useful life and went to his reward. His death left the chaplaincy vacant, and of course Col. Woods felt that he stood committed to the Rev. Mr. Phillips, he having waived his claim to the place at first. He was a good man and a good preacher, but seemed not gifted in preaching to soldiers, and as such, was not a favorite with the regiment; and the good colonel felt that it would be injustice to the regiment to appoint him, and at the same time he felt it would seem hard to take another out of the ranks for the place; so he declined to make any appointment. In the meantime the Rev. Mr. Stockton got the appointment of chaplain in Col. Bushel's regiment, and Mr. Phillips took the ground that the regiment was entitled to a chaplain, and declined to preach under our former agreement, so the burden of the work fell mainly on me; but I kept up regular prayer-meetings in the week, and preached on Sundays at the colonel's request. The kind-hearted men, seeing that it was too hard on me to do all the drudgery of a soldier, and keep up the religious services of the regiment, sent up a large petition to Col. Woods to appoint me, but the colonel was not willing to take another man out of the regiment and appoint him over the Rev. Mr. Phillips, and fell upon the plan of electing one from citizen-life—in fact, he had already made a tender of the position to the Rev. B. Harris, not being informed, in the meantime, of my being chosen by the regiment."

All grades and spheres of human life have their peculiar trials and troubles. The great and the little currents of life have their ripples, their bends, and their curves. In domestic scenes, in the social spheres, in peace and in war, men have their small and their large difficulties. Their aims, their hopes, their interests, and their plans collide, and just there their feelings, their prejudices, and their partialities make a breach. Dilemmas present themselves to them which reason, not fettered by passion, cannot always guide them safely through. In the career of the wisest and the best, there is often just cause of regret as to the past, because of mistakes in the judgment. Errors in conclusions attach to men; infallibility is divine. Great generals, who plan the programmes of great battles, sometimes adopt those which result in defeat. Man is taught to pardon the blunders of his fellow.

Herewith we transcribe the petition sent up by a large list of names to Col. Woods, to appoint Mr. Potter chaplain of the regiment, on the death of the Rev. Mr. Cummings:

To Col. P. C. Woods, Commanding:—We, the undersigned, having learned that a vacancy exists in the chaplaincy, caused by the death of the Rev. J. H. Cummings, which we all regret, we would therefore most respectfully petition the colonel commanding to appoint the Rev. A. J. Potter, of Company K, Thirty-second Regiment, Texas Cavalry, to fill the vacancy. Believing him to be an honest, upright, Christian man, and one who will do good in his calling, we would earnestly recommend him to your consideration.

An honest, upright, Christian man was truly characteristic of the man whose life we are trying to portray. Honest and just, even in that period of life marked with folly, but in the term of his Christian profession truly upright, and honored by his fellow-men. He is always the man for two things, specially—*things that ought to be done, and things hard to be done.* If a camel was to go through a needle's eye, Mr. Potter was that camel; if feats involving dangers of limb or life were to be performed, he was the man to lead in the van; if the sick were in need of a kind nurse, he was called for; if a sermon was wanted, he was the preacher; if the dead were to be buried, he was ready to read, "Dust to dust;" and if an unruly, bad man needed chastising, the whip was in Mr. Potter's hands, both when in the army and in times of peace. That double character of seeming opposites marks his life from earliest boyhood to this day; but as he advances in age he gets farther removed from the tragic and the perilous, though his natural strength seems but little abated.

"Col. Woods was one of the few Confederate officers who went into the war with a Christian profession, and came out with the same untarnished. In all the perplexing cares and sore temptations common to war-life, he ever maintained an unyielding religious fidelity to his God. Through all campaigns the Bible was his book. His place was never vacant at preaching or at prayer-meeting. When I led the prayer-meetings it was my custom to call on him to offer prayer, but the other ministers did not. I called the colonel's attention to the fact, and asked him if he felt free to worship in camp. If he had any reasons for not making his devotions public I would not call on him. He said, 'Brother Potter, I am perfectly free to worship anywhere; do not hesitate to call on me.' Once, when marching through Colorado county, the colonel was quite unwell and sent for me, and said that he was not feeling well, and desired to ride on ahead of the regiment and stop at some house and rest, and that he wished me to accompany him. Captain Homes, who had been quite ill, proposed to ride with us. As we were riding along the road, the colonel said: 'Brother Potter, I wanted to get out from the bustle of camp, and have a good talk with you to-day on the subject of religion, the never-failing delight of a pure, simple heart full of vital religion. It is the grandest theme that men and angels can contemplate.' Here the colonel touched the key-note of my soul, and gave it a grand lift for the upper spheres. About noon we came to a house; I dismounted and went in, and addressed the intelligent lady of the house, telling her that Col. Woods and Capt. Homes were with me, quite unwell, and wanted to rest and get dinner with her. She told me to invite the gentlemen in, and I introduced them to the good lady. She pointed out a room, and told them to walk in and rest. She prepared a magnificent dinner, and invited us out to the table. The colonel and captain did not eat much like sick men. I ate what I thought was a hearty meal, but my sick men were still 'going for it.' I said: 'Madam, I owe you an apology; I have represented these men as being sick, but they do not eat much like sick men.' We all enjoyed a hearty laugh over it, and all agreed that they had done justice to the subject that day. My associations with Col. Woods as an officer, a Christian, and a gentleman, will ever be remembered with the pleasant things of the past.

"The limits of our space prevent us from following the regiment through all its wanderings. In the spring of 1863, we were ordered to Brownsville, on the Rio Grande. In many places we could not get water for our horses, only when we drew it from wells, so the command was divided and traveled in detachments, and our commissary sergeant found it very difficult to get meat. He had orders to kill beeves and give the Mexican owners vouchers, but he could not speak Spanish, and had no little trouble in settling with them; he got so worried over it he feigned sick, and the colonel appointed me to furnish beef that day. We camped near to where the cattle gathered in large numbers for water. I examined them, and found but few fit for beef, except a few two-year-olds. There were four companies of us, and I called on each company for men and ropes; then I pointed out the beeves, and they roped and butchered them. When we had caught three, the colonel came along and said, 'Mr. Potter, how do you come on in getting beef?' I answered, 'Pretty well, colonel; we have three, and the boys are after another.' The colonel smiled, and said I was doing well. So we got our four beeves slaughtered, and the half-starved men began to cook and eat. I reported to our commissary, and called for vouchers for four beeves. 'What!' said he, 'you have not killed four?' 'I have, sir,' said I; 'this is my day to issue beef.' He said it was more than they were entitled to, and that a great deal of it would be wasted. I replied that after four companies had eaten what they wanted, and then cooked enough to take along to-morrow, out of four small beeves, but little would be left; and it was even so."

Among the many noble specimens of Christian character which history has passed down to our day, few have excelled that of Col. Woods, of San Marcos, whose firmness in a conscientious discharge of religious duties, amid all the harassing and insidious temptations of military and war life, which led to the certain demoralization of so many Churchmen and ministers of the gospel, deserves commendation from all true hearts. Years have rolled away since he passed out of the last ordeal of camp-life, and still he maintains all the claims of a Christian gentleman, in all the relations of private and public life as a professional man. In the army he attended the prayer-meeting and preaching, and in his own city home he is at his place in the Church, and ready to serve her interests when duty calls. Such models of Christian faithfulness we earnestly recommend to our young readers, as being highly deserving of their esteem and imitation. A consistent Christian is the highest type of man. Mankind shall not fail to award merit to such a one.

"We were dismounted at King's Ranch, and

marched into Brownsville on foot, leaving our horses in charge of a detail of men to herd them on the grass. Remaining there a short time, we were ordered back. While camping near Brownsville, some of our boys acted a little rudely, going into stores and asking the price of cavalry boots, and when the merchant would say, 'Ten dollars,' meaning in specie, they would lay down a ten-dollar bill in Confederate money, and walk out with the boots. Only a few did so. We received orders to start on a certain day. I had bought me a pony, and being mounted, the colonel detailed me to stay at Brownsville and bring up the mail that was expected to arrive in a day or so; and when the colonel was about to start, he said, 'Mr. Potter, I will not leave you in such a place unarmed; here, take one of my six-shooters.' I took it and buckled it on my person. After the regiment was gone, the paper called the *Brownsville Flag* came out with a most slanderous attack on Woods's regiment, saying they were thieves, having robbed inoffensive citizens of private property. I was sitting on the front gallery of a kind of hotel near where several soldiers were reading the paper. They seemed to be quite elated at something; one said, 'He has given Woods's regiment a hard hit;' another said, 'It is no more than they deserve,' saying that they had a hard name at Port Lavaca. I said, 'Gentlemen, what regiment do you belong to?' One said, 'Shay's Battalion.' I said: 'You belong to a set of the most consummate villains I ever saw. It was you that did the devilment at

Port Lavaca; the people there hate you, while they respect Woods's regiment, and regretted when they were ordered away. Let me see that paper, if you please.' They handed it to me, and I read the slander upon that noble regiment of men. I told them that I would go round and let that editor know that all of Woods's regiment were not gone, and that all were not thieves. Col. Duff's regiment was stationed in the town, among whom I had several acquaintances. As I started to the printing-office to settle with the editor, they hurried through their quarters and informed the men of my intention, and when I entered the office I saw a number of them coming on a run. Approaching the editor, I said, 'Are you the editor?' He said, 'I am.' I told him I wanted a copy of his paper. He handed me one, and I paid him for it. I said: 'Sir, I am going to send this paper to Col. Woods; the regiment is camped only eight miles from here. The colonel shall see what a name you have given his regiment, coward-like, when you thought it was gone.' He said it was as good as it deserved. I slapped him in the face, and sent him staggering back against the wall of the room, and then said: 'Now, sir, a few of the men may have done badly, but a little common sense and a moderate share of decency ought to have taught you not to slander a whole regiment, most of whom are noble, brave soldiers, because a few of their comrades have acted like thieves. I am going to send word to Col. Woods to send me men enough to throw your press into the river, as you surely deserve nothing better.

While they put their lives in jeopardy to protect you and your ungrateful press, you repay them with a tissue of base slander on their good name.' Col. Duff's men cried out, 'We will throw it in the river, Mr. Potter, if you will say the word.' I replied: 'No, gentlemen; Col. Woods's men are the ones to do that work; they have been outraged by this little *ink-slinger*, and let them give it a deserved immersion.' I then mounted my pony and rode out to the regiment. No sooner was my arrival made known, than a general shout went up from the camp, 'All praise to our parson! three cheers for him!' They had heard of my vindication of their good name. That incautious editor went to Gen. Bee and got him to send an order to Col. Woods to put out a strong guard that night to prevent his men from returning to town, to upset his press; and the cowardly 'pencil-pusher' took refuge in Matamoras, a town on the Mexican side of the Rio Grande. I learned that Gen. Bee placed Col. Duff's men on the road, with strict orders not to let any of Col. Woods's men come into town that night; but as soon as the men were informed of the object of their being sent there, they gave a general shout, 'Hurrah for Woods's regiment!' and then they were ordered to return to town."

Having such a colonel commanding as Col. Woods, most of his men must have entertained a sacred regard for the rights of property with the private citizen, and such was their general character wherever they were encamped through the entire campaign. Indeed, many of them were of the highest type of Texan society: men of the learned professions, honest farmers, and industrious mechanics. Seldom has a more worthy set of men been associated in peace or war. But a few black sheep sometimes appear in the whitest-fleeced flocks.

That imprudent editor at Brownsville was indeed rash and hasty in printing that offensive paragraph which called down on his inconsiderate pate the ire of Mr. Potter, who never allowed himself or his friends to be misrepresented, without a defense. In this case, except in a few instances of guilt, that accusation was a public slander. In the common regard of men, a few great wrongs of a minority attach a shade on the associated or kindred majority, for the tacit belief that contact essentially tints in evil things; but there is a philosophic limit to the sentiment, and a public journalist should mark the distinctive line, and never make such an unjust, such a silly mingling of the evil and the good—the guilty and the innocent. He certainly received a competent rebuke for his temerity and indiscretion.

Besides Mr. Potter's readiness to repair injuries or redress wrongs inflicted on himself or his friends, his high social qualities were one cause of his popularity and success through life. He loves society, in cabins or palaces, in times of peace or war—he is "all things to all men;" he is at home anywhere; he is not too rich to be one with the poor, nor too poor to be equal with the rich; not too great to be at home in the private soldier's camp, nor too humble to be equal to the highest officers in the army. He is little, and he is great. He is on a level with his brother in a hovel, but at the same time he measures equal to his more favored brother in a palace.

He is a fine reader of character. He can discern its nice pencilings in the finer lineaments of that noblest thing, "the human face divine." He has also a well-marked perception of the laws and lines of delicate proprieties. He has well cultivated the rare art of not speaking unadvisedly; the art so valuable to man, not to offend, but to please all men for good. He is popular—a favorite among all ranks in the Church and in the world; even those with whom he has had trouble, learning his true character, both respect and fear him.

When in the army, he was a long time both a private soldier and a zealous preacher, passing through all the daily drill and marches of a private soldier, and holding prayer-meetings and preaching to the troops, whenever and wherever religious services could be held in the day or at night. Both privates and officers became attached to him. Not to like such a man was akin to the impossible. In associating with the private ranks he knew just how far to go not to lower the sacred dignity of his profession; he would interchange innocent jokes with them, never allowing such as were, or bordered on, the obscene. He indulged farther in the line of the mirthful and the playful than ministers unlike himself might go, without damage—allowing them to take hold on his person and tussle him a little; but when he called them to the place of worship, they were there, and paid the greatest respect to the rules of order and decorum. He had a fine art of illustrating the truths of the gospel by the scenes and little incidents of daily soldier-life. He heard a strange private from another regiment, who did not know Mr. Potter, telling another soldier that he could tell the preacher when he might come, by his walk; hearing it as he passed, he made it a part of his theme at that hour, showing the importance of a Christian being known by his orderly walk, in the army and everywhere. When the regiment remained at one place several days, sometimes their meetings might have reminded one of an old-field camp-meeting. A great harvest of good has resulted from those army revivals. In all of Mr. Potter's itinerant travels since those memorable days, he has met here and there those fellow-soldiers who ever give him a cordial and a joyous greeting. But in the last great day their reunion shall be jubilant indeed!

CHAPTER XVIII.

Mr. Potter was passing the hotel at Beaumont one day, and saw a young lady sitting on the gallery weeping. He advanced to her and inquired the cause of her tears. She informed him that her relations, living near Seguin, had conveyed her to Houston, and left her there to go on the Central road to Navasoto, and there take the stage to her brother's. She told him her name, saying that while at Houston she had fallen in with an old woman, who had decoyed her to Beaumont, telling her the Beaumont road was the Central. That old woman was the proprietress of a bawdy-house in Galveston, and was trying to ensnare that virtuous young lady to her house of ill-fame. Mr. Potter told her that a number of men in the regiment to which he belonged were from about Seguin, and he would hunt them up, and if they could vouch for her innocence that he would raise money to send her to her brother, as by this time her means were exhausted. On inquiry, he found several men who readily recognized the innocent young woman, and they aided in supplying the money to send her out of the snare into which she had unluckily fallen; but it was with some difficulty that they could get her from the shrewd and false representations of the abandoned old woman, who was eager to hold her valuable captive; she clung to her with great tenacity, but finally they succeeded in rescuing the innocent girl from her grasp, and sent her on to her brother.

Here Mr. Potter was the means of the relief of the captive bird. He was ever ready to aid in relieving human distress. Sight of tears, the fruits of sorsow, ever touched him.

"In the fall of 1863 we were stationed at Beaumont on the Nueces River. Feeling that the burden on me was too hard, that of keeping up the religious services and performing all the duties of a soldier—being a young preacher, I needed some time for reading and study also—I sent a communication to Col. Woods urging him to appoint a chaplain, and not to consider me in the way of any one; that I would do all I could to assist and encourage any one he might appoint; that I could not be longer responsible for the religious services of the regiment. About that time I received a letter from Col. J. J. Myers, commanding Debray's regiment, Twenty-sixth Texas Cavalry. Col. Myers and myself, when at home, lived in the same community. The following is a copy of the colonel's letter:

Rev. A. J. Potter, Thirty-second Regiment, Texas Cavalry— Reverend and Dear Sir: My regiment being without a chaplain, and hearing of your great prosperity and success in preaching to soldiers, and the high esteem in which you are held by the officers and men of the regiment to which you belong, and the high place you hold in the confidence and esteem of the people in the community in which you live, as well as a large number of my regiment; and believing that you have performed the drudgery of a private soldier long enough to be entitled to an easier position, I therefore tender

you the office of chaplain in this regiment. Hoping this will meet your favorable consideration, I have the honor to be your obedient servant, J. J. MYERS,
Lieut.-col. commanding Debray's Regiment, Texas Cavalry.

"To this kind and flattering letter of Col. Myers I replied that I would visit his regiment at the earliest period possible, and have the matter under further consideration. We were ordered from Beaumont to Old Caney. On arriving there, I found that Col. Myers's regiment had also been ordered to that place; and soon we were camped near together. So I visited the regiment, and proposed to preach a kind of trial sermon. I wanted to ascertain, as far as I could, how they might like my preaching. This regiment had been in the service about two years, and had never had a chaplain. Col. Myers was not a religious man, but he was a high-minded and noble-hearted gentleman. Arrangements were made for me to preach at night. The officers got together and made a large fire. Among them was Hon. L. J. Story, now Lieutenant-governor of the State of Texas, to whom I am indebted for many courtesies during my stay with the regiment. Col. Myers inquired of the officers the next day how their men were pleased with me and my preaching. They said that all were well pleased, and anxious for my appointment. So the colonel wrote out my commission at once, as follows:

Head-quarters Debray's Regiment, Texas Cavalry,
Camp Dixie, Jan. 30, 1864.

REV. A. J. POTTER—Sir: You are hereby appointed Chaplain of this regiment, subject to the approval of the President of the Confederate States. You will signify your willingness to accept of that

position by applying (through the proper channel) for the confirmation of your appointment as such. I have the honor to be very respectfully yours, J. J. MYERS,
Lieut.-col. commanding Debray's Regiment, Texas Cavalry.

"With many uprising emotions of gratitude and fear, I began to prepare to take my leave of my old comrades, whose hardships and trials I had shared for a period of nearly two years. Just as I was leaving, Col. Woods took me aside and assured me of his highest esteem and confidence. He explained to me the delicate situation in which he stood, and gave a satisfactory reason why he did not appoint me chaplain. I assured the colonel that I had not, indulged the slightest unkind feeling toward him for the course he had taken."

The parting of Mr. Potter and Col. Woods and the noble men of that honorable regiment could not have been attended with other than sad regrets and tearful emotions. Two long, toilsome years they had been as one family, sharing their mutual privations, toils, dangers, and sufferings, while in camp and on long and weary marches. Now they were parting, as far as they knew, not to meet till the last great meeting of the race at the bar of the final Judge. Not knowing what were to be their destinations the remainder of the war, or what its issues, or when it might close, they took the parting hand with the shade of war's uncertain hopes veiling their future.

Associations of men attach them to each other by ties essentially arising out of the relations involved in the associations themselves, and they are strengthened by length of time and endeared to their subjects by the severity of the hardships to maintain their mutual welfare; and those combined toils, which more clearly bring to light man's single inability successfully to combat his foes, and demonstrate the absolute dependence of one upon another, the more firmly ally them to each other. We see the same principle developed among beasts and birds in the dreary winter's chill, in their herding and flocking together in order to resist the chill of the inclement storm by their unified animal heat. Of all the endearing relations of men outside of the blood-kindred domain, that of the patriot is perhaps the most unifying. It readily cements a nation's heart as the heart of a single man; and well it may, as a nation's weal is the interest alike of all its citizens. In some instances the ties of patriotism have proved stronger than the ligaments of blood relations. In fact, the soldier gives up, in a sense, wife, babes, kindred, and possessions, and becomes one of a soldier or patriot brotherhood for the defense of their common country's life and honor. For the time of the hazards of the war his fellow-soldiers are his greatest, truest brotherhood; and ties of that nature arise between them—ties which hold them in tender remembrance to the portals of the grave. When the writer was a little boy, he remembers to have seen and heard a few old revolutionary soldiers tell of their battles and show their scars. After having been parted many years, they would tenderly embrace each other with tears. A common country's glory and mutual hardships allied them in the dearest recollections of the past. Such scenes of common toils and sorrows, and the uniting cords binding together the patriot bands, can but remind the reader of the allied army of the soldiers of the cross, who are made one body by one Spirit, under one general Head, all being brethren, having their common sorrows and sharing their mutual woes, while "for each other flows the sympathizing tear;" and when life's hard strifes are past, the victory gained, and all the troops get home, they shall meet to hymn the victor's song while the ages roll.

CHAPTER XIX.

"The course I decided upon in entering on my duties as chaplain was to get acquainted with the men, which I did by visiting each company and going from mess to mess, eating and talking with them. I found but comparatively few religious men in the regiment, yet there were some who were as true to their profession as fidelity itself. Prominent among these was Mr. Lee Rogan. He was brought up by Old-school Presbyterian parents, and was a member of that Church. He was a lawyer by profession; modest and dignified, courteous and polite, he possessed all the elements of a refined Christian gentleman, a model of manly virtues. The vulgarity and profanity of camp-life ever grated harshly on his refined sensibilities. He is still living in Lockhart, honored and respected in the circles in which he moves. I ever found him willing to aid in all the religious services in the camp, in prayer and exhortation. Whenever we encamped near a town, which we frequently did, I would preach in the churches, to give the citizens a chance to attend, and would call on Mr. Rogan to exhort, and he always elevated his audiences to heights of religious ecstasy by his almost unsurpassed eloquence. The sacred ties that bound us together through the struggles of a long campaign still hold us in the bonds of a most tender regard for each other. It was proposed that we hold prayer-meetings in each company every week, by rotation; so, one night two men came after me to hold a prayer-meeting in their company; they had made a good fire, which would give sufficient light and heat. On going to the place, I found quite a crowd of men with their blankets spread on the ground, gambling with cards. The men who had made the fire for a prayer-meeting reported to the captain, who, with bitter oaths, said he would move them; but I said, 'Hold on, captain; let me manage that case, and if I fail in moving them, then I will call on you.' Walking up to them, I said, 'Boys, did you know that this fire was made for the purpose of holding a prayer-meeting?' They said they had not heard of it, but finding a good fire they concluded to have a game. I told them to close their services a little while, keep their seats, and we would hold our prayer-meeting. 'Perhaps some of you can sing, and we shall be glad to have you join with us.' They all remained, and some of them did sing, and it all passed off in good order.

"In the spring of 1864, our regiment was ordered to Louisiana, to enter upon that fearful campaign against Gen. Banks, which lasted forty dreadful days, beginning at Mansfield and ending at Yellow Bayou, near Simmsport. Col. Myers had sent his wagon to Navasoto, in charge of the teamster, to remain there until he could come on himself, *en route* to Louisiana. A large number of men who were at home when the regiment marched to

Louisiana were ordered to meet it at Navasoto. The colonel had made arrangements with the quartermaster to furnish corn for his team, and he let the teamster have corn a few times, and then cursed him and told him he had no more for him. Col. Myers sent me on a few days ahead of him to start the wagon, intending to overtake us on horseback. On reaching Navasoto, the teamster informed me that the quartermaster had refused to issue any more corn for his mules, and that every time he went to him he would curse him. In the meantime about fifteen of the furloughed men had come in. I told the teamster to get a sack, and I would go with him to the quartermaster and try him once more; and we approached him, the teamster telling him that his mules were suffering for feed, and that he had come once more to ask him for corn; but the pugnacious quartermaster replied, with an oath: 'Did I not tell you I had no corn for you? Now, sir, do not trouble me any more.' I then said, 'Captain, I am going to tell you the mules must have corn, and you must not curse me.' He exclaimed, 'Who are you?' I said: 'Sir, I am a white man, and I do not allow a whisky-bloat of a quartermaster to curse me; and, sir, I demand corn for those mules. I have about fifteen well-armed men, and if you do not issue the corn at once, I shall be under the necessity of helping myself.' 'I defy you to undertake that; I will put you under arrest.' I said, 'If you do not mind, I will put you under arrest.' Flying into a rage, he said, 'Are you willing to settle this matter with six-shooters?' 'Certainly, captain,' I said; 'that just suits me splendidly.' 'Well, sir,' he said, 'I see you have your pistol on; just wait a little till I can step in and get mine.' Rushing into his office, he was followed by a gentleman who knew me, and who told him that I was the chaplain of the regiment, and came to the door, smiling, and said, 'Preacher, do you want to fight?' 'No, sir, I do not; it is corn I want. I could, however, be provoked into a fight, though it would be unpleasant.' The captain proposed to shake hands over the 'bloody chasm,' and said I could send my wagon and get what corn I wanted."

A determined man, with a strange influence over mankind.

"After the battles had ended, we were camped on Red River, several miles below Alexandria. A man lived near our camp who had manufactured and barreled up a large quantity of rum, and had buried it across the river to conceal it from the soldiers. Our men got an intimation of it from the negroes. The report reached the colonel's ears, and he sent for the man, and told him if it were true he would furnish him a guard, and he might remove it to some place for safe-keeping. He denied having the rum. The colonel told him if he had it his men would find it, and then it would be too late to save it. Our men took their iron ramrods and punched into the sand along a bar, until they struck the barrels, and unearthed about eighteen of them from their sandy graves. They knocked the head out of a barrel, and just 'went for' the accursed 'fire-water.' When the owner heard of it he went to the colonel for help to save his rum, but the colonel told him it was too late—the men were beyond his control; that if he had adhered to his advice he could have saved it. I do not think I ever heard such a racket, or witnessed such a scene. If the lower regions were ever portrayed, it was there. Some were yelling like a band of wild Comanches, some singing merry ditties, some preaching in a solemn manner, some praying devoutly, some cursing bitterly, some laughing, others crying; some were loving everybody, and others seemed to hate every thing. One of them, who was always distant toward me, a young man of a wicked and stubborn nature, became quite social and pious, and declared to me that he was a preacher, a Methodist preacher. Indeed, the confusion was that of bedlam—the scene beggars description. Man's love of intoxicating liquors is as strong as death, yet nothing can be a greater foe to him. It destroys his reason, unfits him for any duties in this life, and disqualifies him for the solemn ordeal of death. It makes him a demon incarnate. Some of them made a raft, and shipped a barrel of the rum down the river a few miles, to Woods's regiment; and after dark they entombed it in the parade-ground, and then they would go out there to play their amusing games. They made a hole in the hidden barrel, and inserted a cane or reed in it, and would kneel down and suck the merry stimulant from its buried home. How wise and good man might be if he was as fond of wisdom and virtue, and would spend equal energy to attain unto them!

"While still encamped on Red River, Col. Myers set out a hook one night and caught a large catfish. I walked down to his head-quarters, and found the colonel and his staff of officers standing around and admiring his fine fish. The colonel said, 'Look there, parson, and see what a fine fish we have caught.' I said, 'It is a very fine fish indeed, colonel,' adding, 'Colonel, I expect to catch as large a one up at our mess in a few days, and if we do, we want you to come up and help us eat it.' That polite invitation started up a roar of laughter, and the witty colonel, seeing where I was driving to, said, 'Thank you, parson; as we already have one in hand, we would be pleased to have you dine with us.' 'Thank you, colonel,' said I; 'I will be much pleased to accept your kind invitation; I shall surely be around in due time.' I enjoyed the colonel's fish hugely, but we were never lucky enough to capture one, to repay his kindness."

Ready wit is one of Mr. Potter's natural gifts. To listen to his sharp cuts of wit, when in an amusing mood, one would think him a genuine son of the Emerald Isle; but he is Missouri's child.

One prominent element in Mr. Potter's ministerial life was that of desiring and courting the respect and good feeling of all men, but not at the cost of truth, candor, or honesty. No man enjoys the reciprocity of kind social feeling with a greater zest than he. Many of his life-joys arise from the genial interchange of friendly feeling with his fellow-men; yet no man is ever more ready to censure and correct their evil deeds. But, too, a more unselfish motive than mere self-enjoyment moved him to seek a tender place in the hearts of men, that he might do them good as the minister of Jesus Christ, which motive is not only allowable in ministerial candor, but takes on itself the phase of duty. Kind feeling with men for a minister of the gospel opens the door of their hearts to his approach, but the opposite closes it against him. A cheerful though grave minister will ever find a hearty welcome into the most sincere regards of all men, who are not of the truly abandoned grade, while one of an opposite type may meet from men a respectful reserve. St. Paul sought to please all men for their good to edification—not, however, at the sacrifice of principle.

The weary four months' campaign along the Red River was one of unutterable hardships and sufferings to the army—hunger, sickness, and unbearable toils in the battle-strife, or standing guard, sorely tried the temper and constitution of hardy men. Many of them fell in battle, others were wounded, and many enfeebled from want of nourishing food and doing extra duties. The armies had well-nigh devastated the country, and but little provisions could be had save bread and sugar until the blackberries ripened, which added a luxury to their commissariat. Bread, sugar, and blackberries, comprised their rations. Such diet was trying on the wounded and sick, and after the hard fighting was ended, many of the men got sick—in fact, the camps were like one great hospital. In all these hardships, perhaps no man realized a greater share than

Mr. Potter. Though not a private soldier, yet he was engaged the while in trying to relieve the wounded, sick, and dying. Now he is seen on the bloody field, where shells are falling like blazing stars, aiding in carrying off the wounded; then he is in the hospital nursing them, and again he is out hunting up food they might relish, which was difficult to obtain. When tears and cries of suffering are before him, he has no personal dignity to fall back upon, to shield him from the drudgery of helping to administer relief. Then he is solely clothed about with the *dignity of pity*. He is preacher, doctor, nurse, and commissary. When the half-starved and feeble troops were on night-guard, you see him along their picket-lines carrying them refreshing draughts of water. Here many of the boys were almost naked, many shoeless. Mr. Potter at one time was without shoes, but a generous sick man gave him his own shoes to enable him to go the rounds to help the disabled. At one time one of the lieutenants was on parade without shoes. Brave men, deserving a better fate.

Mr. Potter, in those days of misfortune and grief to his countrymen, was indeed as an angel of mercy, to relieve the living and to console the dying. Dr. McFall was the regimental surgeon—a great and noble man, a good doctor, and ever kind. He ordered the disabled to be taken back to hospitals, and Mr. Potter is in the lead of those engaged in their removal to better quarters. After their safe removal to the hospitals, the colonel sent him home to rest.

"During my stay at home I preached all through Coldwell county, and collected one hundred dollars in specie, to buy nourishment for the sick in the army, which supplied them until the war closed. In appealing to the people for contributions to victual the sick soldiers, I told them that a large number of the moneyed and leading men started out furiously patriotic, urging every man to go into the war, and helped fit them out, and there were others who were ten-strikers, who pitched in, and were going to kill ten Yankees as an easy job. Some of them had managed not to go at all, or had gotten out of the ranks somehow, and their ardent patriotism had greatly cooled down, and they reminded me of the man who said that the first three months after his marriage he loved his wife so well he could have eaten her up, but before the next three had rolled away she had become so quarrelsome that he really wished to God he had eaten her."

When the war was fairly opened there were many great patriots who could easily put to flight a dozen Yankees, with old flint-lock muskets, and they shrewdly managed by their hot-headed patriotism to get other cooler patriots into the ranks; and if they got in at all, many of them got out somehow, and speculated on the interest of the "war widows," and that of the government they loved so well. They were all over their beloved Confederacy, and hordes of them grew rich on their fraudulent gains—a harvest reaped by the keen-edged blade of their pretended patriotism. Mr. Potter was no braggart—he toiled for the weal of mankind. He pleads for the sick, the helpless, and the needy, not to enrich his own purse.

In the fall of 1864 Mr. Potter returned to his regiment, which was still in the State of Louisiana. On his way, he called to pass the night at a house in Eastern Texas. It was the home of wealth, refinement, and comfort. The lady and her daughter were Episcopalians, who seemed to be alone, except a youthful Baptist minister, who was neatly clad in a respectable clerical garb. He was quite talkative, and seemed to estimate his merits at their highest marketable value. Mr. Potter, knowing that citizens generally in that region did not very cheerfully entertain soldiers, was not very communicative, and really did not care to talk on that subject, and passed the time till supper was announced in reading and listening to the gifted young divine, who seemed to have on hand such a volume of facts in regard to himself and his Apostolic Church, dating back without a broken chronological link to the banks of the Jordan, that he fully occupied all the spare moments in descanting on those important themes to his lone, silent auditor—having told him that his calling was that of a Baptist minister, whose chief business in this case seemed to be to convince all men that his Church was the only true Apostolic Church in the world, having been set up on Jordan's stream by the memorable "John the Baptist" (though he never was an apostle), and to get all the world to join it, and to proselyte other Churches into it. He had greatly annoyed the Episcopal landlady and her daughter from time to time, in trying to unveil their eyes that they might clearly see his glorious Church in the far-removed ages of the past, rising and dripping out of the Jordan, as the glory-attired moon coming up from the bosom of the ocean. With easy, self-stiffened dignity, that inflated ministerial neophyte approached the table, and as usual, soon began his pet theme—his Church, immersion, etc. The polite young lady inquired of him if *immersion was essential to salvation.* He replied that *it was not essential to salvation, but that it was essential to obedience.* The young lady remarked that she was not informed enough on theological subjects to discuss the matter with him, and she would have to call this stranger (alluding to Mr. Potter) to help her, saying, "Stranger, can you not help me?" Mr. Potter replied that he was not in a mood of mind to discuss the matter, having just ended a long day's ride, but that he would not object to ask the gentleman a few questions, if he would grant him the liberty of doing so. "Certainly, certainly, any question you may choose, pertinent to the subject." Mr. Potter began: "Your Church believes in the possibility of apostasy, does it not?" "No, sir; no, sir," was quickly replied. "You know but little of the Baptist doctrine, if you think that." "Very well, I stand corrected," said Mr. Potter. "Well, sir, please tell me how one is to get into your Church." "Why, you have to give in an experience of grace, and satisfy the Church that you are converted—born again—and then be immersed."

"You say you give in an experience of grace, and assure the Church that you are regenerated, and you say that a converted soul cannot fall away and be lost?" "No, sir; a soul born again can never be lost. It is sure to get to heaven." "If, then, I tell an experience of grace to the Church, and it pronounces me a converted man, I am sure to get to heaven, am I not?" "Yes, sir; you cannot fail. None of God's children can ever be lost." "But now," said Mr. Potter, "suppose after you have heard my experience, and called it good, and voted me the right of membership in your Church, then I refuse to be immersed, how will you manage my case? You say I am converted and cannot be lost, but you also say that obedience is essential to salvation, and that immersion is essential to obedience; but I refuse to be immersed; what will you do with me?" The gifted young divine seemed enveloped in a mist—his theological lamp did not dispel its gloom—he looked down on his plate, began to scratch its face with his fork, rose up suddenly, and hurrying to the door slammed it together behind him, and did not appear any more while Mr. Potter remained.

The jubilant young lady arose from the table and danced up and down the dining-room, saying that she would not take fifty dollars for the young polemic's defeat, declaring that he had annoyed her no little for some considerable time with his exclusive immersion, and associated themes. The old lady raised up her spectacles, and said, "Stranger, I would like to know more about you, if you have no objections to speaking about yourself." "I am a soldier, madam, and when we have a little rest-time I get the soldiers together under the trees and preach to them." "A preacher, are you?" "Yes, madam." "What denomination do you represent?" "Methodist." "Well, sir, you are welcome here, and we will ever try to give you a pleasant reception when it may suit you to call."

How beautifully Christian-like is it for all Christians to act in cordial fellowship one with another, and not be ever striving to unchurch each other, and to make the world believe that theirs is the only Church!

"On reaching Woodville, in Eastern Texas, I put up with Dr. McCulloch for the night. I had stopped over Sunday and preached in that town, on my way home, and had shared the generous hospitality of the doctor at that time. The citizens, having heard of my arrival, sent in a petition for me to stay until Tuesday night, and preach for them again. I accordingly did so, and there being such an interest manifested, I concluded to continue the meeting until Sunday; and it resulted in a glorious revival. Among my hearers was an old Universalist. At first he would slip in the door at night, and take a seat in the back part of the house. I noticed that every time I preached he got one bench nearer, till Sunday, when he came to the front seat. When I came in, he said to me: 'Sir, can I sit here? I am a little hard of hearing, and I like your talk, sir, I like your talk very much.' I told him to keep his seat. He wept profusely while I was preaching, and at the close of the services he invited me home with him. I went, and tried to point out to him the errors of his creed, and commended him to the Saviour of men. That night he was converted, and went home shouting through the streets."

Since Mr. Potter entered the ministry of Jesus Christ, preaching has ever been the one great business of his life. Wherever Providence cast his lot he was ready to preach, to any people who might desire to hear, no matter who or where, in the week or on Sunday. If he had no learned sermon "cut and dried" for the occasion, no matter; he ever had enough of religion and theology on hand to comfort Christians, and to tell sinners how to get religion.

CHAPTER XX.

The army now left Louisiana and returned to Texas, and while on the ferry-boat crossing the Sabine River, Brigadier-general Debray had an advisory interview with Mr. Potter on the immoralities of some men in his brigade, saying that many complaints were made against them in Louisiana about their marauding on citizens' hogs and other things. He said that he was desirous of his men demeaning themselves in an upright and honest way, so as to maintain a good character at all times, and now especially, as they were entering Texas. General Debray was a high-toned gentleman, and ever acted with a noble sense of honor. He took pride in hearing his men spoken of in terms of merited praise. He truly remarked that it was not a mere individual concern—that the entire brigade was involved. What a few men might do was charged to them all collectively. It was not what Johnson, Jones, or Smith may have done, but it would be what Debray's men did; and in all after-time, when one of his men might chance to meet with one of those injured citizens, he would share the odium of the guilt of a few men in the judgment of that citizen. He kindly requested Mr. Potter to go through all the companies and messes and remonstrate with the troops, show them the folly and wrong of such conduct, and try to stop their marauding, saying that he would talk with his officers—some of whom he feared had connived at the thing, and, may be, had eaten of the harvest.

Mr. Potter said to the General that those men had been almost necessitated to their ugly habits of foraging on the citizens. Hunger, and almost starvation, had driven them to it. The country over there had been overrun with armies, and rations were more than "short," and the men had undergone incredible privations and sufferings. "And now, General," said he, "if you will allow me to make a suggestion, I will vouch for its being an effectual remedy. Do you order all the tithes brought to your camps, and have plenty of provisions issued to each mess, and I assure you the men will stop their marauding. The people have to haul their tithes to their county-seats to the government tithe-house, and they will haul it to your camps, in each county as readily as to the commissary at the county-seat. These men have hungered and toiled long enough to deserve full rations in their own State, where there is plenty; no waste need be the result—a good supply is all that is wanted." The General approved the idea and adopted the plan, and no more complaints were heard of his men going to smoke-houses, corn-cribs, fodder-stacks, or potatoe-patches, to forage in the darkness of night; but with all the cravings of hunger satiated, they lay down and slept at night with a quiet stomach and a better conscience.

We have heard and read of the hardships of soldiers amid the terrible perils of war. History's page transmits the memory of them to our day. Reading the record, we seem to hear their unmitigated wails echoing along the bends and curves of time's rolling stream. Historians, as sentinels on its banks, seem fond of sending their sad notes to the end of the great river—its merging into eternity. But soldiers of the "Lost Cause" have endured in silent sorrow equal sufferings, and no trumpet of fame tells the story of their woes—their cause was unpopular. The last day shall hang up the picture of that dreadful scene.

On the Christmas-eve of 1864 General Debray's brigade encamped around old San Augustine, and Mr. Potter called on an old preacher residing there to get the use of the Methodist church the next day, which was the Sabbath-day. The minister was a devoted man, but seemed not to have any faith in doing his community any good by preaching to them at Christmas-time. His name was Samuel Williams, a Texan pioneer. He asked Mr. Potter what he wanted to do with the church. He replied, "To hold religious service." "Why," said the old gentleman, "there is no use; you cannot get the people to church Christmas-times; they will be attending dances and parties." Mr. Potter informed him that he was not dependent on the citizens for an audience; that he had his congregation with him —the soldiers. "O!" said the old man, "you can get the house." So Mr. Potter preached on Sunday, and gave out an appointment for night; but the old preacher said as it had rained, and was quite muddy, and would be dark, that few would venture out. The soldiers could not attend in the day-time, and the audience was rather small that morning, so the old man thought it would be less at night—not thinking about the soldiers, who cared little for mud or darkness. Night came, and the streets were illuminated with the lamps of the soldiers going to church; and they thronged the house, and a revival started among them which lasted three weeks, and added sixty members to the Army Christian Association, which was of the nature of an army Church. Sometimes mourners were on their knees in different parts of the church, and would send for Mr. Potter to come and pray for them, and then a similar request would reach him, and he would send for some of those other preachers; but they would say, "No, we want Potter; he has been with us in Louisiana, and ate bread and sugar with us; we want him to pray with us now." O how mutual hardships unite the hearts of men! and a faithful minister of Jesus Christ in times of afflictions and dangers is never forgotten.

At that great meeting Mr. Potter was favored with the help of several ministerial brethren of great ability and usefulness. He got Columbus Sawyer, a private in Woods's regiment, excused from duty to aid in the revival—he was a young man of great promise to the Church; also the Rev. Mr. Burk, P. E., who held a quarterly-meeting there in the meantime; likewise the Rev. E. P. Rogers, P. C., and the Revs. White and Wadkins, refugees from Louisiana; and also the resident minister, Mr. Samuel Williams.

These men at different times labored in the revival to advantage. Mr. Potter had much of the altar labor to perform; he also kept up day-service for the benefit of the citizens.

His labors were wonderfully blessed in getting men to reform their lives during all his campaigns in Texas and Louisiana, whenever he found an opportunity to preach any length of time to his comrades; and between them and their earnest and faithful chaplain and fellow-soldiers there sprung up an attachment which memory shall ever hold sacred till their grand reunion on the immortal plains, where the sound of battle is not heard. That Army Church did much good. General Debray said he was proud of his men then. Full rations worked well.

The following amusing, truthful story is taken from Mr. Potter's manuscript. The lady of this story had been taught by a certain Campbellite preacher that the Methodist Church had been the efficient agent in bringing on the war, hence her antipathy to Methodist preachers. Her object in accosting Mr. Potter as she did was to excite his ire, and get him to leave her house; but she had encountered the wrong man that time. He at once read her intentions, and instantly became fire-proof against all her heated insults. Texas has some rare specimens of feminine pugnacity.

"One day when our regiment was marching through the piney-woods of Eastern Texas, in a heavy shower of rain, I approached a house, and dismounting rushed in for shelter. It was the abode of an aged widow lady, and though she bore the marks of time she possessed much of the vital force of life. Several private soldiers had already called in there, and as I entered the house one of them said, 'It seems to be raining to-day, parson.' The old woman threw her piercing eyes upon me, and said, 'You are a *parson*, are you?' 'I am no preacher to hurt, madam.' 'I do not thank a parson to come into my house.' 'Madam, what have the parsons done to you, that you are so embittered against them?' 'Why, they have been the cause of all this war and bloodshed.' 'Madam, I shall have to attribute that whimsical notion to your want of information. I have been informed that all the men in this piney country vote for Gen. Jackson every four years, for President of the United States, not knowing that he is dead.' 'They have got as much sense as you've got; you need n't think that you know every thing, because you are a parson.' 'Well, madam, have you got some tobacco you could let me have?' She ran to a sack, hanging on the side of the wall, and jerked out a twist of home-made, which she handed to me, saying, 'There, now, take that!' 'Now, madam, I am hungry and want dinner, and I want you to get a chicken and cook it for me; you know Methodist preachers love chicken.' 'No I won't; but I will tell you where you can go and stay all night, and get as much chicken as you want. Go on this road about three miles, and you will come to a blacksmith-shop, and then turn down to the left and you will soon come to a house; tell them you are a parson, and you will be all right, for they are long-faced Methodists.' 'Well, madam, the best of friends have to part. Madam, can you tell me when the stars fell?' 'You are a nice fellow, pretending to be a parson, and don't know what year the stars fell; well, that does beat me!' Taking hold of the shovel, she began to punch the fire, saying, 'I guess I must warm up this parson.' 'Madam, you are very kind. The apostles were driven out, and not allowed to come into the houses, but you allow me shelter, and permit me to warm by your pleasant fire.' 'I would have you know you are not welcome, sir; but you can sit there awhile for all I care.' Then she said, 'Well, parson, you will preach about me when you leave here.' 'No, madam; I do not expect to mention your name only when I am on my knees in prayer. I shall then ask the Lord to bless you in your declining years, and make your closing scenes as bright and placid as the splendid calm of the most brilliant day.' 'I don't want your prayers; I don't thank you for your prayers.' 'I know you don't; but my Bible teaches me to pray for my enemies, and I think you are the worst one I have met. Well, now, you won't cook me a chicken?' 'No, I won't; if you never get a chicken till I kill you one, you will go without one a long time.' I then began to sing:

> Your love to me has been most dear,
>   Your conversation sweet;
> How can I bear to journey where
>   With you I cannot meet?

"I then reached out my hand to tell her good-by;

she instantly grasped it and began to weep, saying: 'Parson, I must own up—I am whipped. I have done all I could to make you mad, but I have not seen the least sign of anger. If you ever pass this way again, call on me; you can preach in my house if you want to, and I will give you as much chicken as you want.'

"I went on, and found the house as she had said. I told the family of my encounter with the old woman. They said that in many respects she was a clever woman, but she had some strange notions; she fed every private soldier that called on her, but never allowed an officer to eat at her table."

"A soft answer turneth away wrath." Had Mr. Potter taken offense, and left that old lady's house showing that he was incensed, it would have strengthened her dislike for his class of ministers.

When the regiment was encamped at Shelbyville, in Eastern Texas, an old soldier went to a house and borrowed a razor. The kind lady entertained very tender feeling for the self-sacrificing soldiers, and thinking that the old man just wanted a shave, and would return it immediately, readily lent him a razor, without even inquiring his name or making any conditions in the loan. The razor was a family relic, and much prized on that account, and after some time had elapsed the good lady became uneasy about the loss of this much-valued heir-loom, and called on the colonel to get him to recover it for her. The colonel told her that he had about six hundred men, and it would be like "hunting a needle in a hay-stack," as he had no name or clew to guide him in the search, but he would be on the lookout for it, and if he found it he would have it returned to her.

The colonel finally thought of his friend, Mr. Potter, who was ever rich in plans to outwit the evil-doer, and he sent for him and narrated to him the razor story, and his promise to the clever lady, and requested him to keep a watchful eye after the lost relic, inquiring if he thought he could make any discovery. Mr. Potter replied, "I will have it before night." "No you won't," said the colonel. "I will have it before night," repeated Mr. Potter.

Remembering to have seen a certain old man clean-shaved, Mr. Potter went to him and asked him to take a walk. They called the old man "Gravy." After getting away from the mess, Mr. Potter said to him, "'Gravy,' that lady is distressed because you have not returned the razor; it is a family relic." The old man said he had kept it so long he hated to go back with it. Mr. Potter got the razor and returned it to the lady, to the great surprise of the good colonel.

While at Shelbyville, the silly citizens would have dances in the country thereabouts, and the soldiers would go to them. At one time a band of them went to a dance, and being short of cooking-utensils they carried off some from the dance-house; but to avoid detection, they had changed their names. They had agreed to call the name of their leader "Brown." The lady called on the colonel to recover her kitchen-wares. Her accusations were made against the name of Brown. The colonel said that he had several Browns in his regiment, and had them all called up and placed in line before her, but she said that neither of them was the guilty party. He then told her that he was at the end of his row—the deed had been done under a false name—and she returned as she came. Just at the time of moving from Shelbyville great rains fell, and made the roads quite muddy. Each mess tied up its cooking-utensils in a sack, and put them into the mess-wagon, and it being heavily laden, mired down just opposite the dance-house from which the cooking-utensils had been taken, and about a half dozen women made a raid on the wagon in search of the stolen articles. They untied the sacks and took out each piece, then returned them and tied the sack up again, till coming to the one containing their skillets, etc. "There!" one jubilant lady exclaimed; "see what bravery can do!" No one disputed her right to renown. Mr. Potter was along, but had no interest in the mess-wagon, and feeling that a just Providence had revealed the guilty party, he had no objections to make either to the ladies' right of property or desert of valor.

"The army marched from place to place till it reached the town of Crockett, where I got a furlough to visit my home, but joined my command again just a few days before the 'break-up,' and then we were ordered to Houston. I learned at Houston that our brigade was held there after other commands were disbanded, to protect the merchants of the city against troops passing homeward from Galveston; it was feared they might break in upon their stores as they passed through. Our rations being poor, I went to those merchants and told them that our soldiers were there for their protection, and I must ask them to supply us with several days' rations. I asked for supplies for two regiments, Woods's and Debray's. I asked for flour, bacon, coffee, sugar, and tobacco. I was told to call in the afternoon, when an answer would be given me. When I called, I was informed that I could get the provisions at Longcoat's establishment. The merchants had made the deposit there, and it was enough to supply the troops, and lasted them *en route* to their homes. I cannot close my account of our three years' campaign without acknowledging my obligations to the officers in whose commands I severally passed those toilsome periods; they were ever respectful and obliging to me as the minister of Jesus Christ, and cordially received me into their head-quarters when I approached them on business or otherwise.

"After the address (herein recorded by Mr. Lee Rogan, of Lockhart), I told the soldiers that if it was convenient I would like to shake the farewell hand with every soldier in the regiments. That was enough; they arose and rushed forward in no orderly manner, and with many tears and sobs we took the parting hand."

That truly was a breaking up. Two or three hundred brave men in tears while looking upon each other's faces and shaking the parting hand, as far as they knew, and no doubt truly so to many of them, for the last time in this world, indeed was a touching scene that would arrest the attention and melt the heart of an angel. For three years, day and night, they had shared their mutual toils and joys; together they had suffered; they had fought side by side in the death-storm of battle; together they had seen their fallen comrades, heard their dying groans, and listened to the painful anguish of the wounded; in moments of rest they had passed their little moods of pleasantry in social interchange of camp-life amusements, and had often worshiped together, till truly they were as one great brotherhood; and now they must part, and worst of all, they must part with their beloved chaplain, who to them was more than a mere man, because he represented to them One who truly was greater than all men. The chaplain was the centralizing object in the army, as he represented the grand centralizing object in the great universe. In the person of a faithful chaplain all hearts unite; all their little likes and dislikes are lost in him—here they are one. Mr. Potter's moral power in that army was immeasurable; by his devotedness to duty he had fixed their faith in the unifying truth of Jesus. They parted in his name, hoping to meet around the great white throne of Him whom their faithful chaplain visibly represented. May they meet him there!

CHAPTER XXI.

When Mr. Potter made his farewell address to the troops at Houston, at their final discharge, a gentleman by the name of Rogan made extensive notes of the address, and while preparing this book, Mr. Potter wrote to him for a copy of the same; but Mr. Rogan having lost the original, he kindly reproduced the main features of it from memory.

Mr. Rogan was a companion with Mr. Potter in the army three years—the place of all others that tries the elements of character to the bottom. He was a lawyer, and a member of the Presbyterian Church, an intelligent Christian gentleman, who duly esteemed true merit anywhere. He was one of the few, like Col. Woods, who came out of that terrible fratricidal war with their religious character untarnished—a clean heart, and "hands unstained with plunder."

He is now an able lawyer at Lockhart, Texas, standing high in the deserved esteem of his fellow-citizens, and the writer is more than proud to have the indorsement of such a one to the high merits of the man whose real character he has striven to truthfully portray in these pages:

Lockhart, Texas, May 7, 1881.

Brother Potter:—Inclosed find my contribution to your book. I have done what I could. The writing has been done in my office, with frequent interruptions. I have no time to revise it. I am not of late accustomed to write much else but legal documents, in which we do not pay much attention to style or punctuation. I have endeavored to follow your line of thought in your farewell address as near as I could recollect. With best wishes for your present and future welfare, I remain,

Yours truly,   LEE ROGAN.

Here follows Mr. Rogan's letter:

In the early part of the year 1864, the Rev. A. J. Potter, a private in Col. Woods's regiment of Texas Cavalry, was appointed by Col. J. J. Myers Chaplain of the Twenty-sixth Regiment of Texas Cavalry, better known as "Debray's Regiment." Although the colonel was well acquainted with Mr. Potter, and knew his sterling qualities as a man, the new chaplain was an entire stranger to almost the whole regiment; but entering immediately on the discharge of his duties, his genial nature and high social qualities ennabled him soon to make the acquaintance of every man regularly on duty in the entire command. Very soon after his appointment, the regiment, with other Texas troops, was ordered to Louisiana to meet the Federal army commanded by Gen. Banks.

Mr. Potter accompanied the regiment in all of its marches, encouraging the men in the discharge of their duties as soldiers, preaching to them as he had opportunity, and availing himself of any clerical aid that might come in his way—thus endeavoring to prepare his charge for any event that might await them in the discharge of their arduous and perilous duties. When actual fighting began at Mansfield and Pleasant Hill, he worked faithfully with the ambulance corps carrying off the wounded and dying, always in the thickest of the fight looking up the brave men who lay prostrate on the battle-field, victims of war's terrible havoc. So through the entire campaign, until the last battle at Yellow Bayou, he was constantly present, doing every thing that he could for the comfort of his men; and doubtless many of the old regiment now gratefully cherish his memory for his many acts of kindness to them while sick or wounded; in fact, "Potter" is rather a "household word" with the "boys," and when they meet and begin to call up old memories, frequent inquiries are made after their old chaplain.

One instance only is now remembered in which the chaplain laid aside the duties of his office and entered into the fight. At a battle fought below Alexandria, Louisiana, near Bayou Beff, the enemy was crowding our men most too closely to suit his martial spirit, and leaving the wounded to be cared for by others, he seized a gun, mounted his horse, and rode to the front, ready to pull trigger with the foremost of the line; but the enemy was too strong, and he with the balance of the regiment was compelled to beat a reluctant retreat.

After the campaign was over and the enemy retired, Mr. Potter obtained a furlough to visit his family in Bastrop County, Texas. While at home, he busied himself in collecting money and other supplies for the comfort of the men, and especially the sick. Returning, he met the regiment in the vicinity of San Augustine, Texas, where it spent a part of the winter and early spring of 1865. While encamped there the men suffered much from sickness, contracted principally in Louisiana. Mr. Potter was there, as ever, prompt in his attentions to the sick, looking for places for some of them among the citizens, and supplying them with such wholesome food as he could purchase. The spring of that year was very wet, and the march of the regiment from east of the Trinity River to the Brazos, where it was ordered, was almost a constant wading through mud and water, and the swimming of swollen streams, both rivers and creeks. Mr. Potter was always in the van, sharing equally with the men the toils and dangers of the march, always cheerful and brimful of good humor; the sight of his smiling countenance, the sound of his cheery laugh, and his encouraging words, materially aided the officers in preserving good order and discipline in the ranks.

When it became evident, even to the rank and file of our branch of the army, that the long struggle was about ended, the war over, and we defeated, the regiment was ordered down to Houston, and stationed on Brazos Bayou, near the city.

In a few days rumors reached the camp that the troops in and immediately around the city were rapidly disbanding without orders, securing what supplies they could, and the men going home. This rumor was soon confirmed, and on May 22 it became painfully evident that the Twenty-sixth was just about to follow the example of others. The regiment was then commanded by Senior Captain John L. Lane, of Lockhart. There were rumors too of disaffection among the men, and of threats of personal violence to some of the officers. Under the circumstances Mr. Potter deemed it prudent to call the men together once more. Accordingly, after dark, with no lights but the twinkling stars and the camp-fires around, many of the men gathered about their chaplain, to hear his farewell words to them. Only a meager outline can now be given of his fervid and impassioned address.

He commenced by reminding them of the cause in which they were engaged—that they had readily answered their country's call; had left home and kindred, and staked their all on the uncertain issues of war; they had endured hardships as good soldiers; they had met the enemy with undaunted courage, and in every contest had shown themselves worthy the confidence their general had always reposed in them. Throughout the entire war they had ever been noted for their cheerful obedience to orders, no matter how hard or disagreeable the duties assigned them; and he now called upon them to show the same spirit of obedience to law and order, and remain in camp until honorably discharged from the service. He said it was true that during the years they had been together there had been many just causes of complaint, but these things did not now afford any sufficient reason for violence or disorder. He had heard too that some of the men entertained feelings of personal hostility toward some of their officers, and now when occasion offered, they were disposed to avenge themselves by attacks upon their persons. If such was the case, if any in his audience entertained any such feelings, he implored them to banish all such thoughts and designs at once. This, he said, is no time to harbor malice or ill-will against any comrade, either officer or private; the war is ended, no longer is the call to arms heard, arousing us from fitful slumbers disturbed with dreams of bloodshed and groans of the dying. Together we have fought for a common cause—we have lost the battle, we have been defeated—but there is another cause which demands that we remain one in heart and purpose, and which requires unity of action; that is, the upbuilding of our country's fortunes, and in and by the peaceful avocations of individual life secure that victory which we have now been unable to win. He reminded them that upon their return to their homes they would find many and great changes, and be called upon to face and endure many hardships and trials to which they had never before been subjected. Many, if not all of them, would find themselves deprived of nearly or quite all the property they had when they entered the service, and they would be dependent upon their own exertions for a livelihood. He exhorted them to go home with the determination to take their places as good citizens, working harmoniously with their respective communities in re-establishing their broken fortunes. He said: "Many of you will find it hard, after four years' absence from your former pursuits, engaged in the active, stirring duties of soldier-life, to accustom yourselves to the duties which will devolve on you as citizens; but as you value your own peace and happiness, the welfare of those dear to you, and the prosperity of the whole country, you must put your shoulders to the wheels and push forward the car of progress with all the force and energy you can command. The past years have been years of trial, the present is dark, gloomy, and forbidding, but these things are to brave men no reason for despondency. This beautiful land is yet our own; our homes have not been blackened by fires kindled by the invader's torch; behind the clouds of adversity shines the sun of prosperity, and if you will faithfully and honestly discharge your duties, obeying the laws of the land, however hard and oppressive they may be, the great Father of all in his own good time will cause the clouds to disappear, and bid the sun to shine upon you. But above all I would remind you of your duties to Him who sits upon the throne of the universe, and controls and directs all things according to his own will. You cannot eliminate God and your duty to him from your plans and purposes, with any hope of permanent success. I therefore beg of you to first give attention to your religious duties, knowing that He has said: 'Seek first the kingdom of God, and all these things shall be added unto you.'" In conclusion, he said: "I say to you again, your duties as soldiers are about ended; your camp-fires will now go out, never again to be lighted; the bugle will cease to sound the reveille, and the roll-call will be heard no more; your companies will be disbanded, and the men who compose this regiment will be scattered to all parts of the State. Many of us, yea, the most of us, will meet no more until the last grand bugle sound shall awake and summon us to meet before the great white throne, to give an account of the deeds done in the body. As your chaplain, speaking to you for the last time, I again affectionately urge you to prepare at once for the last call which shall come to you, and at an hour when it is not expected. Live right, that you may die right. The life of a wicked man is not likely to end with cheering prospects of a happy and blissful hereafter. Live so that when the Master comes and calls for you, you may be ready to answer: 'Here, Lord, am I.' For you my prayers shall ascend to heaven. God speed you in all laudable works in which you may hereafter be engaged, and may He aid you in repairing and building up your fallen fortunes, and in promoting the welfare of our common country."

The regiment remained quietly in camp until the next morning, when the last roll-call was made, and the officers ordered to prepare discharges for their men; and during that day, May 22, 1865, all of the Twenty-sixth Texas Cavalry who were present, and those who were known to be absent, were honorably discharged from the army of the Confederate States, having remained true to their colors to the last roll-call. LEE ROGAN.

We truly prize the strong testimony of a man of such rank as Mr. Rogan as to the high estimate placed on the character we have undertaken to delineate. One prominent trait boldly cropping out in the results of that last wise, patriotic address, made to the remains of a regiment of brave men, when all the disappointment and gloom of defeat was upon them, is his strange and wonderful power over men, even on the verge of panic and in the tumult of revolt. When other regiments had rudely disbanded, and were *en route* to their long-neglected homes and dear ones, he holds the command a day and night in subjection to military orders which truly had no longer authority over them, for the war was over. He also quells their intentions of violence against those they regarded as their oppressors when under their authority, and quiets all purposes of trespass on private property to aid in replenishing their wasted fortunes. In the last days of disaster to their country's cause, he greatly helped the officers in keeping discipline in the army. Religion and patriotism bloom in the close of that address. Nature and grace made him great.

"After the 'break-up' at Houston, I returned home with a company of men who lived at Lockhart, among whom was the Hon. L. J. Story, now Lieutenant-governor of the State of Texas. Soon after my return, my mother-in-law, Mrs. Dorcas Gwinn, who had lived with us ten years, passed to her reward in the triumphs of a glorious faith. She was a member of the Primitive Baptist Church, and a true 'mother in Israel.' The Presbyterian Church in Lockhart, being without a pastor, invited me to occupy their pulpit, which I did very pleasantly for some time. In a certain community in Bastrop County the good people appointed a union-meeting, and invited ministers of different denominations to come and assist in it. They said that the people were giving dancing-parties in welcoming the soldiers home, but they wanted to greet them with a protracted-meeting. I attended at the time, and found myself almost without ministerial help. I carried on the meeting ten days, which ended in a great revival, and many were converted. A confirmed infidel lived in the community, a sporting character, and very fond of horse-racing. He was one of my old 'chums' in the days of my vanity. He attended the meeting, and listened to my preaching several days with marked attention. One day he approached me, and said, 'Potter, I do not believe in your religion, but I believe you do; I believe you are in earnest, and honest in your belief—you will please send over and get a cow and calf from my ranch.' I gratefully accepted his kind offer, and got the cow.

"There was living some three miles from me a man who had been a widower several years, and had reared his children in great ignorance—and some of them were grown. He had lately married a 'school-marm,' an 'old maid.' He was an unfeeling man, and a terrible tyrant to his family. One day I saw one of his sons coming in great haste. He called for me, and said that his ma wanted me to come over and preach his pa's funeral. I inquired, 'Is your pa dead?' 'No,' said he, 'but he is bad off.' I saddled my horse, and rode over and found him still living, but writhing on his bed in great agony, saying, 'My heart will break! my heart will break!' I supposed there had been a family trouble, and took the old lady aside, and inquired the cause of his great mental distress. She said that hearts were not so easily broken, or hers would have been broken; that since their marriage he had been cruel to her, and that on the past night he had taken an ax and ran her and his daughter from the place, and that his conscience had got to hurting him, and he had sent a messenger after her to return, saying that he would die if she did not, and that through mere pity she had come back. I stepped back into the room, and he was still crying, 'My heart will break! my heart will break!' 'Amen! God grant it!' I said. 'You have got a wicked heart, and I hope the Lord will burst it all to pieces and give you a better one.' 'O parson,' he said, 'pray for me!' 'I will do so with all the agony of my soul, sir, for I do not know a man that needs prayer any more than you do;

you have all the attributes of a dog except kindness.' So I read the Bible, and prayed with him. He promised to be a better man in the future, and attend church, which he did. I do not know that he ever embraced religion, but he was ever after a changed man."

CHAPTER XXII.

Not a great while after Mr. Potter got home from the war he was invited to go down on Walnut Creek, some twelve miles from his residence, to preach to the people of that community. The messenger informed him that a party of armed men down there had given the circuit-preacher the lie in the pulpit, and had cursed him, so that the preacher had closed his sermon and left, saying that was the last sermon he would ever preach in that house.

Mr. Potter sent an appointment, and went down at the time and found the citizens there at the preaching-hour. He entered the pulpit, and seeing the armed party there, he told them that he had heard there was some fighting-stock down there that wanted to fight preachers, and that he had come down to fight or preach, or, if need be, to do both. But he wanted a clear understanding and good order in the whole affair. He proposed that all sit still and be quiet till he preached a sermon, as some of the people had come to hear preaching, and after the sermon was over, if nothing but a fight would do, he would be ready for fighting, in the house or out-of-doors, as any of them might choose. He then proceeded to read, and sing, and pray, and preach, no one disturbing him in the least, and perfect good order reigning throughout the entire service. When the worship was over, Mr. Potter said to them: "Now, after dismission, if any one wants to fight, I shall be ready, and we will have it in the house or outside; or we will adjourn to dinner, and let the fight come off in the evening." Mr. Potter was acquainted with the leader of the fighters. After the benediction the leader smilingly approached the preacher, and Mr. Potter said, "Jim, do you want to fight?" "No, sir; I do not want to fight you; I want you to go with me to dinner." He went, and so it ended.

The nature, name, and character, of the man, and his unique manner, give him a strange and wonderful power over men. Many are the spheres and varied are the relations of men, and they are constituted and born with temperaments and capacities suited to each. Some are born to command, while others are constituted to obey. Some are endowed with a ruling genius, and others are possessed of a disposition to submit to authority. A few are made to rule in times of anarchy and terror; to quell the disorderly tempers and raging passions of the reckless multitude, when reason is dethroned, and blind, maddened impulse leads to ruin, as when the steam of high-pressure, without a conductor, drives the train into the awful vortex. A wise conductor cools and shuts off the steam, and checks up the dangerous speed. Mr. Potter was born to manage men—to control them in the absence of reason, by calming and silencing passion, and escorting reason to her rightful throne—born to quiet the most fearful storms of enraged tumults, as Jesus stilled the tempest-winds and quieted the mad, leaping waves of the blue Galilee, by whispering peace to the storm-riven sea. In his nature there is the strange occult magnet, to quell and charm into quietude the antithetic elements of contentious men, even when passion's storms rage to their highest fury. His manner too inspires a quietus in the senseless effervescence of angry tempers, and his words gently command the tempest to cease its rage. Firm and decisive, yet cool as a general in the storm of battle, he displays no wrathful feeling. His pugnacity is not the outflow of temper, but the zeal of reason. He makes no threats, but talks of chastising erring men as calmly as if he were going to eat his quiet meal. His name is a prophylactic against the sins of bad men.

In the fall of 1865 Mr. Potter sold out his home on the head of Walnut Creek, and bought a farm on Seal's Creek, three miles east of Prairie Lee. At the session of the West Texas Conference for that year, Mr. Asbury Davidson, Presiding Elder of the Gonzales District, had Mr. Potter appointed as a supply on the Prairie Lee Circuit for the year 1866. The country being so impoverished by the late war, the Conference cut up the circuits into small, convenient territories, contiguous to each preacher's home, so that he might raise a crop, or do something else to aid the Church in the support of his family; and Mr. Potter was assigned to two appointments, about eight miles apart—Prairie Lee and West Fork, on Plum Creek, now Harrison's Chapel. He did a hard year's work on his farm and for the Church that Conference-year, and his labors were greatly blessed in building up the Church, and in reëstablishing good order in society so soon after the demoralizing effects of the war, which to some extent had inaugurated a spirit of disorder in most all communities. He also greatly mitigated the sectarian feeling, which had no little power in some orders of Christians. All the denominations in that region gladly attended his ministry, and were greatly profited. He also preached to the colored people, and had a good time among them, and even to this day those of them still living love and prize his ministry. In all departments the Church in his field that year was truly blessed, and it is now an oasis to him in memories of the pleasant past, as the first year in his long itinerant career. Here again we copy an incident of that year from his manuscript:

"There being no church-building in Prairie Lee, all denominations preached in an old academy building, but the Methodists and Missionary Baptists were the only organizations there. The Rev. Mr. Powel was the pastor of the Baptist Church, but he was 'an old land-marker,' and a sectarian in the strictest sense. He would not worship with other denominations under any circumstances. I was on good terms with the Baptists of the community, and they came to hear me preach. Mr. Powel appointed a meeting there, to be protracted, and promised the people to furnish ministerial help to carry on the meeting several days, but when the time arrived, he came alone, and was sick. The people had made large preparations, and were much disappointed, and a number of the leading members of the Church went to him, and said: 'We know, Brother Powel, that it is against your rules to worship with ministers of other denominations, but we have been at the trouble of preparing for this meeting, and as you have no help now, just call in Mr. Potter, and let the meeting go on; we all like him, and go to hear him preach anyhow when you are not here.' He replied: 'When I am about my Master's work, I always tell his sort to stand aside.' The meeting closed Sunday night. I attended the meeting. Mr. Powel administered the sacrament on Sunday, and poured hot shot into the unimmersed and baby-sprinklers. When the services closed at night, I announced that I would begin a protracted-meeting there at a certain time, and invited ministers of all denominations to assist me, whether sprinkled, poured, or immersed. The good Baptists approved the deserved retort, and when his pastoral term ended they made another call."

In the fall of 1866 Mr. Potter was received into the West Texas Conference, at its session at Seguin, and it was the first Annual Conference he ever attended. The lamented Bishop Marvin presided. Mr. Potter was returned to the Prairie Lee Circuit, under the Rev. Willie Fly, presiding elder. His manuscripts show that he enlarged his circuit that year down on Plum Creek, Mars' Hill, and Atlanta, at which places he had gracious revivals, and largely built up the Church.

In the spring of 1867 Mr. Potter was asked to

take a lot of horses to Eastern Texas, for a lady near Prairie Lee, an account of which we now transcribe:

"Mrs. Cartwright, an estimable lady, was compelled to raise a certain amount of money at a certain time, to meet a pressing demand. She had a lot of horses and mules, but failing to find some one to take them East and sell them for her, she applied to me, urging me to go for her, as she was not willing to risk every one. I made arrangements to have my appointments filled during my absence, as the Conference had instructed the preachers that year to do something to aid the Church in their support. She suggested that I should go first to Leon County, in Eastern Texas, where she had some relations living, who would assist me in selling the stock; but on reaching Leon County I found that there was no demand for stock of that kind, and made no sales. I remained several days at Centreville, where I found a number of my old soldier-mates, and preached to them several times. Here I met the Rev. Dr. Cowart in the Masonic lodge. He was preaching with great acceptability, and doing a large practice. He is now living at Centre Point, Kerr County, Texas, still laboring in the vineyard of the Lord as a local preacher, but the gray hairs and corrugated features tell how time has been marking off the passing years since I met him fifteen years ago.

"While at Centreville I saw a man looking around my horses. He was a stranger there. He had a six-shooter belted around him, and there was something about the man that attracted my attention.

Finding no demand, I moved my stock down to Huntsville. The young man who was employed to help me drive the stock left me, and I hired a negro. On reaching Huntsville I found ready sale, and sold out rapidly. While holding a few head which I had on hand on the public square, I saw the same strange young man looking around my stock, and talking privately to the negro. Thinking I could sell the few unsold stock on my way home, I concluded to start back in the direction of Navasoto, and, traveling about fourteen miles that afternoon, camped for the night. I had sold all but my saddle-horse and one unbroken pony. About twilight that strange young man rode up to my camp, and said, 'Sir, I am traveling, and it is a pleasant night—if you have no objections I will camp with you.' Believing that it was his intention to rob me of my money, I decided at once to take him in. 'Certainly,' said I; 'light, sir.' As he dismounted, I said, 'Sir, I see that you have a six-shooter, and as you are a stranger, and I have a few dollars, I will take care of it for you to-night.' This was a stunner. 'Hand it over,' I said, in somewhat a positive tone. Being armed with a revolver myself, the stranger thought it best to obey, and, unbuckling his belt, handed it over to me. 'Now, sir,' I said, 'you can unsaddle, and stake or hobble your pony.' The negro soon had supper, but the stranger did not seem to have a good appetite. I tried every way to call him out in conversation, as to where he lived and where he was going, but he left every thing about himself as dark as mud. He said he was tired, and would lie down. I told him if he should have occasion to get up in the night, he had better let me know by calling me. He said he could see no reason why he should be taken prisoner because he had seen fit to camp with me. I told him to be quiet, that my reasons would be given to him at the proper time. My guest did not rest well, but did not get up. Of course I did not sleep a wink that night. I thought perhaps he had made a plot with the negro to murder me that night, and get the money they knew I had. The weary hours of the night at last passed away, and the welcome twilight of the morning came. I gave my guest his breakfast, and told him to saddle his horse, and when he was ready to start I cocked my revolver and handed him his, saying: 'Now, sir, here is your pistol, and we will cut our acquaintance right here. You must be careful not to meet me on my way any more. Now, sir, I saw you looking around my stock at Centreville, and also yesterday at Huntsville, and you followed me out here last evening, and I can place no other construction on your conduct than that you intended to rob me of my money, and perhaps murder me, but I have outwitted you. Now, sir, you must not meet me any more; now be off,' and he rode away, and we have not met to this day. I then turned to the negro, and said: 'Now, sir, we will take a divorce right here. Here is the amount of your wages—there is the road; take either end of it.' About that time some ox-wagons came along, and I tied my led-pony behind one of them, and traveled along with them to Navasoto. I reached home safely, and delivered the money to the lady, who rewarded me liberally."

We cannot resist the conviction that in this case Mr. Potter just escaped the snare of that bandit. At that time many were in Texas, and it is more than probable that there was an understanding between the robber and the negro. But Mr. Potter's cool sagacity thwarted their designs. He was compelled to take in the brigand, or break up his camp and go to a house, or take the pending results. Cautious prudence saved him.

"After my return from Eastern Texas, I again entered on the work on my circuit. I was preaching one day at West Fork, the pulpit being on one side of the door; on looking out at my left, I could see what was going on in the yard, and during my discourse I saw a young man dancing. I said: 'My friends, I think I must be improving; I must be doing better to-day than common. I have noticed at different times my preaching has produced revival effects upon my hearers; I have known them to get angry also; and, too, I have seen them laugh and cry, and get happy and shout, but I do not remember that I ever got them to dancing; but now there is a young man dancing out-doors, and he seems to hold up well and keep pretty good time.' A youth stepped out and informed him that I had called attention to his conduct, and he got into a hurry, and did not wait for the benediction, but mounted and rode away.

"My presiding elder, Brother Willie Fly, was of great help to me this year—a noble, good, and useful man. He has been in local life a number of years, owing to bodily afflictions, but in that sphere he is doing useful labors in the Church. He now lives near Gonzales, but when I traveled the Uvalde Circuit he lived there, and I shared largely in his hospitalities and counsels, which he cheerfully bestows, when asked at his hands, by kindred, friends, or strangers. He has greatly aided in building up the Church at Gonzales in the last decade. The Church of his choice now worships in a splendid new brick building, his influence doing no little in getting it up.

"I closed my labors on Prairie Lee Circuit in the fall of 1867, with as good feeling as ever existed between pastor and flock. A kind and generous people. May we meet 'over there.'"

CHAPTER XXIII.

A NOTED man of color, whose title was Doctor Parker, was lecturing to the colored people in Caldwell County, Texas, on their duty and best interest in the habit of cultivating friendly relations with the white race, and of continuing in the South, where they could get better wages than at the North.

Doctor Parker was a man of some culture, and was a fluent speaker and of good moral character. Mr. Potter was one of a number who invited him to address the colored people in the little town of Prairie Lee. On the day appointed a large crowd of white and colored people assembled at the church to hear the sable orator. The colored audience filled the house, save Mr. Potter and a few others who got seats inside, while many white men were out-doors. That which is great naturally is more admired by mankind than that which is made so by art. A man of great talents unacquired from books and schools excites the curious admiration of men more than one of greater abilities derived more directly from learning and the polish of literature; and the gifts and the oratory of a man from a humble sphere is more esteemed than those of one from scenes of a higher life. The novelty of an African making a political speech just after the close of the war which had so lately unmanacled millions of slaves, created no little interest. A few, no doubt, were deeply steeped in the deep-rooted prejudice that no good could come out of Africa, and may have been a little nettled at the idea that her sable son should have the temerity to make a political speech; but such was not the opinion of the wiser and better element of Texan society. Their surrender of arms in the late war was in good faith—to give all grades, races, and colors, equal civil and political rights under the Federal and State constitutions—and that intelligent and order-loving element in Texan society readily assumed a friendly attitude toward the late freed population, regarding it as an imperative duty enjoined by Christian morals, and interest as well, to aid that people to rise to the *status* of good citizenship. As they must constitute a factor in society, interest demands that they be bettered in their physical, moral, and intellectual conditions, or society must reap the evil contagion arising from contiguity. Mr. Potter has ever entertained that sober and wise view of duty in regard to the colored man. But there were men in the house that day who, perhaps, had different views, and made efforts to disturb the speaker. Mr. Potter, even in his wild days, was a friend of order in public gatherings; he had been schooled in the habit of order in the rigid soldier-drill; and, too, he had invited the speaker there, and felt an obligation to see that he was not interrupted; and, besides, he wished to hear the speaker through, and he therefore politely asked the gentlemen to be silent. But they continued their annoyance, when Mr. Potter informed them

that if they did not desist he should put them out
of the house. One of them sternly asked if he
could manage two of them. Mr. Potter replied
that he should surely try it if the noise did not stop.
They then remained quiet until the address was
ended, when one of them made directly for Mr.
Potter, being closely followed by the other; but just
as the first man aimed to strike a furious blow, Mr.
Potter felled him to the floor. The second man
was caught in his effort to strike by the citizens,
and both of them were rushed out-doors, and directed to their horses, and made to mount and leave
in quick time. But just then a real laughable sight
came to light. Many of the poor colored people
were frightened at the knock-down, and leaped out
of the windows, and ran in wild dismay to their
horses. One of them tied his pony with a long
rope, in order that he might graze, but, being so
alarmed out of his wits, he mounted without un-
loosing his rope, and put spurs to the animal, which
soon reached the end of the cable, and rebounded,
only to make another unavailing effort to get away.
The frightened negro did not for some time think
of the rope.

All laws of politeness and decorum must commend Mr. Potter for calling for silence on that occasion, and self-defense prompted the quick act of
protecting himself against the ready blow of his
antagonist; and pietists who think that religious
ministerial duties oblige a minister to stand still and
allow a ruffian to pounce upon him and beat him
into a mangle may find but few practical adherents

in any age or clime. If that be an essential element in moral action, it has been but seldom observed in any state of refinement. The morality of Jesus is certainly the *pure*, the *true*. His literal saying, if smitten on one cheek to turn the other, surely cannot apply where one's person is attacked in a manner involving life and limb, unless it be in the case of religious persecution.

Before closing this chapter, we desire to call the attention of the careful reader to a few more reflections on the important subject alluded to in its beginning—the *status* of the American negro in our common country. It is a great and unsettled question in its final issues. It once rent the union of Churches, disturbed the peace of the Republic, cost its billions, buried millions of her citizens, and entailed poverty and toil on one-third of her vast domain. But the negro's rightful sphere in the scale of humanity is still a debatable question—with some it is not. Five millions of colored freemen are now legal citizens of our grand commonwealth, and what is to be their ultimate *status* here is a national question. Some have allotted Afric's sable son to the order of beasts, because he is crowned with wool and robed with an ebon skin. But they are few, and their reasons are of chaffy material. Neither hybrid Mexican, the red man of the woods, the black Jew of Malabar, nor the copper-colored Mongolian, is assigned to the beastly grade for his quality of hair or color of skin. Science and the Bible station him as a member of the family of man. God made of one blood all nations to dwell on the earth. Admit him, humanity; he is our colored brother, entitled to the rights of humanity. But his grade on the *homo* scale is still not fixed. Whether it be a low, a medium, or a high one, is not the question we want to impress on the reader now; but it is the duties which a Christianized humanity enjoins on the Government and the Church toward our unfortunate colored brother. Books have been written, and journals published, vindicating the right of slavery *per se*, but they are entombed till the last day. The ruling sentiment of the wise and good in our sunny land now is that it was a great national evil. It was made legal, and slaves styled property, by congressional action. But now the grand work of freedom is settled, and our intelligent citizens are glad that the dark incubus is washed from the skirts of our nation forever; and they now have entered on a new mode of life, and hail all means promising an improvement of the colored race with approval. How high he may be raised from the ashes and rags of ages is not our theme just here; but that he is being lifted up is a certainty, and that it is our duty to aid him in his efforts to shake off the degradation of ages is equally certain—duty of the North, duty of the South, but specially of the South. Our Northern forefathers entailed the bondage of our colored brother on the willing, avaricious South; the North got the price of their sable brother's market-value, and the South grew rich from his unpaid toils. He cleared her heavy-timbered forests, tilled her fields, gathered in her annual harvests, sawed much of the lumber and made most of the brick which built up her palaces, her towns, and her great cities; and now she may not murmur if taxed to help him get up from his low estate—her virtuous wisdom does not. He already shows some wonderful advances in learning and good citizenship—where the chances have been favorable. They have churches and schools, and other moral and benevolent institutions, among themselves, promising good to the incoming generations; but their present means of education and other facilities for improvement are too meager to lead to a hope of extensive progress in the near future. Where they live in small lots here and there among the whites they have no schools, and little or no advance is yet made; but in cities and colonies they have schools of their own, and a marked growth in intelligence, virtue, industry, and enterprise, is the visible result. It is now evident that colonization in large settlements, where they can have schools for their own color, is the surest method of a speedy elevation of the race—not that it is best to isolate him from the white man, but let him be in commercial contiguity with the trading thrift of his white brother. In large colonies they can maintain their schools; in small settlements they cannot, and in dense associations motives of emulation lead them to efforts to follow their advanced leaders. Let us plant the ladder of progress before our brother in the sable attire, and invite him to ascend. Let no low motives of envy and jealousy guide us in our treatment of him whom we have helped to place in his present humble condition. Mr. Potter never owned a slave, nor was he associated with the colored man until he came to Texas; but a sense of just and equal rights among men grew up with him from the cradle; and when he called for order when that colored man was making that speech in the little village of Prairie Lee, it was the outcry of long-fixed principles of equal rights in all grades of society where innocence and virtue rule—that is, where guilt does not abrogate the right. Reader, adopt Mr. Potter's motto on that day—" Let Africa have a fair chance." Not only grant the privilege, but help her son to rise. We must approach this subject divested of all prejudices arising from questions of race, color, or nationality. View it in the lens of a civilization which receives its rays from that Christ-like, world-wide benevolence, which Christianity clearly inculcates. If he can be so lifted up from the dust of vassalage, like the Jews, to dispute, on the grounds of peaceful merit, the crown of superiority with the tribes of men, let it be so. In that case his elevation may not be our downfall.

The writer of this volume, in the years of his youth long gone by, was a missionary to the colored people on the Tennessee River, in Colbert's Reserve. It is now the brighest scene in his ministerial life. He has preached to them, more or less, for forty years, and has had favorable opportunities to form an estimate of the best traits in African character. We can only judge of the natural; their moral and intellectual ideas, being the result of long-inherited effects of their degraded condition, do not afford a safe base from which to reason. But their fondness and adaptability for music and dancing is natural;

it is so with them in their native land. A colored man can tambourine an old Virginia jig with his stitch-down shoes, and make sweet music with his old gourd fiddle. As vocalists they can excel all nations, though untrained. When educated and trained in the arts of instrumental and vocal music, they shall astound the world, and arrest the attention of the celestial orchestra. We venture here the prediction that Beethovens, Haydns, and Jenny Linds, of ebon hue, in the events of centuries, shall minister the sweet anthems of music in the citadels of renown, and in all the great capitals of the globe. In music they must stand on civilization's grand platform, and chant the praises of Him who died to save. Let the Church assume a friendly and a helping attitude toward Africa's alien children, alien from the home of their forefathers. Her mission-field is the world. Preach the gospel to every creature, is the Divine Master's command. The poor are special subjects of gospel grace. See that ye be mindful of the poor. "God hath chosen the poor of this world rich in faith and heirs of the kingdom." Our poor jet-painted brother has not imbibed any theories of an atheistic philosophy. He readily accepts the gospel truth. The arduous work is to teach him Christian morals, and lift him upon the plane of their holy demands in all spheres of life. They have many examples of true piety.

CHAPTER XXIV.

In the fall of 1867 the Conference met again at Seguin, Bishop McTyeire presiding. At this Conference Mr. Potter, by request, was sent to the mountain frontier, and was stationed on the Kerrville Circuit, on which the writer now travels. On entering the Conference, he felt a special call to go into the frontier field, and requested that he be sent there. After Conference had closed, he returned to his home, near Prairie Lee, to make arrangements to begin a work for which a wise and gracious Providence has been schooling him more than half a lifetime, a work which is to engage the prime of his matured manhood, and a work which is to issue in renovating the border world and establishing a vast spiritual empire in the valleys of the mountains. We see him all equipped for his new and dangerous field. Bidding wife and babes adieu, amid a shower of tears, he mounts his noble steed, saddle-bags packed, and a carnal weapon belted to his side, and grace in his heart; he rides away toward the field of his future struggles and triumphs, which lies more than a hundred miles deep into the mountains, where the savage Indian and the stealthy robber nightly roam. Away, away from home and loved ones he is to spend a toilsome year full of the greatest hazards, but none of these things move him;

onward he rides over rocky heights, and rugged declines, and level vales, where the chilling northers pour out their freezing breath, for it is in December's bleak and dreary reign. But on, on he rides, till more than a hundred miles of mountain crags intervene between him and his home in the vale, where dear ones feel his absence. Now he has crossed the Indians' trail, and is within their wild domain. Now he can hear their startling war-cry. But these things move him not from his purpose; he has heard that savage yell in other days, and now he comes to silence its alarming echoes along these crags and vales, and raise up high into these overhanging skies the peaceful victor's shouts of joy. He enters on his work, which then included Bandera and Curry's Creek, quite a territory, but only a few settlers compared with what it is now; only a few old settlers have died, and many others have moved in since that day. Among the stanch members who were in the Guadalupe Valley, were the Reeses, Lowrance, Nichols, Manning, and Powel, and William Pofford, local preacher, who is still a faithful and good man. The Moores and the Burneys were also among the citizens of the county, and friends of the Church. Mr. Potter had good meetings that year; the Rev. W. T. Thornberry being his presiding elder greatly helped him. Mr. Thornberry is a man of great zeal and of wide-spread popularity. This year the foundation was laid for the present Church constituting the present Kerrville Circuit, of more than one hundred members. It now has three other able and efficient local preachers—the Revs. John Gass, Elijah Witt, and J. Jay Cawart—and also a parsonage for the pastor's home. Henry Tatum also was a faithful, good man, but he and his pious wife have joined the holy ranks of friends and kindred dear. Sister Burney, Joshua Brown, and Sister Maggie Vaughan, have also crossed "over there" to their eternal rewards. Unto the end they were faithful, and now the crown of life is theirs. The previous year the Church here had no pastor, and was almost disorganized when Mr. Potter went to it, but it came up with banners unfurled that year. He reconstructed the Societies, and reported an increase of about ninety members at the close of the year.

The Indians were very troublesome at that time, in all parts of his circuit. No one could keep more horses than he used, and he had to lock them up at night, or tie them near the cabin door. One night two Indians walked through Mr. Potter's corn-field and took his neighbor's horse which was tied close to his house. Only a cross fence divided the two fields, and the wild men took out a panel of the dividing fence, and both mounted the horse and rode away, taking a mess of roasting-ears from Mr. Potter's corn-field. Mr. Potter's horses were under lock. Next morning their tracks revealed the thieves, and showed the place where they mounted the horse. Indeed, it was not safe for a man to travel alone, or work far from his house, for now and then they would kill and scalp a lone man, and they sometimes made a raid on a cabin and murdered the inmates, but most of their killing was done when they came upon a person out after stock, or traveling. It is said that the savage Indian would seldom enter a white man's house, or venture into a thicket. They would walk round the house at night, when the inmates were sleeping, leaving the print of their moccasins on the sand or soft dirt where they might tread. It is thought that they marauded after a general conference, for they made simultaneous inroads all along the extended border. At one time, while Mr. Potter was on the Kerrville Circuit, nearly all the horses not secured were taken at about the same time. He and a band of men followed them the next morning, but the cunning raiders traveled on the honey-comb rocks after getting on the mountains, and it was impossible to trail them.

This year Mr. Potter got a dangerous horse—a good work-horse, but he had been spoiled as a riding-horse. He was not aware of that fact, and while on a visit to his home he got on his new horse, thinking him entirely gentle, but he soon learned his mistake. The spoiled horse began to pitch, and though he was a splendid rider, the horse got the advantage of him some way, and threw him, damaging one of his hips; and he lay in bed several weeks, and went on crutches several months. He then got into his ambulance, and made his little son drive him to his circuit, and he preached on his crutches for several weeks. The fall disabled some of the ligaments of his hip, and shortened his left-leg a little, and now there is a slight limp in his step. That is the only wound received through his hazardous life. That horse was a cheat. He had been so spoiled that he would not be ridden: he would lie down if he could not rid himself of his rider in any other way; but he could do such tall pitching that it was next to impossible to stick to him. Some persons cling so closely that it would seem they were a part of the horse, but this horse could dash down the most adhesive riders — he would not be ridden. It is said that all animals pitch in Texas; even sheep, hogs, and oxen, pitch out here, when closely crowded. Our readers out of Texas may not exactly understand what pitching means, and we will now try to explain it. The cow-boys have given it another name now—they call it "bucking." A wild horse is lassoed around his neck, and if he is very wild he is choked till he falls. Instantly the noose is slackened to prevent choking him to death, and his head is held up so that he cannot rise. While he is down, he is tightly saddled with front and flank girths; but if not extra wild he is lassoed, blindfolded, and then saddled in like manner, and the blind is removed, the rider standing on the ground, holding a long rope which is attached to the horse's neck, and head, and nose, so as to answer for a bridle. Then he begins to pitch as soon as he sees the saddle on his back. In that way he is led about until he finds that he cannot get it off by "bucking." Then he is patted, and the blind is drawn over his eyes, and the rider shakes the saddle, and presses on it, ties the stirrups about two feet apart under the animal's body, so that they cannot fly out on either side; then he makes several efforts as if going to mount, to see if he will jump at his mounting, the horse standing still all the time; then he gently but quickly places his left-foot in the stirrup, and swings himself into the saddle like the winking of an eye. There he is safe in the saddle. A horse seldom moves while the blind is on him. The rider then reaches over and slips off the blind, and then the pitching begins. Some run, and pitch as they run; others just pitch and pitch till they find it is of no use, and give it up. Some pitch straightforward, some in a zigzag, called "fence-worm pitching" —that is the most difficult to stick. In the pitch, they stiffen all their legs as if jointless, tuck their heads between their fore-legs, hump their backs, bounce into the air as if going to ascend, but pitch forward, striking the ground with great jarring force; hence, the maneuver is called *pitching*, and the back-humping is styled "bucking." In the meantime, the rider's legs and knees stick so closely to the careering horse that it would seem as if they had grown there, but his body is held more limber, and sways to and fro as the animal may lunge. Sometimes the dashing is so violent as to sling the blood from the rider's lungs, and unhouse his linen from his pantaloons. There is a coarse saying in Texas among the vulgar quite expressive of that violent pitching: they call it "pitching the filling out of a negro's shirt." Once in the saddle, there is no dismounting till the jumping is over, and the blind is drawn over the eyes. No mounting or dismounting for sometime, till the horse is blinded. A leap in the act of mounting, or lighting, is extremely dangerous. This is the way they manage a wild horse, and that is the meaning of *pitching*.

In one of the Indian raids on Curry's Creek that year, an Indian was killed while letting down the fence to steal a horse. Dr. Nowlin, knowing that Indians were in, stationed two armed men in a crib to guard his horses; and two Indians came in the moonlight, and began to let down the fence to get the horses out, and one of the men fired, killing one Indian instantly; the other thief ran off, the other white man being so frightened he could not shoot. The fallen Indian had a string of buttons around one wrist, and a metal cross attached to his hair; and had his little paint-bag, which Mr. Potter gave to Dr. McFerrin several years ago.

Now we copy from Mr. Potter's journal: "This circuit was in the bounds of Brother Thornberry's district, and he had visited it the previous year, and held several meetings, and the people were greatly carried away with him. He was in everybody's mouth. Thornberry was the greatest preacher that had ever visited these mountains. Everywhere I would go it was 'Thornberry, Thornberry.' I preached away the best I could, but it was nothing like Thornberry's preaching. Of course, I would say, 'Yes, Brother Thornberry is a good preacher:' it would not do to say otherwise. At the time I thought it time they were beginning to think that Potter was some preacher—at least some of them. So one night I was preaching at a certain place. I warmed up to a lively temperature, and a good old sister arose shouting, saying, 'Glory to God! hallelujah! somebody can preach as well as Brother Thornberry!' This good sister gave me a lift, and I began to climb upward from that time. Our first quarterly-meeting came on in the same neighborhood, and Brother Thornberry, being the presiding elder, was there. To the great joy of all the people, their great preacher had come again. I was appointed to preach on Friday night, and after preaching Brother P—— overheard a crowd of young men discussing the ability of preachers, one of them saying, 'You can say what you please, but I will bet my horse that Potter can beat your great man, Thornberry, preaching.' It was such a good joke that Brother P—— told it in a crowd of men in the presence of Thornberry. To humor the joke, I said, 'It is a little strange that there should be any dispute about that, as it was now high time all should say that I could just lay Thornberry in the shade.' Brother Thornberry relished the joke, and passed it off in his usual good-humored way."

On this circuit Mr. Potter had quite a unique worldly friend, whom he graphically depicts in his usual style. He calls him "Buck Hamilton." He is now sheriff of Bandera County, and when Mr. Potter was there a few weeks ago, he raised money to present him with a suit of clothes—"Navy-blue." He surely is a remarkably clever, unique man. Here is the description:

"This year I formed an acquaintance with a gentleman named Buck Hamilton, living about two miles below where Centre Point now stands. I preached at a school-house near his house, and it was one of my stopping-places. He was a wicked man, and possessed a large amount of original wit, and a little rough and blunt in his manners. As the old adage goes, 'What came up, came out.' He often said what he did not mean, but just the reverse. Using a common phrase, 'There was no put on' in him. He was a great joker, and the preachers never escaped his wit; and the harder they retorted on him, the better it pleased him; and the more liberties they might take about his home, the more he liked them. I found him to be a great deal better inside than he seemed to be outside. His wife and his relatives are mostly Methodists. When I would stay all night with Buck, he expected to have prayers, but he had a queer way of bringing it about. After talking till time to retire, he would say, 'Potter, it is time to go to bed—we don't have prayers here.' That was his manner of calling up the subject. I would say, 'Well, Buck, if you don't let me have prayers I will not let you sleep.' 'Well, Ann,' addressing his wife, 'get the old Bible, and let the preacher pray.'

"I appointed a camp-meeting just across the river from Buck's house, and the people were very slow about preparing the place, and I went to where Buck was at work, and told him that I could not get the lazy Methodists to erect an arbor, and I wanted him and the other old sinners to build it; and he laid down his tools and raised a crowd, and soon the arbor went up; and Buck furnished all the beef for the camp-meeting. After I moved my family to the mountains, he sent me word to bring up my wagon, and he would give me a load of corn. So, at my appointment at his school-house, I took my wagon, and my wife went with me. He had never seen Mrs. Potter. When I introduced her to him, he said, 'Mrs. Potter, you have crazy spells sometimes, do n't you?' She replied that she might have been a little so at times—about the time of her marriage. He remarked, 'I thought so, or you would not have married Potter.' She had heard of his singular manner, and anticipated the meaning of his irony; hence her answer.

"When he was preparing to move to the upper Medina, I said to him one day, 'Buck, you are going to move into that wild region, and I am afraid the Indians will kill you, and you owe me a half-dollar, and I would like to have that before you go; and perhaps I had better preach your funeral before you go.' He said, No; but he had lost a dog, and thought him dead, and he would be glad to have me preach his funeral. I said, 'Never mind, Buck; may be so; you may die, or get killed, and I can just preach both at once.' Years have rolled away, and Buck still lives, and is still the same noble-hearted, generous man, and I often have the pleasure of enjoying his kind hospitality. I attended a quarterly-meeting at Bandera recently, and Buck and another irreligious man had presented a Cumberland Presbyterian minister with a suit of clothes. I took up a collection on Sunday for missions, and I told the audience that in such collections we had to shear the sheep and the goats too. At the close of the afternoon service, just as I pronounced the benediction, Buck cried out, 'Hold on, friends—I have something to say before you disperse. We goats here have given one preacher a suit of clothes; now come up, you sheep, and give Mr. Potter a suit. Don't delay; bring up your money; don't let the goats outshear you!' That brought the fleece from the sheep—I got the clothes, ready-made."

Indeed, Mr. Potter's friend Buck is a marvel, a strange lump of simple generosity, and the writer can but hope that there may yet be a grace-renewed future for him here, and a glory-adorned state for him hereafter.

At the camp-meeting just referred to, Dr. J. G. Walker and presiding elder Thornberry were Mr. Potter's helpers; and having to leave early, he had to close the camp-meeting with twenty-six mourners at the altar, which was regretted. The last quarterly-meeting at Kerrville was a pleasant time; the financial assessments were all met. In passing down the river to Comfort, Mr. Potter's horse needed a shoe, but the blacksmith could not shoe him. The presiding elder being a good smith, he dismounted, soon put on the shoe, and they were off again. They had appointments to preach, as they passed along the river, at the several preaching-places; and Mr. Potter, having had a good time among the people, was tender, and made a kind of farewell appeals to the congregations, telling them that, though soon rivers might roll and mountains might tower between them, they should meet again. Mr. Thornberry is a cheerful traveling companion, and is fond of "rigging" Mr. Potter. When he would be driving along the long, lonesome roads through the mountains, and Mr. Potter would be in his buggy in the rear, Mr. Thornberry would rise up in his buggy, and reproduce that grand saying, "Rivers may roll and mountains rise up between us;" and told on him to the preachers at Conference. Potter knows the meaning of "rolling rivers and rising mountains."

Mr. Potter sent an appointment to hold a protracted-meeting at a central point between two settlements on Curry's Creek, but on arriving at the place on Friday, he found nothing had been done in preparing a place for worship. He went to a house near by, but the man of the house was absent. Several young men were there, and Mr. Potter asked for the loan of an ax. Getting it, he started off with it, when one of the young men inquired what he was going to do with the ax. He said he was going to preach down there in the grove that night, and there was some undergrowth in the way, and he was going to clear it out; and the young men hunted up other old axes, and aided him in preparing the place for the big meeting. While there, another young man came riding by, and he agreed to ride over the neighborhoods and give notice; and the absent gentleman came home, and hauled poles and puncheons, and arranged seats, and at night the meeting began sure enough, and the grand ultimate was quite a revival.

Mr. Potter visited his family only two or three times this year, and desiring to continue in the mountain work, he sold out his home near Prairie Lee, and made a purchase near Comfort, in the Guadalupe Valley, and moved to it before Christmas. Mr. Thornberry told him that he should return him to the Kerrville Circuit, and that he had better not go to Conference, but move his family on the work during the time of the Conference session, which he did. It was more than two hundred miles from Kerrville to Corpus Christi, the seat of the Conference. The season was late, and many of the preachers endured much suffering *en route*. It caused the death of one of the best divines West Texas Conference ever had—Asbury Davidson.

CHAPTER XXV.

At the Conference at Corpus Christi, Mr. Potter was reäppointed to the Kerrville Circuit, the Rev. J. S. Gillett being appointed presiding elder. Mr. Gillett, like the writer, had a great repugnance at the idea of meeting with Indians, and Mr. Potter was his safe-conduct through the dangerous defiles. He is a tall and a fine specimen of manhood. He had a large horse, and a large pair of saddle-wallets well packed. Thus mounted, with a double-barreled shotgun swinging in front of his saddle-horn and across his horse's neck, and fastened to that horn, he presented a daring front, sufficient to frighten and put to flight a band of Indians. But he was sensitive on the Indian question, and in going to the Kerrville Circuit, a distance of a little more than eighty miles, Mr. Potter always met him at Boerne, and piloted him through to Kerrville, in the upper Guadalupe Valley. Mr. Gillett would venture alone as far as Boerne, but it was not a safe road, for the Indians sometimes ventured in upon the thirty miles intervening between Boerne and San Antonio, a long, lonesome, mountainous road. Uvalde was the extreme western appointment, and it had a dreadful name, which it fully merited; and Mr. Gillett would have Mr. Potter go with him there. To reach that place Mr. Potter had to travel one hundred miles, and more than fifty of them he had to go and return alone though the Indian wilds. He met Mr. Gillett at the appointed time on the Hondo, forty miles from Uvalde, and they journeyed on together. Mr. Gillett preached on Saturday night, and on the same night some one shot into a house and killed a Mexican. That was a little trying to tender nerves. On the Sabbath a drunken man came to the sacrament-table at the close when a song was being sung, but two young men saved Mr. Potter the job of leading him, by taking him by each arm and walking him out. Next morning the preachers started home, but on reaching the Frio River it was too high to be forded, and after remaining on its banks many hours, waiting for it to fall, at last they had to ride eight miles back to Uvalde to stay all night. That was a cross to the tender sensibilities of Mr. Gillett, being hemmed in so far out on the border, where there was little safety in the town or in the brush.

Mr. Potter returned to his circuit in safety, and finished up a pleasant year's work to himself and to the Church. At one of his appointments lived one of an outspoken sort of ladies who was a member of his charge, and she had not formed a partial regard for Mr. Potter at first, but had become greatly attached to his ministry. She called her husband "Tom." As Mr. Potter was about to start to Conference, she was heard to say: "Tom, be sure and tell Brother Potter to try to get back on this circuit. He has done a great deal of good here, and the people all like him, and want him back. I did not like him when he first came here. His eyes looked just like a glass-eyed filly's; but now I want him back, since he has got to preaching good sermons; and everybody wants him back."

On their way to Conference, several preachers were passing through a region of potteries, where the clay was wet from rains, and Mr. Gillett said to Mr. Potter, "The potter has power over the clay; so, Potter, go to work." Mr. Potter said, "Just hold my horse, and I will make a presiding elder, and make a better one than I now have."

From the Conference at Goliad, Mr. Potter was returned to the Kerrville Circuit, Rev. J. S. Gillett being presiding elder, and they kept up a regular correspondence when not together at their quarterly-meetings. There being the tenderest intimacy between them, they indulged in a great deal of amusing witticisms and fun. Both of them usually carry a cheerful class of feelings, and are good at retort and repartee.

Mr. Potter had in some way got into the agency of selling a patent medicine called "Soother of Pain," for which his brethren often took occasion to joke him. In this year Mr. Potter wrote a letter to Mr. Gillett, and signed his name "A. J. P.," and Mr. Gillett replied in poetic measure; but it is lost. It was a scathing criticism on Mr. Potter's medical experiments. He concluded his poetic effusions with something like the following: "Who is 'A. J. P.,' I pray? Is he a quack, that he his name conceals?" Then he made an index-hand with the forefinger pointing down at the phrase, "Soother of Pain," and then signed it "Jack S." Mr. Potter replied:

"Dear brother, I have just received your criticism on the style of my signature. I would just say that letters not only stand for individual names, but titles also—for instance, big 'P. C.' stands for big preacher in charge, and little 'p. e.' for little presiding elder. But who is 'Jack S.?' 'Jack-ass,' I know. I suppose you have just omitted two letters of your name, and I will add them. If 'Jack S.' (ass) comes to my camp-meeting, we will be sure to have some success, as we will not only hear some of the thunder-tones of that voice which reproved the wicked Balaam, but we will be prepared to do battle with that weapon with which the noted Samson gained such a memorable victory over his foes. In either case the 'jaw' will have to be used, and if in the conflict you should lose your scalp, I can bring out a new suit with my 'Soother of Pain.' Since you have tuned your lyre, I shall touch the chords of mine:

>For Attic disorder,
>   Or enlargement of brain,
>You'll find much relief
>   In my "Soother of Pain."
>Just rub well the head,
>   And give close attention;
>It will soften the skull,
>   And make room for expansion.
>   ANDREW JACKSON POTTER,
>   *The Pain-soother.*"

Mr. Gillett and Mr. Potter held a successful camp-meeting this year at Tatum's School-house. Mr. Gillett truly excelled himself in a series of sermons on the vital doctrines of Christianity. After one of those able sermons Mr. Potter exhorted, knowing that the sinners were well convinced, and some of them anxious to come to the altar of prayer. He enforced the prodigal's resolve, "I will arise;" and on giving the invitation, they pressed to the altar in a throng. In a short time one dozen of them were converted. One of them slapped his hands together and said, "Mr. Potter, I feel just as good as I want to." It was indeed a great camp-meeting.

Mr. Potter, by special invitation, went to the celebrated "Sabinal Cañon" this year, and held a noted camp-meeting. He had to travel alone sixty miles through the Indian-raiding region to reach the place, but he made the journey unharmed. The people came as far as forty miles to camp in wagons and cloth tents. Camp-meetings out there were held in the grove, or in a mot of timber; no shelters, but boughs of trees, or brush arbors. Mr. Potter was the only regular itinerant minister there. A local preacher by the name of Smith supplied the circuit there that year. Recently he has been murdered. Two other local brethren aided in the meeting—Mr. Jones and Mr. Newton. It was the first camp-meeting ever held in that cañon. It was a grand time, and long to be remembered by the old Methodists of the Western frontier. Mr. Gillett and Mr. Potter were staying all night at a certain house, and occupied the same room. Mr. Gillett, rising first in the morning, stepped out on the gallery to wash, and there was lying by the wash-bowl a rock resembling a bar of soap, a complete imitation in shape and in color, and Mr. Gillett picked it up, and dipped it in the water, and began to rub it in his hands. Finding it a "sell," he looked back to see if Mr. Potter saw him, when Mr. Potter quizzically inquired, "Can't you make it lather?" He replied, "No; it is a complete sell." Riding down the valley that day with several others, Mr. Gillett was boasting how he could throw rocks. He could hit almost any thing, and was just going to tell of a great feat, and said, "I will venture I have done with rocks what no other man in this crowd has ever done." Mr. Potter replied, "No one will dispute that. I suppose no one here ever tried to substitute a rock for soap." Mr. Gillett was just going to say that he had killed two wild cats with rocks; but that turned the tables. In these mountains there are many strange petrifactions, many of them resembling bars of soap in shape, size, and color, and many petrified sea-shells of the ages gone by.

In closing the toils of three years on the Kerrville Circuit, memory records a vast volume of anxieties, doubts, fears, hopes, joys, and troubles; a multitude of labors, victories, and defeats; but, too, a period of many happy seasons in the cultivation of "Immanuel's land," with Mr. Potter. The Church was established on a foundation which is to stand as the immovable mountains, while the decay of the ages shall wear and waste the works of men and the glory of empires. While clouds and sunshine shall succeed each other in these vales and towering hills, and verdant spring-time shall follow the dreary winter's gloom hovering on height and plain; while wild birds trill sweet music in the leafy grove, and the joyous reapers "sing harvest-home songs" in the golden fields, waving before the mower's blade, the Church-fruit of that grand three-years' sowing shall mature and ripen its successive harvests for the celestial garner.

In the Kerrville Circuit our devoted pioneer has left foot-prints on memory's sands not soon to be covered up by unfriendly winds. "Potter," the immortal Potter, is almost carved on the face of the beetling crags and high, chalky cliffs overhanging the vales where he has traveled, against whose lightning-scathed brow his voice has echoed, telling of the One that saves. There were many friends whose willing kindness he has shared when, toil-worn, he sought rest and repose. Among the dear names of many, with great pleasure he records the names of old Brother and Sister Lowrance, at Kerrville, just awaiting their change to the immortal shore; and also Mr. Daniel Rugh, at Bandera, now ripening for the harvest.

CHAPTER XXVI.

At the Conference at San Marcos, Bishop Marvin presiding, Mr. Potter was sent to the Somerset Circuit, a new name given to the circuit, but ever after it has been called Medina Circuit, or Mission. Mr. Gillett was still the presiding elder.

This year Mr. Potter sold out his home on Flat Rock, near Comfort, in the Guadaloupe Valley, and bought and moved to his present mountain-home near Boerne. It was a year fraught with great hardships to preacher and people, through the scarcity of grass, and water, and provisions, owing to a severe drought in the mountains. He had to give up a part of his circuit in the latter part of the year for want of grass for his horse. In those days grass was the stay and staff of the horse, and without it he could not hold up to carry his rider. It is specially a hard year to the preacher having to move into the woods, without fence, field, or cabin. But withal he had good, religious times. Before moving, his circuit was about sixty miles from home, and he had much hard riding to do; besides going with his presiding elder to most of his frontier camp-meetings, where they had many revival seasons resulting in lasting good to the Church and country. The famed Rev. J. W. DeVilbiss, long an efficient preacher and agent of the American Bible Society, and now superannuated, of the West Texas Conference, just awaiting his Master's orders, lived on this circuit this year. With him and his pleasant family Mr. Potter had many enjoyable social interviews and religious communions. His presiding elder lived in the circuit; and here we copy an account of their pleasant associations:

"This year my presiding elder lived in my circuit, and I had the pleasure of spending many pleasant hours in social intercourse with him and his kind family around his own fireside. There I made one of my homes to rest.

"During the year my wife made a tour with me on the circuit, and of course we called on our presiding elder. Out of mischief Gillett went out and killed a rabbit and dressed it, and had it cooked for dinner. Poor Gillett! he has not yet heard the last of that rabbit. In the year I accompanied him to one of his quarterly-meetings at Kerrville. There being no pastor on that circuit that year, the people paid the elder by public collections at each quarterly-meeting. At this meeting Gillett opened the service on Sunday morning, and just as he finished reading the last hymn I rose up, and taking the hymn-book out of his hand, told him to sit down for a moment. I said to the congregation that I proposed to lift a collection for the support of the presiding elder's family; that I did not ask a cent for him; that he was big and fat, and that the people fed him well wherever he went, but that he had an excellent wife and several interesting children that must be fed and clothed.

I said there were two sides to all public men—for instance: here is Brother Gillett, he is well dressed, and looks like he might be in easy circumstances. He will preach you a good sermon. Here you have the presiding elder; but if you will follow him as I have, you will find a man living about fourteen miles south of San Antonio in a log cabin stuck off in a musquite thicket, and about nine acres of land surrounded by a tolerable brush fence. Here you will see a man wearing a lopped hat and hickory shirt, ax in hand, and also a hammer, dragging around trying to get things in order before leaving home again on a distant tour. Brother Gillett is a good third-rate shoemaker. I have seen him mending his children's shoes. Myself and wife went to spend the day with him once upon a time, and he had to go out and kill a rabbit for dinner. Here you have the husband and father amid the cares and vexations of home-life. By this time Gillett's head had reached his knees. Now while we sing, Brother G—— and Brother R—— will pass around the hat. The collection amounted to twenty-six dollars. Gillett was greatly outraged, and said that two things saved me—I had bragged on his wife and got the money. He said I had slandered him, that he had never worn a hickory shirt in his life—it was checked cotton. He got in a good humor."

Such was the intimate relations existing between these brethren that they took great liberties with each other, and ever took exquisite pleasure in passing upon each other a hearty joke or a keen-edged quiz. On a certain round of quarterly-meetings Mr. Gillett had preached on the subject of natural depravity several times, making it a kind of hobby, till Mr. Potter got a little tired of it. As they were riding along, going down to Mr. Potter's own quarterly-meeting, Mr. Gillett said: "Potter, what must I preach about at your quarterly-meeting?" Mr. Potter could not lose his opportunity; he replied: "Can't you give us items on depravity?" Mr. Gillett said, "I am the man for that;" to which Mr. Potter tartly replied: "You can't do any thing else—at least you have not lately." He did not choose that subject for the pulpit that day.

CHAPTER XXVII.

At the Conference at Leesville, in the fall of 1871, Bishop Marvin presided, and Mr. Potter was sent to the Uvalde Circuit, and J. S. Gillett, presiding elder. It was indeed a *circuit*, being in the form of a circle. It was in many respects the most difficult, the most dangerous part of Mr. Potter's itinerant life. Its nearest point was fifty miles from his home. It is supposed to be about two hundred miles around this circuit as it was at that time, but it paid Mr. Potter in temporalities better than any other circuit he has ever traveled. It gave him five hundred and twenty-five dollars, besides a number of valuable presents. It was contiguous to the Rio Grande, where the Indians could cross over any day; and killing and stealing was almost a daily occurrence. The town of Uvalde was of bloody fame; its record is written in red capitals; but it is now one of the most peaceful towns in the Great West—Sodom is reformed. Mr. Potter was pastor in that town, first and last, four years, and it shows a greater harvest of his ministerial labors than any other place along the extended border-field.

On this circuit he finds many a pleasant home where he is greeted joyfully; and he holds their memories in a sacred niche in its halls, whose names would fill many pages in this book, among whom we record that of Judge Harper, living on the Hondo. He is the father of Methodism in the West, and father of the Rev. John Harper, formerly of the West Texas Conference, and also father-in-law of the Rev. Willie Fly, elsewhere mentioned in this book. There too is the Rev. Irvin Johns and the Rev. A. J. Smith—lately murdered. These brethren knew how to sympathize with a traveling preacher, and to make him feel at home at their firesides. Mr. Johns had been in the Alabama Conference, but has lately spent a useful local life in this far West.

Mr. Potter closed a prosperous year of great benefit to the Church, and repaired to Conference in company with the Rev. B. Harris, in Mr. Potter's ambulance. Here we copy an account of their stopping all night with French Smith, in Guadalupe County—a man of quite a large share of political information, and who has ever been noted for his generous hospitality. He was a special friend of the writer. Once when we asked him for a donation to purchase a bell for the M. E. Church, South, at Seguin, he generously proposed to give me one hundred dollars for that purpose if I would have painted in large capitals, high up on the four sides of the cupola, "French Smith;" saying, "Parson, that is as nigh heaven as I ever expect to get." But he closed a long life last summer, and in his last sickness he had pious songs and the prayers of the righteous—which availeth much—and hope looks higher up in celestial spheres for the spirit of the old Texas veteran than the elevated church-steeple.

The conversion of General Henry E. McCulloch, to which he refers, was a wonderful event, displaying the evident presence of divine power which no spectator could doubt, which Mr. Smith never could forget, and the undeviating life of the general ever after, under the most trying ordeals, clearly stamps his change to have been genuine—divine—fruit of divine operation. Read the following copy:

"It was getting dark and drizzling rain when we drove up to Col. French Smith's, and a gentleman came out to the fence. I asked if we could stay all night. He said he would see Col. Smith. Returning, he said we could not stay; and while we were studying what to do the old colonel came out, considerably in liquor, and said, 'Gentlemen, who in the —— are you, and where are you going? Drive round to the gate, gentlemen; old French Smith never turned anybody away from his house in his life. If you can put up with beef and black coffee you are welcome, gentlemen. Now just strip your horses; and I say, gentlemen, who in the —— are you, and where in the —— are you going this dark, muddy night?' I replied, 'Sir, we are Methodist preachers, going to Conference at Victoria.' He then called out, 'O Shug, Shug [meaning his old lady], kill a chicken, kill a chicken! here are two Methodist preachers. Gentlemen, please tell me your names.' I said, 'Potter is my name, and this is the Rev. Buckner Harris.' 'Gentlemen,' replied the colonel, 'I have heard of you both; come in, you are welcome.' We walked in, and the colonel talked so fast that I cannot recollect half he said;

but he went on to say, 'Gentlemen, I am not a member of your Church. I don't believe some things I hear preached now-a-days. You need not tell me that a negro has a soul; no, he is an anomaly in the universe—he is God's mishap. But I can't help believing that there is a power in religion. I was at the meeting when General McCulloch was converted, and I know that God had something to do with that; God laid his hand upon his heart—he punched him. He is a changed man.' Supper was announced, and he said, 'Now, gentlemen, walk into supper,' and as we entered the dining-room he remarked, 'Gentlemen, let me introduce you to my daughter, Miss Ann Smith, the prettiest girl in Guadalupe County.' After supper he said, 'Gentlemen, I used to hear a good old song, and if either of you can sing it I would like to have you do so.' 'What is it?' I asked; 'if I know it I will sing it.' He replied that it was, 'When for eternal worlds I steer.' I thought that if I could get him to singing it would change the current of his thoughts, so I began to sing.

"Next morning he said: 'Now, Mr. Potter, you must go with me to the stable and see my race-mare, and tell me what you think of her; I am told that you are a fine judge of a horse. I call her Income, and think she is a perfect lamp-lighter.' I asked the colonel to excuse me, as I was in a hurry. 'You are not going a step till you look at my mare,' was his reply. I went and looked all around her carefully, and told him that she would do if she had the bottom. 'She has got it, sir!' and slapping me on the shoulder, he said, 'Now come to the house and have prayers.' We prayed, and bade him adieu.

"Had it not been for one blunder in the life of our friend Colonel Smith, he doubtless would have been one of the leading politicians in Texas—that ruinous habit which so often destroys the usefulness of many men of great and useful talents—indulgence in ardent spirits. His was a house of hospitality. His good lady was one of earth's jewels."

We close this chapter with letters from the Rev. J. S. Gillett and Bishop Marvin:

At Home, June 6, 1872.

MY DEAR POTTER:—I got home in safety, and found all well. I had a good rain on the evening of my arrival, and have a splendid crop. I am thankful to my Father in heaven. I write to ask you to give up riding in your buggy on your circuit, for I am afraid the Indians will get you if you do not. I am much afraid that they have killed Brother Fly. I have heard that he is missing, and there were more than thirty Indians in at that time. I am sad, *sad*, at what I fear is true. You must let me know if it be so. Get you a good horse, Brother Potter, and ride him on your work. Better do that, and let the books go, or take a few on each round. The people had better do without books than that we should lose you. Please, Brother Potter, don't go out there any more in your buggy.

Your friend and brother, J. S. GILLETT, P. E.

As heretofore stated, Mr. Gillett was not one endowed with any anxious cravings to try his valor in the presence of tattooed savages armed with bows and steel-pointed arrows; and it was with no little trepidation that he ventured into the regions so often visited by those heartless enemies of the white man; and he even felt a bosom full of fears about his brethren, whose lives were in jeopardy each passing day and night. Indeed, nothing but a protecting Providence could have saved them from those perils. His love for Mr. Potter is seen in his fears of his loss. It was a squally time, but Mr. Fly came up all safe.

We now transcribe Bishop Marvin's letter:

St. Louis, April 11, 1872.

DEAR BROTHER POTTER:—I was truly rejoiced to hear that you had begun the year on Uvalde Circuit with such fair prospects of usefulness, and withal that you had some assurance of something to live on.

There is no work on earth like God's work. The salvation of one soul is of greater importance than all the wars and conquests of history. I trust the Lord will give you many this year. Live much in prayer; cultivate the feeling of entire consecration to him and total dependence on him. He will never leave you; he has promised to be with his servants even to the end of the world.

I hope your books have come by this time; I have no doubts that you will be able to find sale for them when they come.

I always feel a little solicitation about you on the frontier, but yet when I think that a preacher has hardly ever been killed in that work, I cannot think that you are in much real danger. God will have you in his holy keeping. May his presence be with you at all times! Your brother, E. M. MARVIN.

At the West Texas Conference at Leesville, Bishop Marvin was much interested in Mr. Potter and the wants of the frontier he represented—Potter and the border being identical; which is now an evidence of that departed great man's foresight into character, and the adumbrated future of this extended border.

To aid in the circulation of religious literature in Mr. Potter's mission-field the generous Bishop kindly proposed to indorse a note in bank to enable him to purchase the books. The books were received and circulated—they were the books referred to in the Bishop's letter just transcribed, and also mentioned in the Rev. Mr. Gillett's letter copied elsewhere. Mr. Potter has not only preached throughout this vast mountain-range, but has hauled good books and Bibles all over its valleys and rolling ridges for the benefit of the frontiersmen.

He has been a great Bible distributer, as may be seen in the chapter containing Dr. West's letter. He has piloted the agents of the American Bible Society through this dangerous realm, and then has aided in the distribution of the books by sale and donations. Railroads are nearing the borders of that great mountain-zone, and its vales and slants are being rapidly filled up, and a new work of exploration is being needed, and a supply of ministerial recruits are coming into demand. But the vigilant Potter is on the outlook, and timely sees each opening field, and is now planning for supplies. Already he utters the Macedonian cry, "Come over and help us!" But he calls not worn-out ministerial jades, or the fastidious neophyte who dreams of Indian raids, or dreads a home in Nature's solitudes in tent or camp, but those strong in faith and fearless in zeal for the Master's cause. If the Church will support them, God will send them as surely as he sent Missouri's child to plant the scions of the kingdom of his dear Son here in earlier days.

CHAPTER XXVIII.

At the Conference at Victoria, Mr. Potter had to tell of his Indian fight that year to Bishop Keener and Dr. J. B. McFerrin. After hearing the narrative through, the Bishop inquired, "Brother Potter, what do you do with that scripture which says the weapons of our warfare are not carnal?" Dr. McFerrin replied, "There were no Indians there when that was written."

Mr. Potter was domiciled at McGrew's hotel, where he met a great many stock-men and "cowboys" from the West, and he had an interesting time with them at the hotel, and a more congenial association with his brethren at the Conference-hall. There was a young wag at the hotel who took pleasure in making prominent his non-religious creed. When the subject of the Conference or religion was mentioned, he seemed to think it a duty imposed on him to speak of either in no favorable manner. Mr. Potter endured the silly youth's flirts at sacred things several days. At the table the Conference was under review, and the vain spright was called on to stain the hallowed theme with the slime of his incredulity, and he spit it out as usual, saying that he did not believe there was any truth in religion; that man was no more than a dog; that when he was dead he went to dust like a dog.

That was Mr. Potter's chance: he could not forego the opportunity, and in his cool, shrewd way he said to the youth, "It does not require some men to wait until they are dead to make them like dogs—some of them quite resemble dogs while living." The "take-off" was so apropos that the crowd, leaving decorum out of view, gave way to an uproarious laugh, and the spurred youth had occasion to retire to his room at an early hour that night.

At that hotel Mr. Potter met Mr. "Cood Adams," a large stock-raiser in the West, who knew Mr. Potter's value to society and the stock interest along the western border, by aiding in keeping out the savages, and driving out the clans of robbers, and he presented Mr. Potter with a Winchester rifle, which he carried with him several years when out along the border.

Mr. Potter was ever ready with a suitable retort when occasion demanded. He was at a mill one day, and the miller, being an unbeliever, said to him: "Mr. Potter, you say that your God is a good God; if he is such, why don't he make that old dead cow out yonder, which is so offensive to me, smell sweet as the perfume of the rose?" Mr. Potter readily replied: "Why don't he make a buzzard of you, and make the carrion sweet to your taste, and its odor pleasant to your smell, as to all other buzzards, as it would not take long to do the work—it would require but a slight change?"

At this Conference he was appointed to the Uvalde Circuit, the Rev. Buckner Harris, presiding elder. Mr. Harris passed the year in much toil and great acceptability. He is one of the truest, ablest ministers of the West. He is quite a friend of Mr. Potter. At one of their quarterly-meetings Mr. Potter preached at night, and there was a droll, drunken man in the congregation, who was quite an object to look upon—ragged and filthy, his hair tousled and tangled, his face mottled, his eyes red and swollen, who, when the sermon was over, advanced to Mr. Potter, and said: "Parson, you preached us a splendid sermon, and I only regret that you did not extend the right-hand of fellowship; I would have given you my hand." Mr. Harris, hearing the interview, made his way outdoors to indulge in a hearty laugh at Potter's predicament; but soon the drunken wag got out and got hold of Mr. Harris, and said: "Mr. Harris, I believe we had a superb sermon to-night. Parson and I only regret that you did not extend the right-hand of fellowship; I should have given you my hand."

Mr. Potter made a dangerous swim over the Rio Hondo this year, to get to an appointment. These Western streams, when swollen, move with great force, hurrying away from the mountains to the level plains. He had a large, strong horse. He tied his "Winchester" to his saddle-horn with a long string, so he could hold it up out of the water, threw his saddle-bags around his neck, and moved into the turbid, dashing waters. When his horse struck the bar on the opposite side, the heaving current came near upsetting him, but he narrowly made the landing. When he reached the church he found a congregation, had a good time, protracted the meeting, which ended in a good revival. A man from Alabama had a fine mare, and the citizens of Frio Town made up one hundred and twenty-five dollars, bought her, and presented her to him.

This year the Rev. Temple G. Wools was licensed to preach in Mr. Potter's circuit. Mr. Wools is a native Kentuckian. He is a young man of a polished and finished education. He has been Secretary of the West Texas Conference a number of years, and one seldom equaled. He traveled the Medina Circuit four years, and has filled the Goliad Station three years, with unexampled popularity. He has ever been a warm friend of Mr. Potter. It may seem a little strange that two natures so unlike should unify; but extremes often meet. Mr. Wools is refined and unused to frontier life, yet the attachment between these two brethren is warm and endearing. Mr. Potter has named one of his little sons Temple Wools.

Mr. Potter made a long and laborious tour that year with the Rev. Wesley Smith, Superintendent of the American Bible Society, who was a zealous workman in that vast and important field. The District Conference was held at Midway, on the Cibolo Circuit, and Mr. Smith and Mr. Potter were in attendance. Mr. Smith made a proposition to the audience, when lifting a collection for the Bible cause, to make Andrew Jackson Potter, their pioneer preacher, a life-member of the American Bible Society, and a gentleman by the name of Elam went through the congregation and raised the money in a few minutes. The honor was deserved, for he had piloted the Superintendent through all the hazards along the far-out mountain border.

The general tender regard which a Conference of Methodist preachers have for each other can hardly find a parallel in the world outside the ties of blood kindred; but in special cases it strengthens into attachments like that of Jonathan and David, as in the instance of Mr. Potter and Mr. Wools, and also Mr. Gillett. While, as a class of men, they have their little preferences and antipathies, as one body they are indeed brethren; and at their annual convocations all their little uncementing feelings are neutralized by the general emotion of fraternal love. Their work, their aims, their hopes, are one. If earth anywhere can show some resemblance to the celestial spheres, it is found in the body of an Annual Conference of Methodist preachers. "By this all men shall know that ye are my disciples, if ye have love one for another."

CHAPTER XXIX.

In 1872 Parson Potter was returned to the Uvalde Circuit of the West Texas Conference, a region of country sometimes troubled by barbarous Indians, as was the entire great frontier at that time. The mountains of Texas cover a great area, more than one hundred miles deep each way. They rise up into points, peaks, and ridges, separated by little depressions, and the channels of creeks and rivers making valleys here and there, according to the size of the stream flowing down them. Sometimes the break is no more than a dry, narrow ravine to drain off the water-falls. In places the arable valleys are ten to twenty miles apart, while the intervening spaces are filled with huge cliffs and rugged gorges, fit for naught but the abodes of wild beasts, Indians, and stock-range. The settlements are made in the valleys, leaving wide, unpeopled ranges between them. Along these unsettled belts the wily Indian often made predatory inroads to capture horses, and whenever they came near a cabin they would conceal themselves in the mountain-cliffs by day, and in the night's dead hours walk around the horse-pen, or peep in upon the encabined sleepers, leaving their moccasin tracks to be traced in the sand in the early dawn. But if a horse was about the premises, he fell into their thieving hands; and if they chanced to meet an unfortunate straggler from the settlements, they took his horse and scalp to their wigwamed retreats in some far-off solitude.

When Mr. Potter had finished his last round on the Uvalde Circuit that year, the Indians were then on a thieving raid, in small squads, in that part of the country; and having heard of it, he took the precaution to carry his Winchester rifle with him. He was returning to his mountain-home, traveling in an ambulance drawn by two little Spanish mules, with a like span tied behind the ambulance. His road led him from Frio to Sabinal Cañon, through narrow defiles, steep ravines, interspersed with dense thickets and spaces of prairie glades. In one of these wild, lonely defiles, hemmed in by vast ranges of mountainous solitudes, Mr. Potter met a squad of four savage Indians. Having crossed Cherry Creek, suddenly his keen, watchful eye saw something moving along the deep ravine, and on close inspection he knew that they were Indians aiming to intercept him in the valley below. Instantly he saw that a fight was, perhaps, his only chance to save his scalp from their scalping-knife, knowing that if he tried to return to the settlement he had just left that they could overtake him, and thinking that perhaps a band was already there to cut off his retreat, a fight was the only chance. Wishing to bring on the contest far enough from the ambulance not to frighten the mules, he reined them up to a thicket-mot and made them fast. He then took his rifle in hand, and placing himself so that a mot should conceal his motions from his wily foe, he hastened to reach the mot unperceived by them. Reaching the mot in safety, he cautiously passed through it to the other side, when he discovered the four red savages about fifty paces off, standing near to the road, awaiting the arrival of the ambulance, when they expected to capture driver and all. But they had not seen the preacher near the thicket-mot, which gave him the chance for the first fire; but his gun being rusty, it did not fire. The noise of the hammer called their attention to him, and the two having citizen-rifles fired at him, the bullets passing near to his right-arm. Mr. Potter fired at the same moment, wounding one of them, whose gun fell from his hand. The two unarmed Indians stepped up to the wounded one, one of them taking hold of him, and the other securing his gun, they all retreated down the ravine. The preacher might have slain all four of them when they were passing down the ravine, but he was afraid to risk the firing of his gun; it having been loaded sometime, it had rusted in the breech. He hastened back to his ambulance, and led his team, holding his gun in one hand, looking out for the appearance of other Indians. Obliquing to the right of the road he was traveling, he came to the base of a bleak mountain near to a dense thicket, into which he might enter in case of an attack, well knowing an Indian's precaution never to enter a thicket in the domain of the white man. He now scraped and cleansed his gun, and reloaded the empty tubes, and proceeded to light his big pipe and take a social smoke within the mountain solitudes.

On looking upon the great earthen dome above him, he saw two of the savages looking down upon him. Seeing that he had discovered them, they both fired at him from their high position, but their bullets passed over the ambulance. Mr. Potter then returned two shots at them, when they retreated away into the invisible domain of the unpeopled mountain-world, to meet their antagonist no more, till the last trump shall summon the tribes of all ages and nations to meet at the great judgment, to give an account of the deeds done in the body. Mr. Potter then entered his conveyance and drove like Jehu for a mile or two, when, finding the dangers of another attack improbable, he slackened speed, and traveled on in safety at his usual gait, and in due time reached his cottage-home unharmed.

In the pious minds of those who have attained high plateaus in Christian virtues under the peaceful shades of civilized life, in the olden States, far removed from the blood-stained path of the savage, there is a seeming paradox in the fellowship of the Bible and the sword—the preacher and his rifle, on the frontier borders of Western Texas, where Indian barbarism and quasi-civilization meet and interlap. Amid these far-away mountain-heights, where only a few days agone the untamed Indian's savage yell and startling war-whoop echoed along vale, cliff, and lonely dell, the writer of these pages sits this morning in a little studio erected over blood-stained dust, where fell in battle-strife the brave, dauntless pioneer, the quiet air around his mountain-cottage once thickened by the whizzing flight of their steel-pointed arrows seeking the death and doom of their pale-faced brother. But the peaceful, air-balmed morns of the Eden-like Guadalupe vale cost the life-blood of many an aggressive borderman, whose dust now enriches the growing tree of peace and liberty. It is true that there can be no kinship between the manner of propagating the tenets of the Koran and those of the Holy Bible. The Koran employs the keen, steel-edged sword, but the Bible uses the trowel of persuasive love. It is also true that there is a wide difference between a preacher defending his own life against the brutal assaults of beast-like savages and that of his submitting, like Paul, to persecution for the sake of his religion. Jesus evidently taught his disciples that they must not defend their religion with the sword, telling them that when they were persecuted in one city to flee into another; saying, also, that whosoever might lose his life for his sake should find it in the world to come. But why our Lord Jesus Christ told his disciples to take two swords with them into Gethsemane, the dark night of his betrayal, has ever been a moral enigma to me. It is unlike any thing in all his life, in all his doctrine. It could not have been to defend him, or them, against the violence of the mob, for he was born for that hour—that destiny; and besides, he needed not a sword, or the aid of men, to rescue him from their cruel hate, as all power was in his hands. He too could have called many legions of angels to have delivered him from their hands, as the might of a single angel rendered the guard of a hundred soldiers powerless on his resurrection-morn. Those swords must have been intended to teach them a symbolized lesson, especially the bold and dauntless Peter. When he literally used his sword, and cut off the ear of the high-priest's servant, Jesus healed the ear, and said to Peter, "Put up the sword," clearly showing that his defense was not the object had in view when he told him to gird it about him. That literal sword must have been designed to impress on their minds the armory of God, with which they must be clad to gain victories over the allied enemies of his peaceful religion—"the sword of the Spirit," with which they were truly divinely armed on the memorable Pentecost.

It is also true that our blessed Lord taught the doctrine of non-retaliation of personal insults and injuries, saying when "one cheek is smitten, turn the other also." But there must be a limit to the moral duty of non-resisting submission, where life is imperiled, even with civilized contestants, where the cause of contest is not religion; but if it is a religious persecution, Christians must not unsheath the sword in defense of the cross, but submit, even to martyrdom, for Jesus's sake, as he did for us. But where a man is attacked by a band of lawless savages, or a reckless desperado, who is little if any better than a savage, does moral duty bind him to stand still and quietly yield up his life to their barbarous rage? Shall a man of useful gifts and habits, an able, pious minister of the blessed gospel, unresisting stand still, and let a damaging, brutal wretch, in a moment, destroy his valuable life? This interrogative postulate puts the case in a strong attitude of contrast, but not stronger than true. As it stands, reason revolts against it; and both wisdom and duty seem to unite, and say, "Of two evils, the less must always be chosen." A good man, a useful preacher, had better slay the injurious than to be cut off by their hateful fury—that which is a curse to society had better be taken out of the world, and let that which is a blessing remain.

But, then, it is granted that all possible methods of escape from the dire necessity of taking the life of a human creature must first be tried ere doing the fatal deed—we must be shut up to the point, *life for life*. At that point the law of civilized ages attaches no guilt to the defensive perpetrator of the awful deed; and, too, the law of Nature, which is inborn in all individual humanity, inspires to the protection of life; and that law being *natural*, of *divine* planting in humanity, cannot contravene the *moral code* of the same *original*. Then there must be a limit to non-resistance of evil-doing among men, as there is a bound to ocean's maddened waves, where they rebound in foaming fury to their sky-pent home.

This is the view of Mr. Potter on this delicate subject—the view which has guided him in all his ministerial career, when in contact with Indians or desperadoes. On a subject *nearly bordering on the wrong*, lying just where the fringes of right and wrong seem to meet and part—where one ceases and the other begins, as the colors of the rainbow do—we shall let the zealous minister speak for himself, by appending just here a letter from his own pen, to a Georgian, in answer to certain queries relative to his not fearing either Indians or the devil. Here is the letter:

When I embraced religion and joined the Church, I felt it a duty to use the necessary means to preserve and protect my body as well as my soul. The devil being a great evil spirit, his violent assaults are directed against our spiritual and moral natures, and we are required to resist him with spiritual agencies. In this sphere, it is true, that the weapons of our warfare are not carnal, but spiritual. We cannot fight spiritual foes with temporal weapons, neither can we war against our earthly enemies with spiritual instrumentalities. We cannot attack Satan with a Winchester gun, nor are faith and prayer the divinely-appointed implements to be used in a contest with Indians or desperadoes. I think I believe in the providence of God as firmly as any man, but he has connected the use of means with results in all our natural and spiritual relations. He has given us our persons for a noble purpose, and he has given us the means to feed, clothe, and protect them against all want and violence from men or beasts. When God calls me to travel in a region of country infested with lurking savages, my Winchester gun and a full belt of cartridges shall ever prevent distressing alarms about my safety when meeting a savage foe, feeling that in the fearful struggle for life I have some safe means to preserve my God-given manhood. Had it not been for my faithful "Winchester" my bloody scalp would have long since graced the warrior's victory, and heightened the wild glee of the merry dance in some distant mountain-gorge. I am not so anxious to wear a martyr's crown as to sacrifice my life when God requires me to use means to preserve it. It is no evidence of a preacher's want of trust in God when he carries a gun to shield his life in the time of peril. It would be most sinful presumption not to do so. Indeed, I do not carry my gun because I am *afraid to die*, but because it is a *duty to use means to preserve life*. It is not a sin to resort to the doctor's skill and the virtue of medicine to prevent or cure disease; nor do lightning-rods on homes and churches argue a distrust in Providence, but are the *means of security*. A little experience along this perilous border may greatly alter the views of tender-conscienced men who only see such scenes at a vast distance from their peaceful home-retreats. Time and again have I rode over the ground where its sands have been reddened with the blood of many a noble borderman; there their graves mark the scene of their last battle-strife. I too have gazed on the scalpless head of the dead and the suffering, while the wailing cries of wife and children rent the air around the mountain solitudes.

Such are Mr. Potter's views, and these are the all-inspiring motives which governed his ministerial conduct along the Indian-infested frontier of West Texas for thirteen years of unequaled hardships and untellable perils.

A little personal experience along the track of the savage no doubt would tend to indurate the tender conscience of overscrupulous men about a true missionary preacher striving to save his life from the bloody scalping-knife and the cleaving tomahawk of a brutal Indian. Home-soldiers, who never leave their peaceful, carpeted mansion, to defend their country's name, can well philosophize about the *tactics* used in the bloody battle-day by true men and brave hearts; but in all this jumbling of ideas of right and wrong about moral proprieties and improprieties, it occurs to us that the greatest wrong is to be found in the civil government, in not securely protecting its savage-menaced borders from barbarous depredations, so that people and preacher might fear no harm in the pursuit of their calling.

Mr. Potter closed up a long, prosperous year, and then set out for Conference, with the Rev. Buckner Harris, a distance of more than one hundred miles, as will be seen in the following pages.

CHAPTER XXX.

AGAIN we shall favor the reader with an interesting extract from Mr. Potter's own manuscript:

"I traveled the Uvalde Circuit in the year 1872. The area of the circuit extended west to the town of Uvalde. I was invited to visit San Felipe—about eighty miles west of Uvalde—a large irrigation farm on the Rio Grande River, worked by Mexicans and Americans. Most of the eighty miles was unsettled, and was traversed by Indians and robbers. It was a lonely, dangerous trip for one man; but in September I fixed up my Winchester and six-shooter, and reached San Felipe in safety. I made my arrangements to preach there on three days in the week, and at Fort Clark on Sabbath. As I was the first preacher who had ever visited that region, the people were all agog about preaching. I preached to a crowded house on Wednesday, Thursday, and Friday, at 11 o'clock A.M., and at twilight in the evening. At times the whole audience was moved to tears. I was about to dismiss the meeting, when an old man slammed his heavy fist on the table, saying, 'Hold on; this brother has come a long and dangerous road to preach to us, and he is entitled to some remuneration.' He then passed the hat around. A tall, dark man rose up and said, 'I owe that hat four dollars, and the preacher is going home with me, and I will pay it.' The collection amounted to twenty-three dollars. That night the sad news reached us that a party of men had been in a fight with Mexicans, and that John Pulliam was killed and Tom Evans was mortally wounded. Pulliam's parents lived in San Felipe, but Evans lived in Uvalde.

"Saturday morning I set out for Fort Clark, a distance of thirty-five miles. Within seven miles of the fort I was met by a man who had seen my ambulance at a distance, and hurried forward to ask me to attend the burial of young Pulliam. He told me that Evans had also died in the meantime, and would be buried about midnight that night. When I reached the grave, I found the parents of poor John in inconsolable sorrow over the sudden loss of their noble son. After the interment of the unfortunate youth, I learned the following facts about the ill-fated young men: The old alcalde of New Town, on the Mexican side of the Rio Grande River, about twenty-five miles below San Felipe, had men employed to steal cattle from the Texas side of the river and drive over to him, and he slaughtered them and sold their hides and meat. About eighteen of the Texas boys went over and made an attack on the town about morning twilight, when the Mexicans all fled but the old alcalde, who ran into his adobe house and fired on them. John Pulliam's unruly mule bore him—in spite of all effort to restrain him—right up to the window, when the alcalde shot him in the head, and killed him instantly. They fired volley after volley into the house, and supposing they had killed the old trespasser, young Evans rode up to the window and looked in, when he received a shot through the abdomen. They then set fire to the house, on which the old magistrate ran out, and received his death-shot. They also burned him with his house, and then lashed the dead body of Pulliam to a horse, and the younger Evans set his wounded brother on a horse, and rode behind him to hold him on, and in this way they swam the Rio Grande River. But young Evans soon died.

"It was now nearly night, and the men had hid in the chaparral, fearing the Mexicans and the United States soldiers, and young Evans had no one to help him dress his dead brother for the coffin which was to be there at midnight from Fort Clark. I got him to help me get the dead youth out of the wagon and lay him on a plank, and then procured water, soap, and towel, from a near ranche, and washed the blood and dust from his person, and combed his raven locks, when I said, 'Poor Tom! you look as natural as when I saw you at the camp-meeting in Uvalde a few months ago. But Tom is not here—this is the form—the spirit is gone, and without it the body is dead. Handsome indeed, when living, but soon the grave-worm shall feed on these cold, empurpled lips.' I went into my traveling-trunk, and took from it the linen to dress him for the grave. A kind lady sent me a clean, white sheet, which I folded around his rigid form, and we laid him in his coffin about midnight. By this time the men who had concealed themselves in the thicket had come in, and accompanied us to the burial. A young man held a lamp as I read the burial-service, and while all nature slept under the gloom of night we laid him down to rest beside his fallen comrade, on the banks of the Rio Grande.

"Many fears were entertained of a retaliative raid by the Mexicans. I accordingly set out for Uvalde, and reached there on Monday night, where I found the parents of young Evans in the greatest anguish for their lost boy. Many were the sorrowful questions they asked me about the last of their unfortunate child. I did not intend to say any thing about dressing him, but that was what they wanted to hear, especially the mother—her love nestles over her loved dead in the grave: how he was robed, what kind of a coffin housed her dead son, she must learn. I told them all. The next morning my linen was replaced and a twenty-five-dollar overcoat. On Tuesday night I preached in Uvalde, and some of the good women raised such a shout that the citizens who had not gone to church thought the Mexicans had made a raid on the town, and that the work of slaughter had begun. They all gathered up their guns—some jumped out of bed and came to the scene in their night-clothes and barefooted; when, to their pleasant surprise, the noise was nothing but notes of praise to God. They were not used to that sort."

We have made this long extract because it shows the man. A man's own speech reveals him, and circumstances develop character. As disease tests the tenacity of physical life, so circumstances try the real virtue in the soul. A man may be kind, polite, and generous, when it costs him nothing, or he may be valorous in the time of peace; but the generous, polite, and kind qualities in human nature shine brightest in the perilous scenes of adversity, and true valor glows brightest in the face of dangers. One has said that a good deed in a naughty world shines as a candle on a dark night. In the detail of this tragic story we plainly see three leading traits in Mr. Potter's real character: the lineaments of the soldier facing the imminent dangers of the savage-raided border; the elements of the philanthropist, pitying human griefs, and delving in the menial services of dressing the dead for their long visit to the tomb; and the genius of the preacher, reading the religious formula over the dead at the grave, and preaching the gospel of salvation to the living—just the man for the place. A rough, sagacious, and daringly chivalrous people—among this society he is to show all the tender, valorous virtues of religion, and plant deep in the sparse soil among rocks and shrubs the seeds of a pure gospel. Grave among the more refined, and humble among the poor, as one of them, entering into their sorrows —made all things unto all men—he could slumber on a downy bed, sleep on a blanket on the dirt-floored cabin, or pillow on a stone on the desert mountain-side. Dear reader, see the sympathetic preacher washing the clotted blood from the dead young man's body, while his father and mother are far away. See him clothing the cold form in his own clean linen, then folding it in the winding-sheet; and then, as a minister of religion, he commits dust to dust in the lonely hour of midnight, telling to the sad group of living ones about the fresh grave of a great, coming day, when all of earth's slain shall arise to live forever; and that while all the bright stars are looking pityingly down upon the mourning crowd, fond angels may have clustered there to weep over his tomb for his absent mother.

We once heard of a certain doctor of divinity—now of great Methodistic fame—who in early manhood was stationed at Lebanon, Tennessee. Asiatic cholera raged there during the time, and many died, among them a poor widow, and there was no one to entomb her. That preacher dug her grave and buried her. If we are correctly informed as to these facts, that noble deed shall shine more brilliantly in his diadem of renown than any other gem in his crown of honor in the last day. Had that young preacher chanced to have met our heroic Potter at the bloody wagon in which lay the blood-smeared corpse of Tommie Evans, he would have joined him in dressing him for his long home under ground. The minister of the Man of Sorrows knows how to weep with the bereaved and rejoice with the glad. The world is his home, and the human race his family, his kindred. Wherever he meets man he meets his brother, for whom he has a fellow-feeling and a message of love.

CHAPTER XXXI.

ONE appointment of the Uvalde Circuit was in the Frio Cañon, and a grocery there furnished the whisky which caused most of the strifes of the neighborhood. The moral citizens organized a debating society, and proceeded to discuss the relative evils of war and intemperance. Mr. Potter was appointed principal on the side of intemperance. His opponent was a teacher and a lawyer of some reading and native wit, with a good stock of common sense, and in the course of discussion he indulged in uncouth specimens of humor and repartee, mingled with a hash of argument and dogmatism. He said that Mr. Potter's speech reminded him of a Dutchman who was trying to scrape the hair from the body of a live hog, saying there was more *squeal* than *wool*. Mr. Potter concluded his speech by comparing his antagonist's harangue to a little negro boy who was being chastised, saying unto his master, who was stripping him, "Pray, massa! O pray, massa!" when his master said unto him, "Pray yourself, you fool you!" and the little lad said, "Massa, let us look to de Lord for de blessin', an' be dismissed!" The judge awarded the victory to Mr. Potter's cause. Defeat is not a word in his vocabulary. From his boyish race-riding to his pulpit efforts success crowned his labors. What he did he did to a purpose; and he put forth all his might in the enterprise in hand, acting under the motto that whatsoever ought to be done deserved doing well. He too tried to suit the best means to the best ends. There were few books in this frontier border in those days, and few men of letters had ventured so far along the dangerous Indian trails, but most of the adventurers were men of good mother-wit and energetic enterprise. Men without energy and shrewdness do not migrate into distant, unsettled regions; they usually live and die on the old, trodden fields which have been cleared and cultivated by a more industrious ancestry. The bravest, the most stirring men go to the front, and clear away the rude elements of barbarism, and open up a wide road for civilization's onward march. The first generation growing up under border facilities must partake of the nature of the unpolished, the rude. Cradled and trained up in the unpeopled plains, chasing the mustang, the ox, or the wild game, inspirits youth with a wild, reckless air, unfriendly to a serious life of piety. The little urchin, barefooted and bareheaded, begins to learn his trade of throwing the lasso, or rope in the pen, among calves and lambs, when not more than three years of age; and if there are no other little animals to "rope," they practice it on each other, or cast the sliding-loop over the chair-knob, or bed-post, or any other convenient object. By the time they arrive at ten years of age they can lariat a horse or an ox under speed. There is recklessness about the scene. He makes a sliding-loop in one end of his rope—about forty feet in length—the other end is fastened to the horn of his saddle; then he coils the rope in one hand, swings the loop around his head with the other, claps spurs to his pony, and off they fly at break-neck speed, in pursuit of the horse or ox to be caught. On they go, his lasso sweeping round and over his head till getting in throwing distance, when he casts the loop ahead of his victim, which ensnares its head; then he begins to check his pony's speed gradually, till both are brought to a halt. In that way a boy can capture the wild ox, or the swift-running, affrighted mustang. Such habits give a daring romance to young life unfavorable to a sober, pious cast of mind, and greatly weaken the motives of the fear of death, and the casualties of life, which often prevent men from a headlong rush into sin, or aid them in a reformation from evil habits. Such motives have little effect on an adventurous frontier life. Texan youth on the border are generally orderly at places of worship, and respectful to ministers and the aged, but have a limited idea of the sanctity of a place of worship. As soon as the benediction is pronounced they begin to light their cigarettes, by striking a match, or by the unextinguished lights. They are scarcely capable of sadness—cheerful, merry, and exquisitely fond of the charm of the violin and the dance. But a great reform is fast changing the rude habits into a more settled moral calm. Temperance societies, lodges, schools, and churches, have sprung up everywhere, and their refining influences are instilling more soberness of thought and staidness of habits into the growing generation; while the plow-line is taking the place of the lasso, and the school-master is being substituted for the saloon-keeper; and the clamorous cry is heard all over the land, "Close the bar-rooms." Villages and towns whiten valleys and plains; corn and wheat-fields, like green plains, spread out their broad acres along the rivers and streamlets; and the steam-driven trains bring the crowding strangers into the domain; and a new empire is looming up in the border wilderness. Here our pioneer preacher drove back the savage and planted the germ of empire. His Bible and rifle, his temperance speeches, his pulpit ministrations, watered and nurtured the seed. The harvest is maturing, and the reapers are near. A new era is opening. Its twilight goldens the skies, and its sprinkled dews embalm the sparkling morn. Hail, happy day! Alcohol dethroned, piety and morality holding the scepter! then shall mind mount the car of progress, and the wilderness blossom as the garden of the Lord. But much is yet to be done ere the dawn of that happy day. No time is to be lost, no efforts to be relaxed. The battle rages fiercely. The nearer the moment of victory the more energetic the last struggles of the strong and defiant enemy.

There is a grand temperance movement throughout the domain of our imperial State just now. Our Legislature is in session, and more than one hundred thousand of the moral and intelligent element of the State have memorialized that body to give the citizens a chance at the ballot-box to alter the State Constitution so as to empower the Legislature to pass a prohibitory law excluding the manufacture or sale of ardent spirits within the limits of the State. The bill passed the Senate, but failed in the House to get the requisite majority by about six votes; and it is said that gold, in the interest of the liquor-dealers, did that. It was a bold and flagrant trespass upon the rights of the State for a few paid representatives to lock up the ballot-box against their suffrage; but it is a registered deed, and it has forever entombed those men from political life. The next campaign shall clarion the victory for the great humane temperance cause. A noted lecturer has immortalized his name by his bold advocacy of temperance in this State the past decade. His strong voice has been heard from the mountain-dells to the gulf-washed shore, and from the Sabine to the great Rio Grande. His lectures have awakened thought and stimulated a healthy public pulse on the claims of the modern temperance cause. They greatly aid in troubling the moral waters in their wave-like efforts to wash out the stains of liquor from our State statutes. He is styled Dr. Young—we know not whether it is M.D. or D.D. No difference; he deserves all honor. We do not go high on organizations, but instructive lectures, treatises, and journalistic editorials, leading up the public mind to the sure work of taking temptation out of the way of the ruined and the young—*legal prohibition*.

It is strangely wonderful to see the undying tenacity with which the lovers of the bowl cling to its poisonous contents. They hesitate not to legislate restrictive rules for quarantines against infected vessels, tainted with the contagion of death; but liquor-dealers can run into our ports with millions of the death-dealing spirits, if they can only put a few hundred dollars into the State and County treasuries for the destructive privilege. Better by far shut out the insidious poison, which finds its way into all counties, towns, cities, and rural dells and vales, of the vast continent, and license by taxation the ship-captains to land the infected thousands, rank with the sickening effluvia of "black vomit," for that fearful depopulator of malarious coasts and cities cannot be made epidemic in many regions of the inland scenes. Of two evils, wisdom says, choose the less. Let in "yellow-jack" at a revenue-yielding tax, and lock out alcohol. In the next two years the wisdom, the virtue, and the humanity of the State will not sleep. They may organize; they may look to all the journals of religious and moral tone for aid. Many of them have already done much; and still they shall hoist the prohibition banner. Some hold an even balance, to be turned either way the specific gravity of gold may determine. The Texas *Christian Advocate* has led the van in the moral enterprise, and the clear-sheeted *Journal* has followed close upon its heels. The *Journal* is yet a babe in years, while the *Advocate* is hoary. It has earned a monument at the hands of the virtue of the age. It has for several years made bold and vigorous attacks on the palatial gambling mansions and bar-rooms in the cities, and impartially arraigned their delinquent officials for failures in the line of duty. Its facile and nervous pen has awakened an intelligent and healthy sentiment which is now stirring the heart of society everywhere. Its able reporter, "Cartoon," opened a terrific bombardment on the government officials at the city of Austin last year, unveiling their disgraceful, intemperate habits, which awakened the pride and aroused the indignation of the moral element of the State, which shall neither abate the one nor quiet the other until the land is regenerated and purged of its disgraceful and immoral stains. Wash its garments! make them clean! "Cartoon" wields a caustic quill, and woe unto the poor unfortunate bibulous office-holder, or public functionary, against whose ugly deeds he may chance to point his pen. That pencil, pushed by his fingers, leaves along the lines it marks jewels of wit and gems of humor, all glowing in the string of facts it may narrate. As a newspaper writer, his pen is rarely excelled in this age. His pen deserves a diadem of fadeless hue from the jeweled fingers of Texas. Its dewy sparklings glisten on the pages of the *Journal*.

Knowing from painful experience the direful effects of intoxicating liquors, Mr. Potter has been a bold and steadfast advocate of the innovations sought by all the good of the land to handicap the heartless monster, and imprison him for life in the regions of nonentity. Strife and war, violence and blood, cannot cease in the earth until the deranging *stimulus* is banished and buried from the sight of man. As long as it is made and sold, men will drink it at all cost and hazard, in spite of earth and heaven. They will keep it at home, carry it on trains, in stage-coaches, on ships, in buggies, in wagons, on horseback, and drink it in saloons, in hotels, and in the gaming-rooms, in the face of laws human and divine—at the sacrifice of character, wife, babes, property, health, peace, life—in view of the yawning grave and an open way to eternal woe. No motive reaches the enslaved. *Prohibition is the remedy.*

CHAPTER XXXII.

CONFERENCE met at Lockhart this fall, Bishop Kavanaugh presiding, and A. A. Killough made presiding elder of the San Antonio District, including the border frontier. Mr. Potter was not assigned to a pastoral charge. Mr. Wesley Smith, seeing that a general supply of Bibles along the frontier could not be fully accomplished through the agencies of the regular auxiliaries, procured from the American Bible Society the appointment of Mr. Potter as general distributing or sub-agent to disseminate the Holy Scriptures all over this vast frontier empire, subject to the ratification of the presiding bishop. The bishop confirmed the appointment, and Mr. Potter spent a dangerous, toilsome, and useful year in selling and donating the word of God to the hardy border-men of both the English and Spanish-speaking population.

Traveling near the dangerous regions of the Rio Grande, where the unscrupulous Mexicans would often steal upon travelers while sleeping on the ground, and murder and rob them, and knowing that he was in danger from that class of men as well as Indians, he got him a log of wood about the length and size of an ordinary man, and spread a blanket on the ground near his ambulance, and laid the billet of wood on the blanket, and covered it up so as to resemble a man in sleep; then he made his own bed in a thicket near by, thinking that if the Mexicans or Indians made an attack on the log it would awake him, and then he would use his Winchester on them from his thicket-screen. How cool and cautious that man of unequaled valor! We now transcribe an incident:

"The Rev. A. A. Killough was appointed presiding elder of the San Antonio District, and although I had no pastoral charge, yet as my work lay mostly in the bounds of his district we were often thrown together, and had many long and pleasant tours along the frontier.

"His District Conference was held at Newton's Chapel, on the head of the Atascosa River, in the bounds of the Medina Circuit, of which the Rev. T. G. Wools was preacher in charge. This was Brother Killough's first experience in presiding over a District Conference. It was suggested by J. W. DeVilbiss that, instead of appointing the usual committees, all questions coming before the body should be acted on by the Conference resolving itself into the Committee of the Whole. That method often got things into a muddle. After getting matters tangled and untangled several times, Brother Killough declared that it should be the last District Conference he should hold in the Committee of the Whole; that he could not tell when he was in the 'Whole' or in the Conference.

"There was an excellent old local brother in attendance at this district-meeting who was noted for his long prayers, though of great faith and power.

Brother Killough had never heard him pray, and one night, when there were a number of mourners at the altar, he called on him to pray; and when he had prayed on to such a length that Killough thought that he had covered all the ground, he leaned over and whispered to me, 'Potter, is he never going to quit?' To which I replied, 'I do not know; I do not think he has quite reached the closing clause yet.' Sometimes the old brother would seem to almost reach the point where you would think he was going to say Amen, but then he would branch out again, and make another round. But at last he said, 'Now, Lord, we submit ourselves into thy hands.' Thinking that the long-expected Amen was just at hand, Brother Killough said aloud, 'Amen, amen!' But just then the old man thought of something else he had not asked for, and he started on another tour, when Killough leaned over again and said to me, 'Potter, I take it all back, I take it all back'—meaning the Amen.

"There were a number of penitents at the altar, but they were rather a silent lot of mourners, and Brother Killough seemed to get a little discouraged, and said that those mourners would not have religion if you would hand it round to them in a basket; and after remaining a few days he left us, and Brother Wools and myself carried on the meeting with some gracious results.

"At a quarterly-meeting this year at Uvalde several bar-room men made a private collection, and all came to me privately, saying, 'Mr. Potter, we are not members of the Church, and we don't owe any thing to those preachers down there: if we owe any preacher, you are the man—you have been preaching to us a long time, and this little donation is yours; you have done the country good, and this is yours'—and they poured twenty-five dollars into my hands. I said to them, 'I thank you, gentlemen, in the name of my wife and children.'"

Indeed does all this great frontier owe Mr. Potter more than wordy expressions of gratitude. The great stock-men truly are his debtors in material things. His time, his life, his home-pleasures, have been seriously taxed for their weal, and the safety of their homes and loved ones. "Pay what thou owest."

We now copy a letter from Dr. West, of Boerne, Texas, a man of marked ability and consistent piety, and also a neighbor to the Rev. Mr. Potter many years. He knew the man, and was all the while familiar with his itinerant labors, and the field of his operations:

Rev. H. A. Graves:—Having learned that you are engaged in writing the eventful Life of the Rev. Andrew Jackson Potter, my neighbor and brother in Christ, please permit me to aid you in transmitting to historic fame, for the benefit of the youth of this and coming ages, a few of the many acts performed in the drama of life by that remarkable man.

For thirteen toilsome years he has faithfully preached the gospel all along this Western frontier, looking after the spiritual welfare of a generous, wild, and adventurous people, reaching from San Antonio to the Rio Grande, and to San Saba on the west, going to the outpost of American civilization, and sometimes even beyond it. His path has been beset by wild beasts of the mountain forest, and the still more subtle and deadly foe, the robber, the midnight assassin, supplemented by the savage Indian with his cleaving tomahawk and gory scalping-knife, all gleaming in the light, while his heart-chilling war-whoop disturbs the stillness of the forest vales. But amid all these privations and dangers this heroic servant of the Lord has marched bravely on with a heart full of love to God and zeal for souls, his Bible in one hand and his trusty rifle in the other. To enumerate all the great hazards, privations, hard struggles, hair-breadth escapes, and fruitful victories in his wonderful career along these mountains and valleys, would fill the pages of a volume. We refer you to the immeasurable amount of good resulting from his ministerial labors in this hitherto untilled spiritual field. Many scores of sinners have been converted—many of them great sinners—Churches have been organized in valleys and mountain-dells, and Sabbath-schools to train the mountain-youths, which now adorn every large settlement in this vast West; and in their train is seen the temperance organizations striving to close the bar-rooms from the young of this day. The Rev. Mr. Potter planted the germinal seed, and cultivated the rising crop; but O who can tell "What shall the harvest be?" It is now yellowing for the reapers.

One year he not only preached but acted as a colporteur of the American Bible Society in distributing the Holy Bible by sale and donation—donations made to the poor who were unable to buy.

In a settlement in Uvalde the Indians made a raid and captured every thing belonging to a certain poor widow, and burned her cabin, Bible, and all. A generous old gentleman asked Mr. Potter to ascertain if that poor woman had a Bible. He visited her, and she showed him a few scorched leaves of the old Family Bible which had been saved from the torch of the savage. That dear, blessed old Bible had been given her in other lands, in her youthful days, by the hand of her sainted mother, and she grieved over its loss as a loved one dead. The benevolent gentleman had given the preacher three dollars and a-half to supply her with another Family Bible—a roan, gilt quarto; and after listening to her plaintive story of the old burnt book, the preacher presented her with a beautiful gilt volume, in the name of her kind benefactor. Receiving it with humble gratefulness, she pressed it to her bosom, and dedicated its reception with joyful tears, esteeming its sacred contents of more value to her than all the perishing treasures of earthly wealth and fame.

He passed a night at the cabin of another widow who had lost her only son, and whose home had been burned by the savages. Going to hold prayers, he called for a Bible, when the poor woman gave him a hymn-book, saying that the Indians had burned her Bible with her home. On leaving the next morning, he gave her a small

Bible, and meeting a congregation at church, he told the circumstance, whereupon the kind ladies raised ten dollars to purchase her a large Family Bible; but the brave and generous preacher, desiring an interest in that investment, aided in the contribution. Greatly appreciating her large-type Bible, which she could read with ease, she rendered many joyful thanks to the generous donors. Giving to the poor is to "lend unto the Lord." That was one of Mr. Potter's religious mottoes.

Passing a school-house near Frio City, he halted, when the children were at play, to show his Bibles and Testaments. Soon a crowd were inspecting them. One manly little fellow, on hearing the price of a Bible which pleased him to be only fifty cents, inquired if he would wait till he could run home and get the money. Seeing his anxiety, the preacher told him to go. He soon returned, panting for breath, and bought the sacred treasure, exulting in his purchase as if he had heired an empire. Upon inquiry, Mr. Potter learned that the noble little boy, on a previous Christmas, had bought his two little sisters nice dresses for a Christmas-present out of his own honest earnings, instead of throwing away his nickels and dimes for candies and fire-crackers, as boys most generally do. Texas may yet hear from that manly little boy. Hearing of the generous deed of that man-boy, the preacher gave him a Spanish Testament, in the name of that grand old national and benevolent institution, the American Bible Society, which the lad seemed to esteem beyond estimate. That boy may yet play an important part on the stage of our Mexican mission-field.

Mr. Potter visited an encampment of United States soldiers on the Sabinal, where his reception was a mingling of jest, jeers, and ridicule. He succeeded in selling only five Bibles. Those who bought them seemed to have had devout motives; others quizzed and ridiculed them, saying, in sacrilegious mockery, that those pious ones would soon evangelize the camp. One old soldier attracted the agent's special attention—he approached him, and politely asked if he wished to purchase a Bible, when, to his utter astonishment, he received the following laconic reply: "A —— sight more use for a fine-tooth comb than a Bible." One time the wit of the preacher may have been a little shocked into silence; though he says that a little soap and Adam's liquid warmed might have improved the poor old man's wardrobe and person, as well as the light of the Holy Scriptures in cleansing the errors of his debased intellect, and that a spiritual combing was needed as well. Poor soldiers! hearing little else but military tactics and Indian raids, under which the good in humanity is held in abeyance, while the worst elements are cultivated to manufacture them into soldiers, they lose most of their ideas of moral virtue. They are more to be *pitied* than *blamed*. It is to be hoped, however, that those Bibles may be as bread on the waters, yielding a harvest of good.

The priest-ridden Mexicans on this border, far removed from priests and Catholic cities, have some chance to read and think for themselves. They mostly receive the Bible gladly; some buy it, to others it is donated. These Bibles and Testaments which Mr. Potter has circulated among them are now doing their evangelizing work among that people. Even now there are two Protestant Districts already established in the Mexican Border Mission among that people, and a great work of evangelization is going on among them.

The foregoing sketches from the pen of Dr. West give us a few items in the useful ministerial life of Mr. Potter, but they are not a thousandth part of his labors in the vineyard of Christ. In their detail they touch on some of the ruling factors in his ministerial character: his deep sense of duty in the frontier field, going everywhere inside of the lines of civilization, and sometimes beyond, to the houseless widow, to school-houses, and to meet under the shade of timbered mots to preach Jesus to an audience of rude adventurers—going where no other man would go. They show out his earnest tenderness for the poor, ever obeying the apostolic injunction, not to forget the poor. We see him in the widow's unfloored cabin, praying and donating a copy of God's consoling word to make her heart sing for joy. We see in him the soldier and the minister—his Bible and his rifle—the fellowship of the Bible and the sword—a contest between Christianity and barbarism, face to face. Where the wave of civilization reaches its utmost bound, there he seeks to plant the germinal seeds of the Church. As the new temple-builders under Zerubbabel held their weapons in one hand and wrought with the other, so our valorous preacher held his rifle in one hand and his Bible in the other while planting the scions of religion and liberty along the interlapping border of light and darkness, as some intrepid soldier bearing the standard of his country's banner into the enemy's ranks amidst the flight of death-dealing missiles, and planting its victorious ensign in their assailing camps. To-day many of those germ-seeds are large churches, as great, giant trees spreading out their beneficent shades in the long summer-day to invite the weary traveler to rest under their cooling shadows. Andrew Jackson Potter was the first ministerial visitor there, preached the first sermon there, when the red savage stood on the overlooking mountain-peaks, and hurled steel-fledged arrows at the assembling dwellers of the vale, who had gathered to hear the heart-touching story of Him who gave his life for man. He counted not his life dear unto him only so as to finish the ministry of the gospel committed to him in that valley of spiritual gloom.

The Hon. Mr. Schleicher, representative of the Congressional District of West Texas in the Congress of the United States, when making a speech on the floor of the hall of Congress on the bill of national protection on the frontier borders of Texas, said that the Rev. Mr. Potter and fifteen more like him, of true Texan valor, could do more to protect the frontier than all the troops the Federal Government might station along the outpost. This, possibly, may have been a slight exaggeration, but it involved a great fact: that the adventurous preacher, with his rifle and Bible, had already done much to push forward and protect both Church and State interest in savage realms.

In view of his frontier intrepidity, a gentleman presented him with a fine Winchester rifle, which till lately he carried along with his Hymn-book, Discipline, and Bible. We write not to-day of things done in a dark, north-east corner, nor of a man altogether unknown to historic fame. The Indian-fighting preacher, the immortalized Potter, is already registered on the page of American Methodism, and it shall be printed in the future rehearsal of Texan story when the next historian writes up the victories of her advancing banner. The Federal Government, the State, the wide border domain, and the adventurous stock-men, owe that zealous man more than a simple debt of grateful remembrance, which is not fully liquidated when they have spoken kindly of his labors and triumphs, and have named their most promising sons after Andrew Jackson Potter. The terror of his name and faithful gun have shielded their flocks and herds from the ravages of the *real* and the *pretended* savage, especially the latter, as well as their homes and families. He now goes and returns in peace from his kingdom-like district without his Winchester.

CHAPTER XXXIII.

Mr. Potter was preaching one Sunday night in a certain frontier-town, when a rather amusing incident occurred. The place was thickly set with bar-rooms filled with gamblers and drinking-men; and there was a terrible racket in town that night. He was preaching in the upper-room of a store-house. The steps leading to the room went up from the street. The house was thronged with hearers. He was preaching about Paul and Silas in the jail at Philippi. A drunken man passing the street, hearing the noise above, made his way up to the room, and after listening a short time, said, "Sir, I ask your pardon; but do you think there ever was a Christ on earth?" The humorous preacher replied, "Sir, I am not now discussing that question—I am talking about two preachers being in jail, just where all such drunken scoundrels as you are ought to be, and where you will be in ten minutes if the sheriff will do his duty." The deputy arose, summoned a young man to assist him, and started down the stair-way, but the inebriate refused to go. They threw him down, and then proceeded to lock him up in the jail-house. On returning, the deputy walked near to the stand, and said, "Mr. Potter, that man is in jail, sir." "Thank you, gentlemen," said the preacher. "You can turn him out in the morning, as he may then be sober. Please to take your seats." The service ended in order; but we are here reminded of the cool, unembarrassed mind of the preacher, and his Irish-like readiness of appropriate replies. No circumstances, however exciting and alarming, or amusing, disturb him, or arrest his chain of thought in the pulpit. Besides his natural mental bent toward ready repartee, he was strictly drilled to calm and skillful thought in all the hazards of life and limb in his earliest days, and in the fearful perils of Indian warfare, where preservation of life itself required the quickest and the most dispassionate reasoning. Here he had long years of schooling to acquire a fixed habit of holding the excitable elements of man in subjection to calculating thought, which of all others is the most valuable trait of a true soldier. Dispassionate coolness in scenes and moments of alarm is the main factor in real valor; it is an effectual safeguard against the wild, ruinous rage of panic. Panic is senseless, blind; it knows no strategic plans for safety; it leaps over the yawning precipice, and runs unwittingly into the dangers it seeks to avoid. But the brave soldier's eye of collected thought sees the narrow path of escape from danger, or coolly yields submission to the inevitable. These noble soldier elements, acquired in early life, Mr. Potter has retained as a soldier of the cross, where no less skillful intrepidity is demanded to make a valiant hero in the armies of Him who came to conquer a rebellious world—who said that he who might cowardly seek to save his life by panic-fright should lose it. Never really disturbed by any agitating surroundings, he moved on in the pulpit and along the prairies as if in the land of peace and quiet. Yet he was not insensible of dangers, but ever coolly cautious to avoid or to meet them. At these military outposts the state of society about them is wretched in the extreme. Made up of tradesmen and gamblers, who seem not to care for the virtues and benefits of civilized life, their greatest aim appears to be to gain a living, or to gather in money without manual labor, or some honest method of getting through life. These gamblers collect there to win the poor soldier's earnings, and those traders gather there to supply the gamblers. They are not wanted there to furnish the army—the commissaries do that. So the class of men centering about these posts is made up of those having little or no pure moral motives, being controlled mainly by avarice and an aversion to toil. These were the men to whom Mr. Potter preached, for the most part, at these distant border stations. Among these abandoned men he is to plant the seed of a gospel Church. The gospel is to them as to the refined sinful nabob housed in his palace, and gloating in luxurious ease on his dishonest gains. Jugglers, swindlers, and the stealthy robber, are all alike subjects of reformatory grace. The apostles of our universal Saviour proclaimed salvation to the harlots and smugglers in their day. Simon Magus was baptized, and the books of the Satanic art of jugglery, constituting a great library, were cast into the flames. Jesus issued his enduring mandate, " Go ye into the streets and lanes of the city, into the highways, hedges, and ditches." Yes, gather in the outcast, the vile, the low, the poor, and wash them in the font of regeneration, and clothe them with the wedding-garment, clean and white, and set them up on high with the redeemed, with a new song, "Unto him that hath loved us, and washed us from our sins in his own blood, unto him be glory." In the last day of sainted coronations some cleanly-robed immortal shall sit in that holy throng from the Texan-populated border, through the earnest ministrations of our pioneer soldier of Jesus, who died, to save the worst—the chief of sinners.

Before concluding this brief chapter, we call attention to the callous heart and little regard for the value of human life on the border, by soldiers, and civil officers, and other men as well. When the drunken man did not want to go to jail, the sheriff pitches him down the flight of steps leading from the upper-room to the ground. Regardless of limb or life, apparently in a good-humored way, he throws him on the hard earth as if he were a stone or a billet of wood. That was heartless cruelty—it partook of the nature of heathen barbarism to the helpless, the prisoner. Cruelty to the captured is incompatible with the moral sentiment of a Christian age. A reformation among the civilized governments of the world as to the treatment of convicts in prison-life is a moral necessity. "Man's inhumanity to man makes countless thousands mourn," in all grades and spheres of life, in the culprit's dungeon as elsewhere. Man is not a mere animal; he has a soul of great faculties, capable of a deep degradation or a high elevation, ranging at all times within the possible limits of a thorough reformation. The design of penalty of law, of prison-life, is not malignant—not to torment the subject, but to prevent farther trespass, and to reform. Deprivation of liberty for life is a competent punishment for all crimes, save that of murder, for which the moral law demands *life for life.* Humanity is due all captured, imprisoned violators of law.

We must also invite attention to the almost total disregard of the civil institutes on drunkenness and gambling about the military outposts. These rank gardens of vice flourish under the strict eye of the military, and no officer, civil or military, seems to regard their presence as an infraction of law or good order. There is a dead fly in the Government ointment-can just here. Drift-wood floats out on the margins of swollen rivers, so the drift and *débris* of society incline to lodge around the border outposts. But law should be enforced on the extreme limits of organized governments as faithfully as in the great, tumultuous centers of commerce and trade. Lawlessness there breeds the contagion and infection of disloyalty, and sends their poisoned virus back from the extremity into the center of life, mingling its sickening effluvia with all the life-blood of the body politic. Disobedience to law, like the infectious gangrene, is dangerous anywhere, even on the remotest extreme in nature and in political economy. Law—order, peace; no law—confusion, terror, carnage. These constitute opposite tripartites. Law and gospel join hands. Law obeyed becomes gospel in results; gospel disobeyed turns into law, and condemns the guilty. The preacher and the civil officer mutually aid each other. The preacher represents the gospel, and the civil officer personifies the law. Religion gives the disposition and the motives to obey law, but the Government carries the penalty in its hand, and says to the unwilling as well as to the loyal, "Thou shalt." Religion persuades, law compels. Religion requires both internal and external conformity to law, but simple law exacts mere outward rectitude. Where good laws are strictly maintained religion has an open field, but it works under disadvantages where law is defied. Most of Mr. Potter's ministerial life has been passed in regions where law held a slack rein.

CHAPTER XXXIV.

SEVERAL years ago, before Indian raids ceased in the upper Guadalupe Valley, Mr. Potter was traveling alone on horseback one quiet evening along the road running near the river between Centre Point and Comfort, when some unknown stock-man, on the top of the mountain verging on the road, undertook to frighten him with a make-believe Indian attack upon him. At that time the sure-enough Indians did really come into that region each full moon, and sometimes oftener, and all settlers and travelers were duly armed and on the outlook. So the stock-man on the elevation concluded that he could have the pleasure of seeing the valiant preacher try the speed of his noble horse, by making him think that the Indians were upon him. In those days he rode a superior and fleet horse of the hardy half-breeds, which could scent the Indian as the wild ass snuffeth the scent of water from the plains of the wilderness, and had in moments of peril carried his valiant rider with dashing speed from the precincts of danger. Seeing the preacher riding quietly alone in the valley below, the man above got near a thicket of scrub timber where he could conceal himself, and tried to startle his unsuspecting traveler by mimicking the awful Indian war-whoop yell. Hearing its terrifying echoes falling along the vale from peak to peak, he drew his revolver, examined and found it all right, then looked in all directions to find the source of that startling yell, but could see no one. Presently that frightful clarion broke on the silence of dell and vale, ringing round from curve to bend, and crag of mountain-heights. He looked, and saw the person of a man on horseback, half hidden in the brushwood on the earthen pile above him, whom he took to be the front leader of an Indian squad. Knowing that he could advance and fire on him, and get out of the way of danger by the speed of his horse, ere the Indians could descend into the valley for pursuit, he reined in his warlike steed, whirled his revolver round his head, gave a loud, menacing squall, and dashed on toward his assailant, when the white man wheeled out to show the trick he was trying to play off on the preacher, and hurriedly rode out of danger; but it well-nigh cost him a taste of the leaden hail from the preacher's well-tried revolver. The event of the Indian mimic's effort to frighten the preacher to see him run ever sealed the stockman's mouth on the subject, as it has never been found out who the make-believe Indian might have been.

In 1873 Mr. Potter was traveling alone, returning to his mountain-home from the Uvalde Circuit. He was on horseback, driving a mule and a horse yoked together by a rope tied round the neck of each. When about fifteen miles out from the settlements, he stopped to "noon it," in Texas phrase, which is simply to rest, eat a lunch, and grass your horse. The place was a prairie, dotted here and there with small mots of live-oak timber and underbrush thick enough to conceal any one. He had unsaddled and "staked his horse to grass," which is to tie one end of a long rope to the horse's neck, and fasten the other end to a tree, stub, or bush, so that the horse can get his dinner by grazing; and just as he lifted his canteen to his mouth to take a drink of water, bang went a keen rifle-crack, and a bullet whizzed by his head. Thinking it might be huntsmen shooting at game, who had not seen him, he cries out, "Ho, there! do not shoot this way!" But no one answered, which was in evidence that it was robbers or Indians, hidden in or beyond the thicket, from which came the report and the ball, about one hundred yards distant from the preacher. By this he knew that something was wrong; that he was in imminent danger from some unknown hands; and being ever fruitful in precautions, he went to his horse to bridle and mount, and enter another thicket near by, to give him an equal chance in the strife of balls, which he then began to anticipate; but as he was bridling his horse, bang went another gun from the same direction, the ball cutting the tip of a bush near to the preacher's head. It was a dangerous moment. He then pointed his "Winchester" in the direction of the mot, and cried out, "Come out of that thicket and fight me like men, you cowardly scamps!" at the same time lying down in a little gulley just deep enough to shield his body, awaiting a dashing charge from his cowardly foes, but no advance was made. Remaining there about one hour, he arose, saddled his horse, rode all round and inspected the premises, but finding no one, he drove on his coupled stock, and reached the settlement unharmed.

Possibly it may have been a small band of poorly-armed Indians who in this case fired the two shots at Mr. Potter from the far side of the thicket, and, on finding him armed with a "Winchester," took alarm, and sped away into some mountain-dell. An Indian is said never to go into a thicket in the territories of a white man. The greater probabilities are, however, that it was a small squad of scantily-armed robbers of Mexicans or Americans, who saw that they had attacked the wrong man, and concluded that the better part of valor would be to take their heads out of the range of that dangerous rifle, and hastily fled to a sure retreat.

How wonderful the many escapes from danger, in moments of the greatest peril, in the life of our strange hero! One is made to think him not born to be cut with the madman's knife, hit with bullets, or smitten with an arrow. Ever an angel's electric shield is over his head, to turn away the arrow's point, or glance the bullet from his head. "Hurt not mine anointed."

CHAPTER XXXV.

Mr. Potter was returned to the Uvalde Circuit in 1873, and the region of country it embraced was infested with a number of men called desperadoes— a kind of fearless, reckless men, who have little or no regard for life or character—for the most part refugees from other States, and fugitives from justice—desperate men. But that day is now passed with Texas. The speedy methods of travel and rapid manner of transmitting news, by railroads and telegraphs, and the ceaseless influx of immigration of a class of intelligent, moral, and enterprising peoples, have initiated a state of society unsuitable for the stay of lawless men, and the mountain fastnesses of Mexico are now their sheltering retreats from law and justice.

Among that class of madmen there was a certain youth who made bold pretensions to high antecedents, claiming to be the son of a governor of a great State, while he fearlessly stated that he had killed a man in said State, and had made his escape to West Texas; which perhaps was true, as the sequel may show. In Texas he was quite dissipated, living a corrupt and vicious life. He was regarded as a dangerous young man; and all who knew him dreaded a personal rencounter with him, expecting in that event to have to kill the desperate youth, or fall a victim to his murderous rage. That daring young man became enamored with one of West Texas's charming beauties, and notified some of her friends of his earnest intentions of addressing her. Man, in all conditions of life, civilized or uncivilized, in the deepest depths of infamy and shame, may be attracted by gentle woman's charms. As the sweet concord of melodious sounds thrill all the tender chords of the soul, so innocent beauty's "witching smile" embalms the roving heart of restless man. She becomes to him the attractive center of all his aims and hopes. That imbruted youth, with a soul immersed in angry passion's bloody waves, was arrested by sight of the native adornments of innocent virtue, redolent with the glow of youthful woman's charms. Surely there must be some occult magnetic attractive force betwixt opposite characters of the youthful sexes. It is often seen that young men of the most debasing habits are captivated by the highest types of womanly virtue, and many a dove-like creature readily unites her temporal, and also her eternal, destiny with a degraded debauchee, a *fac simile* of her own opposite. Perhaps an undefined feeling of romance may sometimes lead to such strange alliances, or may be innocent womanhood, in the full gush of inexperienced youth, may admire the gay, the reckless activities of young manhood. We know too that affection and passion are eyeless—blind: only reason sees the light of character, and weighs it in the scale of merit.

Mr. Potter, being a special friend to the young

girl and her family, was urged by the sense of duty to advise her as to the great risk of uniting her life with such a desperate youth. Where the path of duty lay, the preacher stopped not to think of the perils and dangers which might lurk along it, and had no sense of fear in the face of the greatest causes of alarm. A sure conviction of *duty* was his guide—it nerved him to action in all the strifes of his ministerial life. Whether the flattered girl informed her admirer of the preacher's counsel, or whether it reached him through other channels, we are not informed; any way, it reached his ears, and he did not hesitate to utter some serious threats in a public manner, that he should surely "shoot it out" with the preacher when they might chance to meet. He seemed greatly enraged; and, knowing his character, great excitement prevailed in the community as to the safety of the preacher. But the preacher was not of a timid species. Hearing of the murderous threat of the pugnacious youth, he took the precaution to arm himself with two good pocket-pistols. Not long after, they met at a private house. The family was greatly excited, expecting a fatal encounter between the preacher and the offended young man. The youth had a cavallard of horses penned near to the place, and he walked out to the pen and returned with a "six-shooter" belted to his side, but seemed intimidated in the brave preacher's presence, but finally said to the preacher that he had been wanting to see him for sometime, and that he had some horses in a "corral" just out there, and invited him to go out there with him. In the early twilight, when night's dusky curtains began to drape the mountain-heights and shade the deeper vales, side by side walked the dauntless preacher and the menacing young man. But the cautious preacher's keen, eagle-like eye was on every motion of his antagonist as they slowly strode away into the deepening mountain-shades. At length the young man said, "I guess we have gone far enough. Mr. Potter, I do not wish to take advantage of your defenseless position. I am armed, and you are not." Mr. Potter quickly replied, "Mr. P——, you are mistaken, sir; if it be a question of arms, I am armed to my full satisfaction." Here the courage of the pugilistic youth seemed to desert him, and he said, "No, Mr. Potter, it is not a question of arms—I only wanted to have a friendly talk with you. I wish to retract certain threats I have made regarding you, and to apologize for the same." He said that he was greatly enraged on hearing of the preacher's interfering with his courtship, and made those threats in the heat of passion, but on calm reflection he saw that the preacher was right; that he had only discharged his duty to a friend; that he knew he was not qualified to be the husband of such a noble woman, though he was devoted to her. To all this the preacher remarked that he was truly glad that he had at last taken so sensible a view of the subject; and although he never desired or sought difficulties with any man, yet there were men with whom, if nothing but a personal encounter would satisfy, he would measure off distances, and " shoot it out" with them; yet he would not put his life on an equality with him, as his habits had rendered him hurtful instead of beneficial to society; and that if he had first asked him if he were armed, he should have shot him in the twinkling of an eye, regarding his own life as of some worth to the world, and having heard of the youth's menacing determination. The dispirited youth then said that the preacher was right—that he regarded him as a Christian gentleman, and that he intended to return to his native State, stand his trial, and return to Texas, settle down, and make a good citizen. The preacher advised him to carry out that good intention.

Thus ended the dreaded interview, but how changed the lion! When Daniel was in the lions' den an angel tamed them into lambs till the coming morn. The quieted young gent afterward said to some of his associates that it was his intention to "shoot it out" with the preacher, but that when he mentioned the subject to him, he gave him such a piercing look that his purpose failed him; that he could easier face the mouth of a Winchester gun than that awful glance of the preacher's eyes. The eagle, in his arrow-like flight after his prey, never held a steadier, keener eye on his intended victim, than our determined preacher when he fastened the wondrous, fiery orb through which his incensed soul looked on him who had stirred his ire by wrong-doing. Conscious guilt can no more endure their fixed gaze than the eye itself can look on the unclouded sun. We learn that the fugitive youth did return to the scene of his crime, stood a trial, but put an end to his own life by cutting his throat, seeking relief from the results of sin in this life by immersing himself in its dread effects in the boundless future. Surely the road of evil-doing is a rugged one in this world, and virtuous habits are the better, if there is no hereafter to good and bad men. But let us "awake to righteousness, and sin not."

As a faithful biographer we must state *facts*, regardless of theory or character; but when character or theory get in the way of facts, they must take care of themselves. As a moralist, writing for the instruction and edification of mankind in the elements of the true and the good—the *real moral philosophy*—we must not trench upon the true Christian rudiments of a scriptural morality, the only infallible standard of human conduct in the present life. Scriptural casuists may be inclined to censure the conduct of the dauntless preacher in the premises in the foregoing story; but it admits of great palliation. An error of action in one case may not be an error in another. The habit of self-protection was of life-long standing with the preacher. At ten years of age he was thrown out into a contesting world upon his own resources for a living and for protection, having spent all his early manhood in soldier-life. Always kept on the guard for defensive self-security, it was fixed in him to protect his own life. Besides, the licentious youth had placed himself in the attitude of a dishonorable, a murderous, and a lawless character. Lastly, at that time there was little security in appealing to the officers of law for protection against such characters. They were, indeed, *lawless*. Sheriffs had been slain outright in trying to arrest such desperate men in other parts, till sheriffs, bailiffs, and jurors, seemed to fear them. If arrested, they escaped the penalties of law by a sham sort of trial, "jail-delivery," or forfeiture of bond; and then in some ambush take the life of their informant, and flee into parts unknown. If then the preacher had appealed to the law for security of life against the murderous menaces of a reckless man, he would have been in great uncertainty of getting it, and in the end may have fallen a victim to his antagonist's demoniacal fury, in open combat, or from some hidden retreat in the mountain solitudes.

CHAPTER XXXVI.

The vast territory of Mason District was formally included in the San Antonio District, and when the Indian-fearing presiding elder of that district or the agent of the American Bible Society came into the mountain regions, they called on Mr. Potter and his faithful "Winchester" to pilot and protect them through its dangerous gorges. American settlements were far apart, being mostly confined to the water-courses, and the wide, unsettled belts intervening were infested with marauding Indian bands. Across these unpeopled zones Mr. Potter was the pilot and the shield. Below we copy an account of one of those trips to guide Dr. Walker, a presiding elder of the then San Antonio District:

"I have just returned from a tour with the Rev. J. G. Walker, P. E. of the San Antonio District, along the line of his frontier appointments, having held quarterly-meetings at Centre Point, in the Kerrville Circuit, and in the Sabinal and Uvalde Circuits. The Bandera Mission Quarterly Conference was held in connection with mine at Centre Point; but it will be held separately in the future. Although our visit to the several-named places was not marked with any revival movements, yet we can say, to the praise of God's grace, that we had many sweet seasons of divine worship. Crowded congregations assembled at every appointment, eager to hear the word of life. Dr. Walker preached to them with the divine unction on his ministrations. The Quarterly Conferences were closely inspected. All hands seemed inclined to meet their obligations to sustain all the interests of the Church along this border. Nearly all this region is Methodist territory. Methodist preachers were the first to enter this frontier field for many years; but such has lately been the rapid increase of population that important changes in the work are imperative. Bandera Mission has already been taken from the Kerrville Circuit. Uvalde is a growing town of much importance to the Church. For a number of years it has been like a faint sunbeam struggling to penetrate thick clouds, but now we look up for a brighter dawning. The Sabinal Circuit is now set off from the Uvalde; so you see how the field enlarges. Uvalde has a melancholy history; it has been the scene of many a fearful and bloody tragedy; but a great change has come over it. It is now one of the most civil and respectable towns in the great West Texas. At its first quarterly-meeting the people anticipated our arrival, and we found Brother Denton, with his signal-fires blazing high, looking out for us. The house could not seat the congregations. Several joined the Church. On Sunday night there was a great shout in the camp. One young man was converted—said to be the first ever converted in Uvalde. May it be the first sheaf of a great harvest!"

This brief sketch will give the reader some conception of the *status* of religion in this border-land the first of the present decade, and of the diocesan-like toils of Mr. Potter, and the beloved confidence reposed in him by his brethren. Indeed, all West Texas is proud of her toiling, dauntless Potter. He labors on his own circuit, and guides and helps his superiors in office in their perilous way. He is at home with them, and at home when alone wending his pathless way to the cabin of the hardy pioneer.

When we read the itinerant missionary life of Robert Newton, of England, in the days of our youthful ministry, we thought him almost illimitable in labors in modern times. His field of operations lay within the limits of an enlightened empire; vast multitudes of the refined and wealthy, of the purest elements of civilized life, waited on his ministry in villa and city, in proud-domed religious temples; palaces adorned with the splendors of art sheltered him at night, and easy-going wheels carried him from place to place by day—invited and greeted by fond friends and true lovers of Jesus, at all times and places. Not needing staff or scrip, his wants supplied by generous hands, he moved on in his grand enterprise for the Church of Jesus—a man of great zeal, and deserving all honor for his works' sake. But the man of whose mission-life this little volume speaks, gives a counterpart of labors; his sphere of action the vast, untilled domain of the mountains of West Texas, stretching over an area nearly as large as the English Isle itself; not covered with the fruits of Christian civilization—peopled only here and there with rude adventurers, living in tents, huts, and cabins; few villages, widely separated; few public roads—only stock-paths and Indian trails—leading through valleys and over mountain-ridges where wheels can never go; no churches—worship conducted under shading mots, in private cabins, public shops, or store-rooms; few sheltering cottages at nightfall, where merry hearts tell of happy days gone by, or of hopeful ones to come, but the cold earth for his bed, on the bosom of the vast, unsettled prairie, or in the lone, wild hills, where the prowling wolf trots by, or the fierce night-hawk screams and swoops down upon his prey. No easy-going cushioned coach to bear him gently on in that early day; but his proud, trusty, mission-horse carries him over the prairie's wide solitudes, and the steep, rocky mountain sides. Few friends to hail his welcome approach; but the savage Indian seeks his horse and scalp, and the robber his purse. His rifle and Bible in hand, onward he goes in the face of all toil, suffering, and danger, to meet not the great, the rich, the good, but to meet men in a semi-savage state; men without a religion, without churches, without a Sabbath; men in grog-shops and gaming-rooms; men armed with butcher-knives and pistols—a heterogeneous mass of men from all the nations and islands of the globe; men too, in soldier-life, who can think of little else than battles and blood. In this agglomerated concrete of fallen humanity he is to plant the seed of the future Church, the growing Church of to-day. Wherever a group of men were found in that early day, from the Colorado to the Rio Grande, along the great frontier belt of three hundred miles, there the daring preacher went to tell the story of that wondrous grace which had saved him from the drunkard's grave and the gambler's hell. That good old song was his favorite, "Amazing grace, how sweet the sound!" He sung it in the congregation and along the way; when alone, he made the air vocal with its sweet strains, when none but the forest-birds and wild beasts could hear its heart-felt melodies.

Late one afternoon he reached a military outpost, where a quiet village of several hundred traders had settled, and, it being the time to pay off the soldiers, quite a crowd of gamblers had congregated there from other posts to game with them for their money. Many of them knew Mr. Potter, having met him at other posts, and some of them had been with him in the dark days of his gaming-life. Seeing him coming near, they recognized him, and gladly hailed him in their earnest rude style: "Ha! yonder comes the fighting parson." "Hold on there, old fel." "And to be sure, we hope ye are well." "An' can't ye give us a relegious send-off to-night—that is, a sarman?" "I shall with pleasure, gentlemen, if you will provide a place, and hear me civilly." "You bet we will be all eyes and ears." The open gallery of a saloon-man's dwelling was selected as the place of worship, and the saloons were robbed of their seats; benches and chairs from private dwellings also made up the preparations for worship. The place was literally stocked with drinking and gambling-rooms, and the soldiers' camps, near at hand, altogether made up quite a little city far out in the wild Indians' broad domain. The news was soon spread in store, saloon, and tent, of the arrival of the strange, eccentric preacher, and at an early hour some began to assemble, and there being no bell to tell the hour of beginning the service, a man made proclamation as follows: "O yes, O yes, O yes! there now, do you hear? There is to be some spang-up religious racket on Mr. F.'s gallery, by the 'fighting parson,' a reformed gambler, but now a celebrated gospel sharp. The racket will begin in fifteen minutes. All you old rummers, and whisky-guzzlers, and card-sharpers, come out and mend your ways, or you will all go to hell as sure as you are born." The preacher was in the prime of his manhood and the flower of his ministry, and his stentorian voice made all the attentive crowd hear his message of mercy and warning, and no doubt some good seed was sown in productive soil.

The style of the proclamation just narrated indicates the rude character of society at most places visited by Mr. Potter at an early day along the extreme border. No doubt there were some gentler natures mingling with the huge mass, as a few grains of good wheat are mixed with the chaff and defective ones; but the ruling elements of society were of a crude and unrefined species. Among them he must mix, share their hospitality, listen to the village and neighborhood gossip, and the little jealousies and envies peculiar to a people limited in their spheres of reading and means of information. He had but little time for reading himself. The immense field over which he had to travel occupied most of the time he was not in the pulpit. He read when an opportunity offered. He *read some*, but *thought much*. He digested what he read, and utilized it in the pulpit. He had the gift, by nature, of a keen perception, a strong memory, a vivid imagination, a good stock of wit and humor, a marked decisiveness of character, and an unconquerable will where the right was plainly involved. He "shunned not to declare the whole counsel of God" to friends or foes, yet he was polite and kind to all men in social life. He seemed conscientiously devoted to one great work—that of reforming the bad and building up the good of mankind: to this end he preached, held all sorts of meetings (protracted and old-time camp-meetings), organized Sunday-schools and temperance societies, and lectured and debated on the great temperance question. He was well-nigh a stranger at home. His wife said that she had given him to the Church, and tried to manage the home. He was truly "in labors often," and he desired not to build on any other man's foundation. He had a kingdom of labor of his own on the vast border, and a new Christian empire in that region is the fruit of his toils.

CHAPTER XXXVII.

Boerne is a beautiful little German town on the head-waters of the pretty Cibolo, and is the county-site of Kendall County, Texas. The mountain-home of Mr. Potter is within four miles of its outside limits. It is closed in on all sides by mountain-points and long rides, save along the hard-trodden stage-road leading from San Antonio to Fredericksburg, and the military outposts along the Indian border, and also a few neighborhood roads leading out into the little settlements among the hill-coves and small creek-valleys.

German towns are generally well supplied with spirits and malt beers, and men of drinking habits, in passing, often get intoxicated and tarry a time to indulge in draughts of the stimulants. A kind of itinerant desperado—a strange, reckless man—halted at Boerne a few years since, and Mr. Potter went to town the same day. The unknown man, being excited by liquor, was passing up and down the street, cursing the Dutch, and throwing rocks at them, and ran his horse along the main street in great speed in defiance of all the citizens. While Mr. Potter was riding homeward that furious creature ran by him twice, and to avoid contact with him he alighted and called at a friend's house on the street; but the aggressive man rode around the

house a time or two, then hitched his horse and
rudely walked on the porch where Mr. Potter and
two ladies were seated. Taking a seat, he began
asking impertinent questions, then used a mess of
vulgarisms, when Mr. Potter arose, took hold on
one of his arms, and placing his other hand at his
back, sent him a tilt into the yard. The enraged
man ran to his horse, snatched a revolver from his
saddle-wallets, and returned to seek revenge on
the brave preacher. In the meantime Mr. Potter
stepped into the house for some implement of defense.
Finding only a hatchet, he stood beside the
door, awaiting the approach of his antagonist,
hatchet in hand. The daring man turned around,
walked to the street, and led away Mr. Potter's
horse. That was more than the preacher could endure—to
stand still and see an offending stranger
lead away his own trusty steed. He would not
have been Potter had he not tried to regain his old
circuit-horse. He followed on till the man halted
near a store down the street, when he got over into
a side lot, so that his approach might not be discovered,
and having no arms, he advanced cautiously;
but when within a few yards of him the drunken
man saw Mr. Potter, and instantly presented
his six-shooter. Mr. Potter was too fast for him—
he instantly leaped at him, and wrenching his pistol
from him, gave it to a bystander. Then the astonished
man seized Mr. Potter, and a fearful tussle
ensued. The struggling preacher got hold of a
stone in the affray, and brought his antagonist to
the ground with it, and held him until an officer

arrested him and brought him to trial. On trial the evidence was clear that he had made two assaults on Mr. Potter with intent to kill, and had taken forcible possession of his horse. Knowing that if the magistrate bound him over to the District Court he would likely be sentenced to the penitentiary — which Mr. Potter did not desire — he asked the court to levy a small fine and release him, to which the court consented, and fixed the fine at ten dollars and costs; but he was remanded to jail till payment of the fine, and while *en route* to the prison he abused the court, and waved his fist at Mr. Potter, saying, "I shall see you some time." Mr. Potter asked the sheriff to "hold on," which he did, when he gave the prisoner the following lecture: "Sir, I was forced into a difficulty with you by protecting respectable ladies from your insults. I have exercised a great deal of patience and forbearance with you; I have put my life in peril to save yours; I ran on your pistol, and why you did not shoot I cannot tell. I could have killed you with your own weapon while it was in my hands, and the law would not have hurt me. Through my advice the court fined you instead of putting you under bond, which, if done, would send you to Huntsville: you have gotten off quite light. Now, if you ever make another pass at me your stay on earth may be short." Next morning that unfortunate man, being discharged from jail, rode out of the little town a vanquished desperado, never to visit more, we reck, the scene of his sudden humiliation by an ineffectual contest with the "Indian-fighting preacher." Perhaps this was the most critical, the most trying scene in his ministerial life. The excited moments of quick surprise instantly spring into vigorous activity the elements in the strong character of our wonderful hero, his pure gallantry leading him to act as quickly as powder to guard securely innocent and unprotected woman's virtue, even while putting his own life in extreme hazard—his profound sense of his own personal prowess to meet in physical antagonism the most powerful men, and his want of fear in moments of the risk of life, though coolly cautious to avoid harm—his lively sense of duty to protect and secure his personal rights when they are in jeopardy, and his real sympathy for a vanquished foe when at his mercy.

This critical affray puts the pugnacious tendencies of our ministerial hero in their strongest attitude. No other event in all his contests with bad civilized men, after he began to preach the gospel of love and peace, was so violent, or involved so much risk of life and limb; and as it is likely to disturb the delicate sensibilities of the extreme moral æsthetics of regions serene in peace, where law and order reign, we shall pen a paragraph on that subject just here, though we have glanced at the moral principles involved in another chapter of this book.

It may be urged here that the preacher should have called on the officers of law to have arrested the lawless brigand. At the private house where he insulted the lady and her daughter there were no officers at hand, and when he was leading off the preacher's horse no official protested. In fact, the officers had allowed him to lord it over the town, cursing the citizens, throwing stones at them, driving them, officers (perhaps) and all, into their houses for security. Truth is, it is clear, they were not extremely anxious to tackle the human demon. If Mr. Potter had depended on citizen or officer for relief at the suburban home of those insulted ladies, he surely would not have obtained it, for no other man was near, and that orderly process would have ended in a severe drubbing or loss of his life by the hands of that reckless debauchee. It was plain that all his aims were directed to the point of a personal encounter with Mr. Potter, as he seems to have been the only man he found riding in the street—being determined to ride rough-shod over the entire town. It is highly probable that Mr. Potter would not readily have regained possession of his horse had he depended alone on the officials to recover him.

The life of man in those times out here was of little value with such men—preacher, judge, or sheriff, must stand out of the path of their deadly missiles. And to escape the collision, Mr. Potter called at that private house. Had he mildly requested the beastly man to walk quietly away from the presence of the insulted females, and then have striven by force of moral suasion to change the lion into the lamb, it would have been as casting pearls unto the swine, and have more likely ended in the rending of the moralist, as it would have given the vantage-ground to the braggadocio's designs—a personal difficulty.

Whether this cruel and rude specimen of humanity had any knowledge of the man whom he strove to encounter, we are not advised; but in any event he intended to defeat any man he might chance to meet in the town at all hazards. And it is equally true that in this case he had met the wrong man.

After all, the moral of the question involved turns on the right of a good man to save his own life by the destruction of the life of a bad man, when there is no other way of security. The God of Nature is the God of the Bible, and his laws in the one do not contravene those in the other. Natural law gives to all animal creatures the right and the means of self-defense, either by stratagem, flight, or force of contest; even the silly sheep is armed with a stone-like head to defend his person. Man is more highly endowed with rights and implements of self-defense and protection than any other earthly creature, and an extreme penalty is annexed to the crime of murder, on account of his confessed superiority. If man is allowed to destroy the life of a beast, a bird, to preserve his own, on account of his superiority over them, surely a good man may be innocent in destroying the life of a hurtful man, when there can be no other method of escape from violence. If all men are of more value than the lower animals, good men must be of more value than evil ones; and on that process of reasoning, when the lives of both are in peril, it is wise, right, and best, to save that of the good, the beneficial, at the cost of the hurtful. A skeptical lyric poet sung:

> He sees with equal eyes, as God of all,
> A hero perish, or a sparrow fall.

That contradicts reason, nature, facts, and theology. The Immortal Teacher said of man, "Ye are of more value than *many* sparrows." So also is the life of a virtuous man of greater use to the world; therefore it should be preserved at the cost of the other, when there is no other way to elude the violent hand. Will the sensitively pious reader pause and ask himself the startling query: "Would I sit still and let a heartless ruffian take away my life when I might save mine by destroying his?" *That's the point of the pivot at issue.* Do not evade it—face it. Will you die in the career of a useful life rather than kill a dangerous man who is already damaging the race? Mark you, your death is not to save the *already ruined* and *injurious* wretch from further sinning in this life, or from the penalties of evil in the life to come; for after you have allowed him to beat you, and take your life, he may go on destroying human happiness here, and finally fall by disease, or some other hand, and realize the doom of all evil-doers in the world to come. If your tacit submission to abuse and death should result in the present reformation and ultimate salvation of the poor creature, then the point of issue is changed. But no such effects are anticipated in the premises. St. Paul says, "Evil men and seducers shall wax worse and worse." They usually go on in their destructive way to the bitter end. If it be right to seek the destruction of the causes of disease and pestilence, to kill venomous reptiles, ravenous birds and beasts, and the raving mad-dog, which endanger human life, then too the *desperado*, who puts himself on a parity with them, forfeits his claim to life, both to the civil law and to the individual whose life he may attack. The equitable civil code attaches no guilt to deeds done in strict defense of self-life. The doctrine of self-abnegation at the peril of life finds no foundation in the catalogue of human virtue, as no human action is meritorious, or suffering vicarious, as in the case of Him who was more than man—above the demands of law.

CHAPTER XXXVIII.

Conference met at Gonzales. Bishop Keener presided, and the Rev. John S. Gillett presiding elder of San Antonio District. Mr. Potter was reäppointed to the Uvalde Circuit. It was a year of the severest trials of his life, occasioned by the affliction and death of a beloved son—a young man in his sixteenth year, and of great promise. He was taken early in the spring of 1875, and just gradually declined under all kind of attention and wise medical treatment. His medical adviser told him to travel with his son, as he could do him no good with medicine. Mr. Potter carried him around his circuit with him, but he did not improve; and he then took him over into Mexico, to try the virtue of its elevated altitudes, and the reviving qualities of the Hermanos hot springs, and San Lucas cool mineral springs—remaining five days at one, and eight at the other. But he did not improve, and he returned to his home in Texas. There was a company of about twenty-five or thirty persons—men, women, and children—and they all met and rendezvoused on the west bank of the Nueces River on the Fourth of July; and they crossed the Rio Grande at Piedras Negras and Eagle Pass, which is on the east side of that river, passing through San Juan, and San Juan Sabinus, and other Mexican villages—the whole distance from the Rio Grande to the springs being about one hundred and fifty miles. "The spring bursts out of the base of a small mountain, and runs off into a considerable creek. It is surrounded by a rock wall about eight feet high, and has no entrance except where the wall had been thrown down to make a gap. One mile below the spring there was a *hacienda* and a large farm watered from the creek, where we got most kinds of vegetables. No accommodations at the springs, and all visitors had to camp and supply themselves. It is said the reason that no improvements are allowed at these springs, it gives the poor an equal chance at their healing virtues."

After getting into Mexico, their route led along a level plain, with the grand ridges and wave-like heights of the sublime Santa Rosa Mountains running parallel to the right all the way. Mr. Potter says in all his sights of the grand mountain-ranges he has ever beheld, the Santa Rosa's excels all in picturesque loveliness. The water when drunk hot was pleasant to the taste, but when cool it was sickening and offensive. The temperature was a little burning to one in health, but Mr. Potter's son, in a delicate condition, could bear its heat when applied to the surface. Mr. Potter stripped for a bath, and stepping on a rock, put one foot in, and it felt so hot he jerked it out, and said, "Tom, I can't stand it!" Just then the rock slipped, and in he tumbled, and he said he thought he was scalded. The manner of bathing is to go into the water and drink as much of it as you can well bear, and after remaining in about ten minutes, come out and roll up in a blanket about five or seven minutes, then rub with a coarse towel, and dress. The sweating in the process is profuse. This is done twice or thrice per day.

The party then went to the San Lucas spring, about fifty miles distant—passing a *hacienda* about four miles before reaching the spring—then up a narrow cañon you will reach the spring, which does not run off, but is truly in a cave. You enter the cave at the spring, and then, with a light, descend along a rocky declivity over which the water rapidly flows deeper into the bosom of the earth. The water is cool and pleasant, and must have curative virtues, as when you bathe in it you can find the precise location of the disease. The sediment and mud taken from the crevices about the spring and applied to the surface is almost equal to a blister. It will eat holes in the clothing. Many of the party received great benefit, but their time was limited, and they could not remain. Lung affections were alleviated.

Returning, they came by the old town of Santa Rosa, of historic fame, reaching back three hundred years. It is a mining town, and its prosperity was like the tides, ebbing and flowing, and was at a low tide at that juncture. It is on no river, but is watered by a number of springs coming out of the mountains, sufficient for irrigation in the valley. They lay there one day, intending to visit the mines about four miles distant, but rains prevented their doing so. A remnant of Kickapoo Indians came into town, and Mr. Potter's son being desirous of seeing an Indian, he drove with him into town. About twenty-five of them were there on horseback, and the young man thought them the grandest sight he had seen in all the trip.

After a tour of thirty days, the party returned to Uvalde, where they parted, each going to his own abode. But Mr. Potter's son was not improved. Depositing him at his mountain-home, he returned to his circuit with a heavy heart. Having traveled near a thousand miles with his beloved son, and feeling so deeply attached to him, with but little hope of his recovery, he felt the shading of that pall of sorrow which, sooner or later, must fall upon his paternal heart.

From Frio Town Mr. Potter, Mr. Rutledge and his wife, and Mrs. Kingsbury, wife of the Rev. Ichabod Kingsbury, got into Mr. Rutledge's ambulance and drove out on a fishing excursion in the Frio River. They stopped at a crossing, and got a Mexican to ride to a house not far away to get some fishing-tackle. Mr. Rutledge turned out his horses to grass, but in a few minutes here came the Mexican riding at rapid speed, saying, "Indians! hitch up and get to the house as quickly as possible! Indians are close by, and have shot a man!" They harnessed in quick time, and drove in good speed, reaching the house unharmed. Mr. Potter held his "Winchester" and revolver in his hands, ready for battle; Mrs. Kingsbury was cool, but the other lady was a little nervous, and frequently said, "Whip up, Ed! whip up, Ed!" They all had, indeed, just made a narrow escape. The Indians, about fifteen in number, had crossed at the precise point where they had halted to begin their fishing, about fifteen minutes before their arrival, and had passed on about a mile and shot at young Newton, who was herding stock, and hit his horse, but the horse lived long enough to carry him home unhurt. The fishing-party heard the report of the gun.

This year the Rev. Ichabod Kingsbury, then living in Frio Town, was licensed to preach. He is now a member of the West Texas Conference, and pastor of the San Antonio City Mission — a true man, and faithful in his work.

Learning that his son was rapidly declining, Mr. Potter came home early in the fall. Seeing that his son was nearing his end, and feeling the need of fraternal sympathy and condolence, he wrote to the Rev. T. G. Wools, then on the Medina Circuit, to come, if he could, to the scene of his trials and sorrows. When Mr. Wools received the letter he was under pledge to deliver a Masonic address at Pleasanton, but, like a true brother and follower of Him who ever comforted the sorrowing, he laid aside every thing, and soon passed over fifty intervening miles, and reached the home of his afflicted friend and brother. His coming was greeted by the sorrowing family. He remained with them several days, consoling the family and the sinking young man, and then returned to his circuit. Mr. Potter had a favorite pony, which he gave Mr. Wools to ride and keep through the fall and coming winter.

Mr. Potter's son gradually declined, and Mr. Potter could not attend the session of the Conference at San Antonio. He became anxious to die in the Church, and when Mr. Kingsbury came home from Conference, he received him into the Church in the disciplinary form; and from that time he was full of joyous grace, admonishing and encouraging all who might enter his room, asking them to meet him in heaven. In the light of eternal joys he passed away on the 11th of November, 1875. Death chooses a shining mark, as little hands love to pluck the prettiest flowers. That young man was truly a noble youth. Fond of reading, he had stored his young mind with a knowledge of books not often surpassed by those of his age; but alas! as a flower blooming lovely in the morn, he fell into decay ere the coming of the evening. The family sorrow not without hope. They express grateful remembrance too of the kindness of the Rev. H. W. South, who wept with them in the days of their great grief.

CHAPTER XXXIX

We have already said that Mr. Potter did not attend the session of the Conference in San Antonio, owing to the affliction of his son. He had now been sent far from home for four successive years, and he was sent to the Bandera Mission, which included Boerne, near to his mountain-home, that he might have some chance to adjust home affairs, as his long absence had a little tangled up his finances. Dr. J. G. Walker was the presiding elder. It was to Mr. Potter a laborious year. His unimproved home demanded much attention, his stock were to be looked after, and all the duties the Church imposed on him to be met. We have nothing of marked interest to record of his mission this year, but an enjoyable feast with the Christian portion of society, and some increase in membership. Much of the towns of Bandera and Boerne are of the German element, and most of them are infidels or Roman Catholics, and cannot be reached, because they never attend Protestant preaching, except a few who attend through the respect they have for Mr. Potter.

This year he made a trip to the Sabinal Cañon, with his presiding elder, J. G. Walker, to aid in holding a quarterly-meeting. The preacher in charge objected to having preaching on Saturday night, saying that there was a horse-race near by, and many of the men were drunk, and that they would be at church at night and create a disturbance, and have a row. Mr. Potter was in favor of having service; his motto was, never to give way till defeated in the contest; but Dr. Walker consented to making the appointment for night-service if Mr. Potter would preach. Preach! certainly he would—that was his calling; and too to preach to all men, good and bad; and to preach he had traveled sixty miles through frontier dangers, and no time was to be lost through fear of molestation of wicked men—that was not his method. He consented to preach, the appointment was announced, and at night the house was thronged, and those drinking, racing men were there. But look, dear reader, and you will presently see that which may be a strange sight to you, though common out here in those times. Mr. Potter enters the crowded house, and gravely walks down the aisle with the belt of his revolver hanging on his left arm, and his well-tried "Winchester" in his right hand; and on reaching the stand he hangs the six-shooter on a nail in the wall behind him, and leans the gun against the wall near to him, and proceeds to read, sing, pray, and preach, and dismiss the crowd in order, and all go home, no one disturbing in the least.

It was not fear of the fire-arms alone that kept that audience in order—it was a partite mingle of curious respect for the wonderful preacher, and fear of arousing his valor. Mr. Potter never returned any one for misconduct at his meetings—that entered not into his plans. County-sites were too far removed from each other, and officers of law not at hand, and his travels were too extensive, and he had no time to waste in attending courts as a witness; and besides, when you go to law you raise issues, and partyize communities, and often do harm. He managed his own congregations, he was law and gospel, he was preacher and sheriff, and if he could not govern his people, he never went to law about it. He always notified his congregations of his manner of operations, and told them if they created any disturbances they must meet his remedies, which were mild or harsh, as occasion might demand, even to the dexterous use of his carnal protectors if need be; and if in his methods of chastisement for evil-doing he defeated them, they must abide the issue; but if they mastered him, he made no appeal to law.

At this period of border history there were a number of refugees out here, and they did not much fear the civil law, and that mode of dealing with them was the only plan promising success. Mr. Potter had two threatening difficulties in carrying out his rules, but, fortunately, all ended without any thing serious; and we decline narrating them here, as the parties are living, and the healed wounds need not now be probed. In fact, after he had been known, his name was ever a guarantee for orderly crowds, and, for the most part, the worst of men would befriend and defend him, and would listen to his preaching when they could not be induced to pay attention to the ministrations of any other man.

Many little cuts of wit, displaying the high social class of feelings he ever carried with him, in the parlor and along the road, might interest the reader, a few of which we here mention. He had appointed two amiable young ladies to raise money to purchase Sabbath-school literature, and they brought up sixty dollars. There was a nice gentleman there —a bachelor—by the name of Stewart, who was a great gallant, and had, perhaps, aided the fair Misses in raising the money. Mr. Potter could not let the chance to make a pun on the phrase "steward" pass him, and after tendering his gratitude to the young ladies, he said that he thought it a wise plan to appoint them *stewards*, and looking at Mr. Stewart, he said, "Not that I mean to insinuate a change in the name to *Stewart*, unless that be desirable under certain circumstances." That ended in quite a general, hearty smile in the audience.

One night Dr. Walker had preached one of his close, logical sermons, and there was a minister present whom the Doctor esteemed as a man of rather uncommon talent, and he imagined that his gifted brother did not indorse all he discussed that night. Mr. Potter knew the value the Doctor placed on the opinions of that able preacher, and when the Doctor said that the greatest man at church last night did not sanction all his theology, Mr. Potter said, "I don't know that you have heard me speak about it." The Doctor saw the point, and joined in a hearty laugh.

When traveling along the road one day he picked up a six-shooter, and soon he met a man returning on the hunt of it, and instead of inquiring if he had found such an article, the gentleman said, "You didn't find a six-shooter?" Mr. Potter remarked, "You tell a lie: here it is," handing it to him. The gladdened man could but smile.

A full-blooded Hibernian would meet a full match in ready wit and retort when he encountered Mr. Potter, and he seldom ceased his witticisms till victory perched on his standard and amused the listeners. His memory was like an encyclopedia, and a gazetteer printed in large primer type.

This year the district-meeting was held at Pleasanton, in Atascosa County, and here Mr. Potter met with the Rev. T. G. Wools, his intimate friend and brother, to whom, in the previous fall, he had loaned a favorite pony. Having learned of Mr. Wools's strong attachment to the pony, he intended to give it to him, but had never even intimated it to Mr. Wools; but at that meeting he made out a bill-of-gift, and presented it to him; but when Mr. Wools discovered the nature of the bill, his heart-tenderness melted into grateful tears, and the Rev. J. W. DeVilbiss, who was standing by, finished the reading of the bill, when Mr. Potter said to Mr. Wools that, knowing his great fondness for the pony, he felt that it would be a species of cruelty to take it from him—telling him, at the same time, that he had fifteen or twenty other ponies, and that he could give him any one of them and not feel it, but that he *felt* the giving of that one, as he had bought it for his own riding, and money could not buy it. "But now it is yours, all yours, as fully as if you had paid in coin its real value; you can feel just as grateful as you may desire, but you owe me nothing for it in the future. When some people make a gift, it requires the favors of the remaining lifetime to repay it; but you and I are now even, and if ever in the future we may have any trading, it is your dollars and mine, but this pony is not to come into the account." Mr. Potter held to two maxims about giving—viz., that a gift you did not prize was truly no gift; that it was not a sacrifice unless you felt that the giving had deprived you of something of value; and that such giving is a loan to a remunerating Providence. In this valuable donation, too, Mr. Potter felt that he was in some sense meeting a debt of gratitude for fraternal attentions and sympathies given him in that day of dark sorrows, when he was called to bury a dearly-beloved son. Attentions to the sick, and tender kindnesses to our dying loved ones, are seldom forgotten; they endear us to each other as if we were indeed a common brotherhood. It is when the iron is infused with a great heat that its integral parts are closely welded into one. So hearts, in sympathetic contact under the melting of a great sorrow, readily fuse into one. The ties existing between these two brethren, having been cemented together in the furnace of a deep affliction, will outlive the waste of time and the toils of life. "I feel this gift, but it is yours." What an immortal strength of sincere attachment does that phrase contain!

Mr. Potter was ever ready to help the poor and the needy. A man by the name of K—— lived at

Boerne, near to him. He had been in affluence, but misfortunes had reduced him to want. Knowing his tender sensibilities about his humble condition, Mr. Potter called on him one day, and said, "Mr. K——, I have a large beef running in a thicket, and I can't get him out to sell him, and he will have to be butchered in the woods, and if you will accept of him I will have my boys butcher him in the thicket and bring him to you." The needy, grateful old man said, "A thousand times grateful to you, Mr. Potter; send me only half of it—I hate to receive all of your large beef without paying you something, which I am unable to do." "No," said Mr. Potter, "I don't need it, and it is cool, and you can salt it down and keep it securely." So when Mr. Potter was leaving home, he said to his eldest son, "John, if you will kill that big beef in the thicket, and take it to Mr. K——, you may have the hide," which at that time was worth about three dollars. John slew the wild ox, and delivered its meat agreeable to orders.

Mr. Potter was absent a long time on his mission, but while engaged in his Master's work of distributing Bibles, on parting with a Christian lady, she dropped two ten-dollar gold coins in his hand. He asked, "What is this for?" not knowing but that it was a donation to the Bible cause. She replied, "It is yours—your own." Tendering gratitude to the donor, he thought, "Double price for my wild beef"—ten dollars being its market-value at that time. After his return home he went to see Mr. K——, and remained to dinner, and Mr. K—— remarked, "This, Mr. Potter, is the last of the fine beef you gave us, and I must tender you many earnest thanks, till you are better paid; for I do not know what we would have done without it." "No," replied Mr. Potter, "I have already received a double price for the ox," telling him how. The old gentleman, though not a religious man, indorsed the doctrine of a retributive providence.

Mr. Potter was going to town one day, and a poor widow hailed him, and handed him one dollar, saying, "Please get me a dollar's worth of coffee," adding, "That is all I have in the world, and I do not know where the next is to come from." He bought the coffee, but, like Joseph in Egypt, he put the dollar back in the sack. While there, the widow sent her little daughter to parch some of the coffee, to make her a cup, and on opening the little bag, she found the dollar, and ran to her mother with it. The mother understood it, and began to weep a widow's grateful tears, and Mr. Potter mounted and rode on. But on his next round he was called on for his taxes, and the evil spirit said, "There, now, where is your dollar?" He met a half-drunken man, who said, "Mr. Potter, the Lord has converted my soul; I am a changed man. Here is five dollars for friendship." "Giving to the poor is lending to the Lord."

CHAPTER XL.

"In 1876 the Conference was held in Seguin, Bishop Doggett presiding, and I was sent to the Kerrville Circuit, and Dr. J. G. Walker was the presiding elder. I had been set down to a circuit in another district, but when the Bishop proposed to return Dr. Walker to the San Antonio District, which included so much of the Indian-infested border, the Doctor said that he could not consent to take it without me, saying that he was an old man, and must have me to accompany him through the dangers of the frontier, and the kind Bishop changed me to the Kerrville Circuit. My having to make the general tours with the Doctor that year was no little drawback to the work on my own circuit, being absent so long on those district-trips; nevertheless, we had some glorious revivals, and the Church was greatly built up in the faith. We had a camp-meeting just below Centre Point, on the Guadalupe River, and the people mostly brought their provisions on the ground in the day, and returned home at night; but I could not consent to be defeated, and I hitched up my own wagon, provided myself with sufficient provisions and bedding, and a full outfit for camping, and was the first on the ground. But there were four ladies and gentlemen who had come from a distance to be entertained that night, and my wagon was the only tent. Now, what to do was the puzzling query with a man who was used to house-keeping in the great open world. But I stretched my wagon-sheet for a tent, and laid down a mattress crosswise, so as to give space for the four ladies, and they occupied the tent. Brother Kingsbury and myself rolled up in our blankets under the shade of a live-oak. Sister Kingsbury was one of our lady-guests, and was ever full of humor with, and merrily criticised, my culinary arts; but at eating-time she displayed commendable appreciation of my skill in that line. Dr. Walker was entertained at a private house. People came in from a distance and camped, and Sister J. D. Brown bought cloth and soon stretched a large tent, and plenty of supplies were brought in; and the meeting continued over the second Sabbath, with an extensive revival and glorious results."

Dr. Walker refusing to be returned to the San Antonio District unless Mr. Potter was stationed in its bounds, with instructions to guard him along the belt of the dangerous border, quite forcibly displays the value of Mr. Potter to that frontier region. Dr. Walker had been there, and knew of its hardships and its dangers, and also the importance of being piloted by a brave, cautious guide. He had spent years of his early ministerial life with the friendly Indians, nor was he wanting in either skill or courage, but he was then physically frail, and is now really superannuated, but will not be in fact. Mr. Potter is now presiding elder of the same territory, reaching deeper into the Indian domain, but carries no longer gun or pistol. The voice of the savage sounds out no more along its dells or vales. Songs of praise now go up to heaven all along the border-line. And though Kerr County is now the last organized county on the western limit of American civilization, the hardy shepherds keep watch, unharmed, over their flocks on the unpeopled pastures on the prairie wilds, far away from human habitation. If the gospel advances, the frontier recedes, as clouds disappear before the shining light; but if the gospel retreats, the border lessens the sphere of civilization's reign.

This year the District Conference was held at Selma, and Bishop Doggett presided. The Bishop preached one of his magnificent models of an evangelical sermon on the Sabbath, on Ezekiel's dry bones in the valley. Dr. Walker wanted a preacher to follow the Bishop at three o'clock; he knew that most preachers were sensitive about following a bishop, when he has crowded the mind with a volume of theological facts just a few hours before, and after the people have also loaded their stomachs with a mess of condiments: heads stored with great ideas, and stomachs crammed with meats, do not enable a congregation to hear any thing to a sense of vivid appreciation. At best, three o'clock in the afternoon is usually regarded as a hard hour to enlist the thoughts and feelings of an audience on any theme.

Dr. Walker said to Mr. Potter, "I generally say to my preachers when I want them to preach, You must preach at such a time; but I won't do that now.

But, Brother Potter, if you think you can preach this afternoon after the Bishop, I wish you would do so." Mr. Potter replied, "I do n't know but that I can preach after the Bishop as readily as after you;" and at the hour he stood before a large, intelligent congregation of citizens, preachers, lay delegates, and the Bishop. His theme was fidelity to conviction, as in the case of the blind man who received his sight. He had the spirit of preaching upon him, and the hour was one of great refreshment to the Church. The brethren responded with hearty amens, and the good old Bishop commended the sermon, saying it edified him. Noble old Bishop! His toils are over now! When parting with the writer, the last words he uttered were, "Glory to God! let us meet in heaven!" Potter is not afraid, yet he is a modest and a sensitive man.

21

CHAPTER XLI.

"In the fall of 1877 the session of the Conference was held in Corpus Christi. Bishop Wightman presided, and a new district was formed, covering all the border circuits from the Rio Grande to the Colorado River. W. T. Thornberry was the presiding elder, and I was appointed to the Uvalde Mission, covering quite a large territory, which had never been occupied before, except the town of Uvalde, which was detached from another circuit, and connected with this new mission, to give the preacher a little support. It was the only place on the work where there was an organization. The appointments were, Uvalde, Eagle Pass, Fort Clark, and San Felipe. Some of these points were sixty miles apart, and the nearest one to my home was a hundred miles. I found only two members at Eagle Pass, a town of several thousand inhabitants, except among the Mexicans, who were supplied with a preacher speaking the Spanish language by our Conference, but among the English-speaking population I could find only two Methodists.

"Here I must record an affecting incident. An invalid lady in the town had been lingering sometime, and was approaching her dying moments, and she sent a friend to search for some one to pray for her, and no one could be found that would pray in public. The sick woman said that there was an old Methodist lady living in the outskirts of town—'go after her, and tell her that it is my dying request that she come and pray for me.' Being delicate and timid, she at first refused to go. She had never been asked to utter a public prayer; but she finally went and took up the heavy cross; and it soon became light, and He who said, 'Where two or three are gathered together in my name, there am I in the midst of them,' was with them, making the dying-room the antechamber of heaven. It is said that 'It is good to be there.' How blest the spot where the good man meets his fate! it is honored above the common walks of men. God and angels deign to meet him—there earth and heaven meet. Heaven clothes the earthly with its radiant glories, and the death-bed becomes the gate to fadeless joys. In this case the dying woman prays, and Israel's sainted mother prays, and the celestial minstrels touch the key of joy in the penitent's heart, and it thrills out a new note of praise, and heaven begins just at the verge of the grave. No priest nor preacher are there, but the great High-priest himself is near with his angel-bands. That benevolent Jesus, whose tender heart held him still at the blind beggar's cry, heard the tearful wail of the helpless penitent, and the earnest pleadings of the aged saint, and instantly, quick as the speed of thought, he comes to the scene of want. Amid the grateful anthems of angelic millions he hears the cries of sorrow, and sees the falling tears of earth's afflicted children. Once he was a man of sorrows, shedding tears. He is man's brother, touched with a feeling for his infirmity—his brother exalted and endowed with power to save.

"The scene is away, away in a Sodom-like city, where no one lived who prayed audibly to God; but one lone, delicate woman ventures to utter a cry to the Mighty to save, and the answer comes. Gentle reader, think of the charm woven around the name 'Methodist!'—a sincere, a devoted Methodist, as its immortal Founder was. The dying penitent woman said, 'There is an old Methodist woman living on a certain street—go tell her that it is my *dying request* that she come and pray for me.' That plea touched the Methodism—the religion—in the heart of the good lady, and, like her divine Master, she repairs to the death-chamber. The revolutions of the wheels of fortune had borne that mother in Methodism to the extreme limits of the domain of the American Republic. From her little home-room on the bank of the Rio Grande she could look out upon the hills, and hear the bell-chimes of a benighted nation. Did not an *all-wise* and gracious Providence station her there to open the gate of paradise to that penitent one?"

The name of Methodist is now almost identical with that of religion. It has been fitly styled, "Christianity in earnest"—*Christianity in harness*. It is carrying Christianity's saving institutions to the nations. Mr. Potter was the first evangelist to visit that Sodomic town, and no doubt his visit there revived the name of Methodist in the memories of the English-speaking people; and we now hear of at least one redeemed spirit passing from its sinful haunts to that region where sin is not. O who is not proud of a pure Methodism! It is now in all lands, and is identified with all people; and its genius is inoculating all hearts, and is being whispered by all tongues of the babbling earth. Its arms are, like a Saviour's love, embracing the world, and her noble missionary evangelists shall soon mingle their love-toned voices at their meeting on their voyage around the globe. Now they are almost within hearing of each other. When the gospel of the kingdom is preached in all the world, then the end cometh. Our grand old Methodism leads the van. Potter on the border, and Lambuth and his valorous crew in China, Patterson in Mexico, and Ransom in South America. Drive on its cars.

"After making a tour of about two months in my distant field, having carried the gospel to the utmost limit of the United States, my voice having mingled with the sounds of the church-bells of another nation, I returned home to my family. In my travels I had followed up the Rio Grande River to the remotest settlements. While on my homeward trip I met my presiding elder, W. T. Thornberry, making his way out to the north-west portion of the frontier, and he proposed that if I would go with him on that trip, he would make a whole round with me on my large circuit, to which I consented. Remaining at home only a few days, I met him at Centre Point, and we started over a territory entirely new to us both. It was about the first of March, and the weather was very pleasant. Our first objective point was Junction City, Kimble County. It took its name from being at the junction of the north and south prongs of the Llano River, sixty-five miles from our starting-point. On reaching Junction City, the place for holding the quarterly-meeting, we found that the appointment had not been circulated, the preacher not having reached the work. Meeting an old friend who was not religious at that time, but is now a steward in the Church, he said he would hurry round and let the people know, and in about an hour he had convened a good congregation. He pointed out a house to us, saying that was the only one in the place large enough to take care of us. We drove there, but the gentleman refused to take us in, and we returned to the church, and found the audience ready for preaching. After the sermon, we were invited to dinner with our old friend. The town was just being settled, and they had erected a few small log-cabins, and scarcely had room for their own families. But a vast change has come over the place: in the last three years they have constructed good and comfortable houses; they now have a neat court-house, where all the preaching is done; and a large congregation usually attends. Our old friend A. J. Allen has erected a large hotel, where preachers are ever welcome to his munificent hospitality."

How true the promise to the minister who leaves home and friends for Jesus's sake, that he shall find both home and friends to welcome his coming! How large the promise to him who gives shelter and food, even a cup of cold water, to him for Jesus's sake! His reward is sure; if not here, it is "over there." But how terrible the threatening to him who refuses him hospitality, and closes his door against his approach! It is to be more tolerable in the day of judgment for Sodom than for him. Even the dust which the minister's rejected feet leave on his door-step shall witness against him in that day. The preacher is on the King's business, and demands entrance into all climes, homes, and hearts. He carries a key of command which is to unlock the empaneled doors of the palace and unpin the clapboard shutter of the cabin, and woe to the man who denies him entrance in his official attire. He comes in Christ's name. Jesus said of him, "Whosoever receives him in my name receiveth me." Dear reader, is your generous home ever open to the faithful minister of Jesus Christ? Then are you blessed. He is about your family altar in the name of Jesus, and to him it is as if you had received him in person. Even on the frontier God touches hearts to shelter and feed the evangelical pioneer.

CHAPTER XLII.

Mr. Thornberry and Mr. Potter then proceeded from Junction City to Brady City, the place of holding the quarterly-meeting. Here they met Dr. Tucker, who then took charge of the two missions—Mason and Brady. Here they had a pleasant time, but leaving Brady City, they passed down through Mason and Fredericksburg to Centre Point, their first starting-point. On this trip they stopped a day or two to rest. The lady of the house was an elderly Methodist, and in her early life had heard many of the able preachers of the older States; and she was fond of discussing the relative merits of the great divines. Mr. Thornberry said: "Sister, you have never met Brother Potter and myself before, and you have never heard either of us preach. Now, judging from the appearance of the two men, which would you think uses the best rhetoric in the pulpit —that is, which is the abler preacher?" The old sister elevated her glasses, and looked at one and then the other, and replied: "I don't know much about rhetoric, but I think that Brother Potter can make the best *display*." Mr. Potter was careful to be silent, and the heavy end of the joke rested on Mr. Thornberry's shoulders, as he was the presiding elder, and he had asked the question. He, however, did not venture another query on that subject on that trip. That gave Mr. Potter the long end of their joke-rope, and it was just to his hand.

In this journey these two brethren traveled across the entire border of the West Texas Conference, from the Colorado to the Rio Grande, a distance of three hundred miles. Mr. Thornberry, according to promise, went with Mr. Potter an entire round on his great mission-circuit, making in all more than one thousand miles, ending at Eagle Pass, on the Rio Grande River. But they crossed over the river, and stood on Mexican soil, and then returned into their own land. Here they passed into the domain of another nation, and when on the Colorado they had entered the bounds of the North-west Texas Conference.

Ministerial brethren traveling together through such a vast, partially-settled region, beset by the frequent incursions of blood-thirsty savages and the wayside robber, learn to feel more sensibly man's dependence on his fellow to aid him in defeating his foes; and their sense of dependence strengthens their fraternal attachments for each other. Besides, Mr. Thornberry is said to be a most excellent traveling companion—always in a cheerful good humor; never murmuring at any thing; at home in the wild prairie, or in the forest-dell; sleeping alike on the cold earth, sprinkled with night-dews, or on a downy bed; feasting on "jerked beef" and "black coffee," or banqueting on luxuries in a mansion—no matter where or what, all was ever right with him. In these things he and Mr. Potter were true yoke-fellows. They could do justice to a good dinner when they might happen to overtake one of that kind; but in the line of jest Mr. Potter usually carried off the laurels, though they were well matched.

The reader is now invited to read from Mr. Potter's manuscript an account of his Christian fellowship and fraternal intercourse with a minister of the Baptist Communion—the Rev. W. W. Harris—who, no doubt, now holds fellowship with the "Church of the first-born" in heaven:

"In 1878 the Rev. W. W. Harris, a minister of the Missionary Baptist Church, was suffering from pulmonary consumption, and he made a tour with me to the Rio Grande, for his health. He was, I think, a native Texan, and had great pulpit notoriety. He was educated at Independence, Washington County, Texas, under the auspices of that noted educator, Dr. Rufus Burleson. He began to preach when quite young, and was for some time called 'the boy-preacher.' He was also styled 'the young Spurgeon,' or 'Spurgeon Harris,' on account of his almost unsurpassed eloquence in the pulpit. He was a stanch Baptist, but nicely respectful to all other denominations, and he was welcomed to all their pulpits. He also was a strong defender of Baptist doctrines, but he had a nice regard for times, and places, and the Christian feelings of other people. He could preach a week, and it would be difficult to tell what denomination he belonged to. He gloried in the cross and its connected truths, and seemed to lose sight of all other themes. He combined in himself a number of singular characteristics. He was cheerful and witty, grave and dignified;

his gestures in the pulpit were somewhat theatrical; he could make heaven with his smile, and hell with his frown; he was a 'man of one work;' he never gave an hour's study to secular affairs in his life; he was never married. I first formed his acquaintance in Caldwell County in 1862. He was then young and vigorous, and was preaching with enlarged popularity. In 1877 he came to the upper part of Kendall County in search of health. His furrowed cheek and gray hairs told how time had been rapidly marking off the passing years with him. His wasted form and brilliant eye indicated that his useful career was hurrying to a speedy close; but his heart still lingered in the Master's work, and still he could and would bear his witness for Jesus with an energy that would not yield to disease. He assisted me in two revival-meetings, and preached with great power, 'though his outward man was perishing day by day.' In 1878 my circuit lay mostly out on the Rio Grande, and he made a tour with me, to test the virtues of that genial clime. He had to take charge of a small Baptist Church in Kerr County. When he was taking leave of his little flock for his Western trip, I told them after I had got away from them that they had all as well join the Methodists, for I would have him in my Church before our return. He replied, 'Don't you do it. I will plunge Potter in the Rio Grande as soon as we get there.' Mr. Harris had no experience in frontier-life, and the journey was novel and romantic to him. There were but few Baptists in that country, and he would always be introduced as a Baptist minister. He was a Baptist in earnest. I put him forward to preach as often as I thought him able, and the people would flock to hear him in large numbers. I left him at San Felipe until I made another round on my circuit.

"The Mexicans were committing great depredations by stealing and driving stock over the river into Mexico, and there was great excitement all along the line on the Rio Grande River. On my return to San Felipe with Master George Griner, a boy about twelve years old, the weather being intensely warm, I concluded to make a night-drive. Leaving Fort Clark about sundown, we set out for San Felipe. We traveled till about midnight, and halted for a nap until early morning. I hobbled out my ponies to grass, and lay down on our blankets 'to nap it.' Mesquite-brush, prickly-pears, and almost any other thorny thing you might imagine, were all about there. Just before day George awoke me, saying that some one was after the ponies, driving them off in the brush. The moon was shining brightly. I jumped up, drew on my shoes, having no time to draw on my pants, but seized my faithful 'Winchester,' and hastened in pursuit of my ponies. On arriving near them, I saw the thief loosing the hobbles, and fired upon him, and he disappeared in the brush. The ponies, being frightened at the report of the gun, jumped off a few paces, but I got around them, and drove them back to camp; but in running through the thorny thicket I had filled my lower limbs with thorns. I pulled out the larger ones, hitched up my ponies, and a drive of fourteen miles brought us safely to San Felipe. With the aid of a small pair of tweezers I drew out the remaining thorns from my flesh. I learned that the Mexican I had shot belonged to a thriving band who had driven a large amount of stock into Mexico from the Texas side of the river. When I was running after my ponies, I did not know whether it was Mexicans or Indians, or whether there were many or few of them; but I intended to fight for my ponies.

"Mr. Harris had now been at San Felipe about six weeks, and had gained several pounds; but he became so nervous over the Mexican troubles I had to bring him to Uvalde, where he was quite sick, but kind hands administered unto him until he was able to travel again, when he came into San Antonio, and thence to San Marcos; but his health continued to decline till some time last year, when he went back to San Felipe, on the Rio Grande, where he ended his sufferings, and passed into the radiance of eternal day. The Baptist Church in Texas has never mourned the loss of a minister so universally beloved by all denominations of Christians. My associations with him will hold a pleasing room in memory's hall. Dear departed brother, we call to mind all that was lovely in thy character in the days of thy sojourn with us; but thou hast gone to mingle with the spirits of the just made perfect, whilst thy silent body rests far away, where no tombstone marks the place of its repose, but Infinite Wisdom sees all its dust, and shall know where to find it in the last great day. O may the green grass carpet, and the gentle zephyrs blow peacefully over, thy far-off grave!"

How strong the Christian attachment of Mr. Potter for real good men! His religious fellowship was not confined to the limits of a Church creed; he readily associated with any good man, and indulged for him the most ardent brotherly regards. Where the light of piety shone, he laid aside distinctive tenets, and joined the fraternal hand. What God approves he never calls common.

Mr. Potter's last quarterly-meeting for 1878 was held at Uvalde about the 1st of September. Mr. Thornberry was the presiding elder, and was present. At the close of the meeting Mr. Potter took his reluctant and tearful farewell of his host of warm friends. He had been their pastor four years, and their attachment was indeed of a vital type. He has not met that people since, but he often speaks of those happy days, now gone forever. Mr. Potter then accompanied Mr. Thornberry to his quarterly-meeting at Frio Town. There Mr. Potter was among his old friends, and two saloon-men captured him, and boarded him at an hotel, furnishing him a neat room, and paying his fare; and these two gentlemen —Lester and Harkness—furnished the wine for the sacramental occasion. When Mr. Potter was about to leave, he went by the saloon to tell the men good-by. There was a side room, where visitors could enter, and not go into the saloon, and Mr. Potter went into that room to have a little parting talk with his benefactors. He had put on an old duster to drive in which was considerably torn. In their interview Mr. Potter said, "Gentlemen, I do not think myself better than others because I may chance to have on a better suit of clothing." Just then Mr. Lester tore off his old duster, and took down a nice silk-alpaca coat which was hanging on a nail, and said, "Here; put this on." Mr. Potter replied, "Mr. Lester, I can't take your coat; my old duster was not worth any thing, and that is a fine coat." But Lester said, "Take it along, Mr. Potter; you are welcome to it. We catch men drunk here every day, and take their coats off of them; we will have plenty more hanging up there in a day or two." And the fine silken coat adorned the preacher and the pulpit. What a wonderful man! How strange his power over all classes of men and grades of society! Gamblers and saloon-men seem to claim him as their preacher, not merely because he was taken from their number into the Church, but he ever made it a special duty to preach to them the same religion that had saved him; and too he was ever polite and kind to them. All men have an interest in the Bible and in the message of mercy he proclaims from its pages.

We close this chapter by calling the reader's attention to the inestimable value of true Christian fellowship among all religious people. "Behold how pleasant it is for brethren to dwell together in unity." Ministers of the various orthodox Churches may hold various views of ceremonies, and even doctrines; but in heart they may be one, unified in love. Love is the all-essential grace, the never-failing charity; it fulfills the law. Mr. Potter was a real

Methodist, and Mr. Harris was a true Baptist, yet they loved and respected each other as did Jonathan and David of old. They rejoiced together as brethren of a common cause, and when death intervened the grave between them, Mr. Potter mourned his loss as a brother indeed, and still fondly cherishes the memory of his virtues. "Jesus, the Corner-stone, did first their hearts unite," and with all Christians the love of Jesus in the heart should be the end of all strife. Mr. Potter's motto is to cultivate kind feelings for all men, and to deal justly and tenderly with all with whom he may chance to meet. Polite kindness, dear reader, is cheap, and it pays well in the end—blesses the mind of receiver and giver. Love is union, and union is strength; but sectarianism tends to strife and disunion, and that leads to weakness. As sure as contending winds rend and tear down, so sure does contention disunite the good which God and man may have joined together, and poison that which grace may have healed. To take a stone or brick from one part of a great temple, and place it in another part, does not add to either the symmetry or growth of the general structure. Ministers whose ministerial works seem to indicate a call to contend with the members of other Churches, and take them out of the Church of their choice, and initiate them into their own Communions, may help to build up a certain sect, but may add nothing to the cause of Jesus Christ in this world. Such ministers are usually dogmatic advocates for some pet "ism," or stanch ritualists, or rigid ceremonialists. If Mr. Harris had devoted his great talents in trying to proselyte affusionists, and to fix in their minds the cold, separating belief that they had no right to Church fellowship and communion, unless they would allow him to immerse them in some stream, pool, or tank of water, his higher, nobler ministry would not have left such a sweet odor in the memory of all good people who knew him. Like the Apostle of the Gentiles, he spread the cement of love on each layer of the great temple, while others of his less noble brethren spend their efforts in private and public in doing the ceremonial business of plunging people into water. St. Paul said his commission was not to baptize, but to preach the gospel. Baptizing, then, is not so essential as ceremonialists would have it to be. While the good man sleeps, the living cherish his memory.

CHAPTER XLIII.

Rev. H. A. Graves—*Dear Sir:*—Your card has been on my table for some time, but business-cares prevented an earlier reply. You ask for incidents and facts in the life of the Rev. A. J. Potter, as I have known him, and his relation to such occurrences. Since my acquaintance with him we have both been engaged in the itinerant ministry, and I cannot say that any thing exceptional or phenomenal has come under my observation. Knowing the man, however, as I do, I have thought that I could detect in his character those elements that furnish the solution of a career remarkable in many of its features. The striking incidents and passages in his life are known to you, probably, as well as myself, and hence do not need repetition at my hands. Persons now living have mentioned to me many a strange occurrence, and narrow escape, bold adventure, striking display of cool daring, and intrepid courage, and wonderful events on the tented field, on the wild frontier, or in the sphere of home-life, which illustrate his character and endowments. All that I could furnish you would be something in the way of an essay, and that, I think, would not comport with the style of your work. His has been a most remarkable career, full of thrilling adventure, and replete with instruction to all who are given to the study of that profoundest book, human nature, especially as exhibited in an original and unique character. "Truth is stranger than fiction." Who that knew A. J. Potter in those days spent in the sports and excitement of a wild, stormy, and reckless life, would have seen in such a man the possibility of the humble Christian and minister of the Lord Jesus Christ? He was then a terror, if not to evil-doers, at least to all who sought to deceive him to his own hurt, or who openly or secretly plotted to do him injury. The evil upon which he was bent was open to all, and though not charged with those crimes which excite abhorrence and disgust, yet he was felt to be inimical to good order and the well-being of society. But withal, even in those days, he could be trusted—he was never known to forfeit his word, and he would abide by his engagements at the cost of life itself. He was trusted by some of the best men of his acquaintance. An aged man and blameless Christian was imposed upon by a younger and unscrupulous neighbor, who, with threats of using the horse-whip, sought to deter the old man from the legitimate use of his own property. The old man—who always acted from pure motives—knowing his inability to redress his wrongs, sought the counsel of A. J. Potter. Mr. Potter accompanied him to the scene of the trespass, and the arrival of the plaintiff and counsel settled the dispute at once, and in favor of the old man. The threatened horse-whipping was stoutly affirmed to have been only a piece of pleasantry.

From what I have learned of those who knew him in those days, there was a boldness and openness in his violations of law and good order that in some degree commended him to the peaceable and law-abiding. When he committed an act that seemingly merited the penalty of the law, there was no want of testimony as to what he had done. He acted openly, and in the light of day, and would frankly admit the deed. When arraigned for any misdeed, his cool and collected manner, and shrewd mother-wit, and power of exciting the mirth and good-will of the court, often mitigated the penalty, which was never more than a petty fine, and that before a magistrate's court—his offenses never reached the dignity of the higher courts.

The gospel is to be preached to every creature, and A. J. Potter is a wonderful exhibition of the reasonableness of the command of our Saviour, and the motives to obedience upon the part of those charged with the high commission. The gems and diamonds are often concealed and imbedded in the coarse clay. The "ore" was in the man. We do not depreciate the grace of God, we magnify it. Only by the divine method of redemption could he have been saved and plucked from the burning. But the materials were of the best. There was a patent of nobility in the man, blurred and marred by sin, which needed the retouching of the grace of redemption to bring out all the letters in clear and bold relief. Those who have known him only as the humble Christian and devoted minister of the Lord Jesus, feel that he was a man, even in the days of his recklessness and abandonment to evil. He was a giant in that cause, for it was in him to do nothing by halves; but the courage and desperation of the man were inspired by original but perverted attributes of character, and a sense of manhood that never failed him. His native abhorrence of meanness and baseness has more than once, as your pages will testify, prompted him to the use of carnal weapons, and the infliction of penalties, which seem, in him, to be legitimate. I believe he has never been arraigned for these things. It seems generally to be accorded to A. J. Potter to do some things which would meet with due censure in others, and would subject them to ecclesiastical pains and penalties. Had some of us, his ministerial associates, committed some things to which he pleads guilty, we might have suffered severe censures from our brethren, and been damaged in our usefulness. But Potter has done some things for which he is not censured by his brethren, and for which, as I have knowledge, he is commended by peaceable and law-abiding citizens.

How exceedingly fertile the resources of our Church in supplying the masses of the people with a living ministry—a ministry seemingly classified and adapted to the wants of the age and the country. The frontier of Texas on the west has had the services of A. J. Potter. It has been often remarked that the economy of our Church is peculiarly adapted to a new and formative period of society. Potter is indispensable to the advancing lines of the westward move of our population, and the peace of the Church in providing for this movement. To the frontier people he carries the bread of life, he protects helpless families from the incursions of the savages, and is a terror to bad men. A ceaseless care and anxiety for the welfare of wife and children are among the unpleasant features of the life of the frontiersman. Those people are attached to the man who, as a shepherd, protects their folds from the incursions of spiritual foes, as well as guards their homes from savage raids. To those who have not a personal acquaintance with the subject of this sketch, it may be proper to say, that although accustomed to rough and exciting scenes and a hard life, yet there was in him a true refinement of manner, and a heart full of love for mankind, and the tenderest sympathy for the sorrows and sufferings of others. He was a most valuable counselor to those in distress. The writer bears testimony to his strength and power of sympathy and prayers in days of sorrow. His own experience would supply him with facts, a recital of which would greatly commend the grace of God in the subject of this brief sketch, but we refrain in the presence of a great sorrow of years now passed. B. H. HARRIS.

Luling, April 12, 1881.

The author of the foregoing letter — the Rev. Buckner Harris — is a learned, able, and popular minister of the West Texas Conference, now pastor of the M. E. Church, South, at Luling, Texas, and some years ago was Mr. Potter's presiding elder on the frontier, and had to be piloted through the most perilous regions by that brave pioneer and his trusty "Winchester." Having been so intimately associated with him, as a brother minister, and many years members of the same Annual Conference, he had a good opportunity of reading those ruling traits in his Christian character pointed out in his short letter. He never knew Mr. Potter in the years of his profligacy, but he has touched at some of the rudiments lying at the bottom of his formative life. They were "diamonds in the rough." Having these constitutional elements, Divine Wisdom marked him out as the man for the place he has filled so befittingly in later years. The sublime image was in the rough marble, and the chisel and mallet of the Divine Artist has developed it into beautiful features. A grace-refined sinner becomes a saint in earthen robes. The gospel-displayed power among the lowest grades, and the chiefest of sinful men, is nothing else but the power of God unto salvation from the most debasing habits of vice. Truly does it regenerate men. Then they are born again, begin life anew; changed in heart, man reforms his outward life. No material agencies, no moral motives, can remodel his moral nature, can change the internal forces which control a sinful life. The African cannot change the color of his skin, nor the leopard his spots, neither can the sinner turn back his nature's evil tide. Internal salvation is of God. Man's good intentions and firm resolves, under the dictation of an illumined reason, pass away like chaff before the first impassioned storm of evil desires, often made doubly strong by the long force of habit. But when grace has cast out the strong-armed man which nature and habit have intrenched in the citadel of the heart, it is an easy task to turn away from the long-pursued path of sinful associations, and enter into the habits and alliances of a new and opposite manner of living. The fountain cleansed and opened up, the stream flows readily to its great estuary. Love is the motive-force of a new heart. Love makes all things easy, even the toils and hardships which duty may enjoin. The sinner promptly gives up his sinful deeds because grace, or religion, has taught his heart to hate them, and has reversed his affections and placed them on divine things. What he used to love he now hates, and that which he despised he now loves. That is a new heart—it is being born again. That, dear reader, is "experimental, heart-felt religion." St. Paul styles it being made a "new creature"—"changed in the spirit of the mind." That is the wonderful secret agency which suddenly turned about the entire course of Mr. Potter's life, and so devotedly attached him to the Church which instrumentally rescued him from the deep mire of the pit.

Mr. Harris mentions some acts in the Christian term of Mr. Potter's career as being censurable in other men, and perhaps objectionable in him, though looked over by both civil and ecclesiastical courts. We suppose he made reference to his knocking down a man in the church at Prairie Lee, his contest with the desperado at Boerne, and his difficulty with the young braggart—all recorded in separate chapters in this book. These events were severely trying to his ministerial graces, and as much as the circumstances leading thereto may be cause of regret, yet we have not met any one familiar with them who has administered a censure on him for the deeds. *Manner* and *motives* have much to do in making up the moral coloring of human conduct. Not that the old Romish doctrine that "the motive sanctifies the deed" is true. It is true that no deed is virtuous without a good underlying motive, but good intentions do not sanctify unlawful acts. To do evil, hoping for good results, is not admissible; but there are some deeds of men along the border, where the distinctive line runs, marking the parting of good and evil, where one ceases and the other begins, about which men may not agree as to their moral type, that good motives and a Christian-tempered manner may so palliate as to deprive them of guilt and rob them of censure. Such were the acts alluded to by Mr. Harris. His motives were good, and his manner was not of vengeful wrath. He only sought to protect himself and secure his rights. Any good man may have good motives, but the spirit of the manner of doing things may materially differ with men, and greatly alter their character and results. Even a deed of charity may lose its pleasant benefits on the recipient by the ostentatious manner of its bestowment. So likewise inflictions of chastisement on a rebellious child in the temper and manner of kindness is a good deed, but the same punishment administered in an ill-tempered spirit and malignant manner partakes of the evil. In all Mr. Potter's administering merited retribution on bad men, his manner was not spiced with any bitterness. When he knocked a man down it was only to prevent his doing a greater injury, and he never went farther than that. There he ended his strife. He could have bruised, mangled, and killed, but that was not his motive; he had no raging temper to satiate. When his antagonist was secured against farther harm to himself or others, he was ready to pity, to forgive, and to relieve. His attacks were never made on the unoffending; good men never feared him.

We have treated at some length in another chapter the scriptural doctrine of retaliation, or resistance of evil; but the subject demands our attention in relation to some allusions in this chapter. We here state that the notion of total non-resistance of the evil efforts of wicked men to injure our person or property, cannot be the doctrine of the New Testament. It is true, however, that non-resistance in all minor matters is there plainly inculcated; but in things which materially endanger life, limb, health, and our living, or property, it cannot be intended to be therein taught. When our Saviour said that if smitten on one cheek we should turn the other also, he could have meant no more than the lesser insults and minor injuries entailed on us by our fellows. He also said, If sued at the law for your coat, let your cloak go also. But the apostolic Christians did not construe that moral teaching of Jesus to deprive them of legal redress for wrongs, for they went to law for a righting of their claims; and St. Paul never entered up blame against them for the act of going to law, but for lawing before unjust magistrates when there were Christian judges before whom they might settle their differences. But Jesus never said, Let a man take your horse, and do not resist him: he only said, Let your cloak go. There is a difference between some horses and some cloaks. That desperado at Boerne was taking off Mr. Potter's horse, and surely his religion did not bind him to let him go on without an effort to regain it. The immortal Teacher also said, in the same connection, If compelled to go a mile, go two, which gives unto that memorable paragraph the coloring of a symbol—that is to say, that in all things where greater evils are likely to result than good, it is best not to resist, but to submit; and where I am asked to be kind, to be liberal, and do more than petitioned for, if need be. Liberality is safe in deeds of kindness, but not so in acts of anger. St. Paul said, In understanding be ye men, but be children in the evil. So also we may say to all men, Be ye giants in the good, but infants in the hurtful. Not that it is truly needful that a man must inflict some pains and penalties on his fellows in passing through the world, but that there are times and conditions in which it is best and proper to administer painful but temporary injuries on some men to prevent their greater damage to you or to others. The penalties of all laws root in this principle. To guard against harm to one's self, and wrong to others, law deprives men of liberty, and even of life. In organized and refined society the individual is expected to give up his personal right to self-defense, or redress of injuries, to the civil law. But what is a man to do where he is endangered, and there are no agents or officers of the law at hand to give him security against harm, or where the custodians of law do not care to execute the mandates of law to shield the innocent? Is he to cry out for help when none is in hearing, or when help has not an ear to hear? In the frontier-wilds of West Texas, in the days of Mr. Potter's pugnacious contacts with pugilists, population was sparsely strewn along her vast plains, and in many places officers of law were not inclined to tackle such dangerous outlaws as Mr. Potter coolly encountered. In those instances he took the place of deputies of law, and all law-abiding citizens felt the benefit of his semi-official acts, and approved them. So circumstances, motives, and manner, have much to do in giving a moral coloring to otherwise unallowable acts of men, especially with those called to officiate as ministers of religion—that religion designed to save men, not to destroy them. But what Mr. Potter could do, and remain uncensured for, would attach guilt to the writer, because not the man for the place. He could bruise the body and whisper peace to the soul.

In Mr. Harris's letter he tells us that he has personal experience of Mr. Potter's ability to counsel and comfort the afflicted in days of gloom and sorrow. He there refers to that dark day of years long fled, when God took from him the wife of his youth, and the young mother of his little ones, in the city of San Antonio. She was a noble Christian woman, of whom the world was not worthy; but she has joined the holy ranks of friends and kindred dear on the immortal shore. Mr. Potter visited her in her last days on the earth, and prayed and talked with her and her disconsolate husband. She was happy, and when he parted with her, he told her that it was probable they might not meet again till the joyous greeting on the other shore. "And now you are happy, but when you pass into Jordan's chilly waters, leave me a message as to your prospects then." When she was far out in the cold waters of that last river, she feebly whispered, "Tell Brother Potter all is well!" and the angel-bands on the other shore sent that message back into their shining ranks, "All is well!" Truly, to the young husband that was a day of great sorrow—its gloom veiled his heart as the shadow of a dark storm-cloud on the bosom of the sea. Earth's bereaved millions have seen its darkness and felt the pressure of its weight of griefs. The writer has passed under its dismal shading. For twenty-one years his youthful companion has slept with strangers near the bank of the Brazos, where its gulf and mountain-waters mingle, and where the waving, long gray moss sprinkles her grave with rain-dripping tears. O what a dread catastrophe has befallen earth! Why that parting of love-unified hearts? In some sylvan home may earth's sorrow-riven children meet to die no more! Reader, be of that number of happy ones.

After writing the foregoing, Mr. Potter's notice of the occasion, in the Texas *Christian Advocate*, has come to us, which we here copy:

"How happy are those who die in the faith of Jesus Christ! What sacred peace! what divine transport! what emotions of love, of joy, and of confidence, do they then experience! As the outward man perishes the inward man gains strength and vigor. The death-bed distinguishes the believer, and renders him an object worthy the notice of men and angels. It is there that he appears victorious over the world. He is in the world without taking part in its concerns—he is in the body, not being attached to it. He rejoices in hope of the glory of God. He walks with tranquillity through the valley of the shadow of death, and fears no evil, amid all its objects of dread, for his God is with him, and sustains him in the final hour. His faith too penetrates through the clouds of mortality yet surrounding him. He looks within the veil, and beholds his glorious Redeemer ready to receive his unimprisoned spirit; he sees the eternal inheritance for which he has so often sung and sighed in the land of shadows. He is nearing the heavenly home —'city of the living God.' Even now he is filled with the glorious presence of the Divine which holy souls enjoy in the fadeless realms unseen. He is now on the borders of 'the beautiful land,' 'the inheritance of the saints in light.' O how near to the holy ranks of angels and kindred dear! He can hear the immortal harpers chanting the 'song of Moses and the Lamb.' He longs to join the celestial symphonies. Now 'the clouds disperse, the shadows fly,' and immortal day dawns upon the soul. So our lamented Sister Harris passed into the light of endless day.

"No words spoken or written linger with such tenacity about memory's heart as the last message of a dying loved one. The last lines traced by a dear hand, now cold in dust, print themselves on the unforgotten page—mementoes left us by the long-absent dead which ruthless time cannot fade.

"These reflections were called up by meditating on the triumphant death of Sister Harris. The consoling message she sent to the writer from near the celestial bank of the mystic river, comes as a herald from regions immortal. Raising her hand in token of victory, she whispered, '*Tell Brother Potter all is well!*' That message was delivered to me in sobs and tears by the bereaved husband, after his departed Georgia had joined the 'Church of the first born.'

"Here we laid our hand on her grave, and looked up to heaven and implored a death like hers, knowing the unseen heavens contained her departed spirit, too pure for an earthly tabernacle now. Faith almost sees her in her glory, and hears the sweet notes of her lute of heavenly tone. O may we, when far out on the chilly wave, be permitted, like her, to send back to weeping friends, '*All is well!*'"

The foregoing pathetic outflow of a Christian heart indicates the deep tide of pure sympathy which ever flowed from that devoted man of God about the couch of suffering and the abodes of sorrow, and at the same time reveals the strength of his faith in the consolations of that blessed gospel he was commissioned to preach to the living and the dying. He had an inward knowledge of the saving power of that gospel. He felt in himself some of the prelibations of the hope he commended to the acceptance of others. Under its heavenly fruitions he could sweetly sing:

> In hope of that immortal crown,
> I now the cross sustain.

CHAPTER XLIV.

THE reader is now invited to read an interesting chapter from the pen of the Rev. J. S. Gillett, the presiding elder who "killed the rabbit," as seen in another chapter. Mr. Gillett wrote this chapter, not knowing what incidents the author had already inserted in the book; and we put it in type in Mr. Gillett's own handwriting, without any alteration, as it will serve to confirm the exact truthfulness of the many incidents narrated in this biography. The minor differences in Mr. Gillett's detail of the incidents narrated by him and those of the author do not affect the leading primal facts. Mr. Gillett wrote from memory, after the lapse of several years, and the author wrote from the direct verbal or written statement of Mr. Potter. Indeed, the entire volume of incidents and facts, as relating to Mr. Potter, are penned after Mr. Potter's verbal statement or recently written diary. Mr. Gillett has the leading facts all right. He and Mr. Potter are truly brethren and friends, and while memory holds her throne they can never forget the many pleasant seasons they had together while passing alone through the wild solitudes of this vast Indian-infested land, when they did not know at what moment the heartless savage might claim their scalps. Dangers endured together endear men to each other with ties that the erosions of time can never fret away. O dear reader, these border preachers, who have toiled and suffered together, are indeed *brethren!*

"Both in theory and in practice the Christian system is without a parallel in the history of the world. In theory, it is faultless; in practice, it aims at and, where unobstructed by the human will, attains perfection. There is no deformity here. The one is the counterpart of the other. There is nothing merely theoretical in all that grand philosophy which had its origin with the incarnate Son of God. In all its details it was the divine intention that Christianity should be *lived, enjoyed.* Hence its universal adaptation and its personal approach, its all-encompassing invitations and its individual encouragements. Nor is this all. In point of fact, the divine origin and value of Christianity has been attested as often as the guilty have come in God's own appointed way seeking salvation. It is the boast of our religion that it saves. Regeneration is its central idea whence radiates all good—the new life. These are the promised, the expected results of faith in the Son of God. These are the fruits, in brief, which come to all who are 'justified from all things by the faith that is in them.' This is no new doctrine. It is as old, at least, as the ministry of Jesus Christ; yet it has all the vigor of youth; it bears none of the marks of age or infirmity; men are saved *now* as in the ages past. The living, as well as the dead, are the witnesses. Let us take two: About a quarter of a century ago there were two young men, boon companions in vice, without wealth, or refinement, or culture, bent only upon making provision for the flesh to live after the flesh, and wholly oblivious to the high and holy purposes of human life and destiny. They were Alexander A. Smithwick and Andrew J. Potter. In the midst of great recklessness of life the arresting hand of God was laid upon the former, and from his sick-bed he saw his duty and his danger. The impressions of that hour were never forgotten. Its divine convictions, its holy inspirations were followed up, or he was rather led by them into the marvelous light and liberty of the children of God. The transformation was complete: he lived in another world; he was a new creature in Christ Jesus. But Potter was not there. When he heard of his friend's (to him, unaccountable) change, he was like one bereft. Sadness took possession of his heart. He was alone now. But he had confidence in Smithwick. He knew he would tell him the truth. He would see him, and hear the story of his conversion from his own lips. If religion, according to Smithwick, was true, Potter must have it. They met; the conference was short and simple; the witness was willing, direct, positive. Potter's decision was taken; he must know for himself, and it was not long until he did know: the friends rejoiced together. Both were moved by the Holy Ghost to preach the gospel; but here was a difficulty: They had only the grace of God, good minds, and strong bodies—no mean factors, to be sure, in such a work; ay, indispensable to it, but by no means the only conditions of success. There must be training, thought, culture, the very things these young men lacked, if the largest results are to be expected. Friends doubted, the Church hesitated, and finally, in the case of Potter, refused. But the call was imperative: they must preach, and they did. In the fall of 1859 Alexander A. Smithwick was admitted on trial into the Texas Conference, and transferred to the Rio Grande Mission Conference, and appointed to the Helena Circuit. He gave great promise of usefulness, and was full of zeal, but the next year, 1860, God took him. He fell, ere he had reached the zenith of his usefulness, beloved by his charge, and in full prospect of heaven. His remains repose in the churchyard at Sandies Chapel, now of Rancho Circuit.

"In the year 1865 Mr. Potter was received into the West Texas Conference. He was now fairly committed to the work of his life, and soon developed into a first-class frontier Methodist preacher, which, by the way, is no mean distinction. Dangers, privations, and toils, among the hardy frontiersmen, have such attractions for him, that he stands a constant volunteer for that very work which most men instinctively shrink from. Of course, his wish has been gratified, and in consequence he is known and respected in almost every neighborhood and village throughout the whole extent of our Western border. If he glories in it, who shall censure? if he is proud of it, who shall say he has not the right? And let it be put in this permanent form, that he who in times past was addicted to almost every form of vice, has not only been actively employed in 'spreading scriptural holiness over these lands,' but has furnished, in his own person, one of the brightest illustrations of the power of divine grace to renew depraved humanity, and keep in the way of life the trusting soul. One such illustration is of priceless worth. A good life is the best argument. In the presence of purity even blatant infidelity is dumb with silence. 'Who shall lay any thing to the charge of God's elect?' But there is nothing somber in Potter's piety, nothing ascetic. His whole life, with all its surroundings, forbids the very thought. He is Nature's own child, as blithe as the birds, and as joyous as the lambs that skip in the sunlight. Yet he knows how to be severe. and, upon occasion, to stand up manfully for his rights. This last remark may be taken in a two-fold sense, for he is lacking in neither moral nor physical courage: he is a true friend and a determined foe. But he is not a stirrer up of strife—he loves peace, he abuses no man's privileges, takes away the rights of none. Still, it cannot be denied that sometimes, when he is for peace, they are for war; and when nothing else will do, Potter knows how to fight. This is now so well known that he comes and goes at pleasure, no man forbidding him.

"For the purpose of illustrating his fighting capacity, and to satisfy those who may be disposed to criticise this propensity of his nature—to show, in a word, that there is 'method in his madness,' and that he does nothing in this direction without cause, the following incidents are inserted:

"On one occasion, happening to be at the house of

a friend who was from home, a rough came in, and began to use obscene language in the presence of the ladies of the family. Potter unceremoniously put him out of the house. The man went to the gate, obtained his revolver, and came back. Potter, who was unarmed, would have gone forth to meet him, but was restrained by the ladies who, seeing the danger, drew him into the house, and shut the door. The desperado, finding himself foiled, left, coolly taking Mr. Potter's horse with him. This was too much. Potter got out, ran across a lot, and intercepted the would-be thief, who dismounted, pistol in hand, and advanced upon him. Nothing daunted, however, Potter seized a stone, and, before his adversary had time to shoot, knocked him down, and leaped upon him. Then came 'the tug of war.' It was now a hand-to-hand conflict, and Potter was hardly a match for him physically. But stones were abundant, and as often as he seemed about to rise, Potter would knock him on the head, and settle him for awhile. In the meantime the sheriff and his *posse*—all Germans—came in sight. They had been after the man who had whipped out the town, and seeing the preacher with their man down, cried out, 'Hold him, Mr. Botter! hold him, Mr. Botter!' which he did until they came up. The man was jailed. Next day, at the trial, appeared Potter, unsolicited, and without fee or reward, to plead for him who but yesterday sought to take away his life.

"Such is the man. It is not contended that in all cases the cause is as just as in this instance, but when Potter fights, to *him*, at least, there is reason for it, and to others, as a rule, there is room for ample justification. Still, he regrets these experiences, and thinks, and *says*, as often as they occur, 'This shall be my last.' This statement is made with special pleasure, for while it may be necessary sometimes to fight, yet no man, and especially no preacher, should defend the practice, or glory in it. Rather, 'let him that glorieth, glory in the Lord.' In the work, however, to which our brother is committed there are dangers as well as difficulties, and a man of less spirit might be appalled in their presence. It cannot be doubted that the very traits of character which fit a man for a work like this, would prompt him to deal summarily with all offenders. The country being new and uninhabited in many places, save by predatory bands of savages, of course there must be long trips, with much exposure, both from inclement weather and unscrupulous foes, and Potter has experienced the hard contact of both. Once, as he crossed from Frio Cañon to Sabinal Cañon, a rough and uninhabited mountain region, where already slept the dead victims of savage barbarity, he saw several Indians passing down a ravine, with the evident intention of intercepting him. He quickly tied his horses, and taking his Winchester rifle in his hand, ran on until he came near the place they were aiming for, and took his stand. He did not have long to wait. The stalwart sons of the forest came out into an open place, and paused to listen for the rumble of his buggy-wheels and to make observations. Potter tried to shoot, but his gun missed fire. One of the Indians then shot at him, almost striking his arm. He tried again, this time with better success, for, as he fired, the Indian's gun fell from his hands. The savages beat a hasty retreat. Potter ran back to his buggy, and, taking a good position for defense, awaited developments. Two Indians soon appeared on the mountain, and fired at him from a very safe distance. He took out his pipe and smoked while they exchanged shots, but he has since confessed that it was more for the moral effect than for enjoyment. It was not indeed a tender of the calumet of peace—it was simply to say, 'Who's afraid?' The effect was fine—he 'bluffed' them, and they left. Potter claims that he 'got meat;' he knows that they did not.

"The two cases given above are typical of the rest. In all there is the same dash and the same show of justice, at least in part. There is also a touch of the serio-comic in Potter's nature. He can appear to be serious, and yet do the most amusing things. At one of his appointments there were some young men who persisted in going to the mourner's-bench for their own sport; they had done so for a long while. Potter found it out, but they were ignorant of his knowledge of their conduct. So they agreed that at the next service they would go in a group to the altar of prayer. One of their number was to lead the way, but when the time came he alone of all the group had the courage to venture. Alone he knelt at the mercy-seat, practicing a lie. The singing over, Potter said, 'Brethren and sisters, here is a poor sinner who has sought religion a long time without success: come, let us gather around him, and help him to the Saviour. And now, Dick [addressing the penitent], you have been a great sinner, and if you want salvation you must pray. While we pray for you, you must pray for yourself. Pray, Dick!' said he, with great emphasis of voice and fist—for he delivered the whole strength of his right arm full upon the back of the crouching mourner. Then followed other exhortations with peltings, until the sham mourner was not a sham sufferer, in the flesh at least. He stood it for awhile, but at last his powers of endurance could hold out no longer. He arose running, and made his escape, a sorer and a wiser man.

"He also enjoys a joke, and that must indeed be a dry case that furnishes Potter no occasion for merriment. Witness the following: He and his presiding elder were personal friends. They were often together exchanging views, talking of things they knew and did not know, or discussing questions social, domestic, and private. In one of those free and easy conversations, in which the question of food was being discussed, Potter remarked that he was fond of rabbits. The remark was not forgotten by the presiding elder. So hearing one day that Potter and his wife would dine at his house that day, he took his gun and shot a rabbit, and had it dressed, especially for his guest, intending to serve the rest of the company with other meats, of which there was an abundance, and to have a good laugh at his friend's expense. Dinner came, Potter ate, and said nothing, and the matter was forgotten by the crowd. Some time after this they attended a quarterly-meeting together, in a distant charge, and Potter begged the privilege of taking up a collection for the support of the ministry (as was usual in those days), which, being granted, he proceeded to do. He took his presiding elder for a text, and spoke in substance as follows: 'Brethren, the presiding elder comes to you once a quarter; you see him well dressed; he preaches well, and attends to the duties of his office, and you may think he is in need of nothing; but you should see him as I have,' etc. Then followed a graphic description of the man at home, surrounded by his wife and children, of his dress, his multitude of duties accumulated in his absence while serving the Church, of his house and little patch of ground, and whatever else was necessary to complete a picture of extreme poverty. By this time the congregation was in tears; but he did not reach the climax until, in the midst of mingled tears and smiles, he cried in tones of thunder, 'Why, my brethren, wife and I dined with him a short time since, and he had to go out and kill a *rabbit* for dinner!' Then came out the secret of his great interest in that special collection: he had been weeks in laying his plan to get even, and in preparing that speech, which, it must be confessed, was successful, for he got the cash.

"There are many things of interest which might be called up, and which would appropriately occupy a place in a book, but which must, of necessity, be excluded from the brief limits of a chapter; but let this suffice. His record is on high. No doubt 'the day' will reveal many an essential fact in his eventful life, passed over in silence here, and which shall constitute, in part at least, his crown of rejoicing forever; for the things which attract the eyes of mortals are not always the most valuable, while the little and despised assume at last the proportions of stars of the first magnitude. Of one thing, however, we may be sure: nothing shall be lost, for God will group together in that day love and labors, toil and triumphs, and out of these shall come 'a large reward.'

"Who can tell how wide-extended is the work of his own hands? how potent for good! how capable of evil! But the time will come when he shall know. Ay, in advance he knows that this brings life, while that brings only death. Yet eternity alone shall reveal the length, and breadth, and depth, and height, of all his doings. In the final summing up, when life is under divine inspection, when character and work shall be thrown together into the crucible, may there come forth immortality and a crown! J. S. GILLETT.

"San Marcos, Texas, June 3, 1881."

CHAPTER XLV.

In the fall of 1878 the Conference was held at San Marcos, and Mr. Potter was sent to the Mason and Brady Mission, with the Rev. I. K. Waller as junior preacher, and the Rev. W. T. Thornberry presiding elder, and there were two able local preachers in the bounds of the mission—the Revs. J. D. Worrell and J. T. Williams. Mr. Worrell settled there twenty years ago, when all that frontier was a vast wilderness, and has aided in planting and cultivating the Church amid all the extreme hazards of those early days, and is now almost a necessity in Zion's field. He is a merchant, and still preaches along the border. He is fast ripening for that golden harvest-day when angel reapers shall gather in the ripened sheaves. As he says in his letter, to heaven it is hoped he shall be gathered into that eternal garner. The Rev. Mr. Williams is a lawyer, but he is likewise a faithful minister of Christ, and during this year he did great service in aid of I. K. Waller, who, after the opening of spring, was left alone on the mission, as will be seen.

The mission was a hundred miles from Mr. Potter's home. The long winter's travel, and camping out on the cold earth, in the norther's chilling blast, caused his health to decline; and the mission was poor, and the appropriation small; so it was discovered that, all in all, the two preachers could not get a support. Mr. Waller being a single man and a good preacher, Mr. Potter's health threatening, and the charge so far from his home, Mr. Thornberry, the presiding elder, excused him from the work the rest of the year, except to attend the camp-meetings and the quarterly-meetings, and to keep an account of the work, and report to the Annual Conference, which he did.

Mr. Waller did a good work, with the help of the local brethren just mentioned, and left the Church in a growing condition. In the meanwhile, Mr. Potter traveled largely as an evangelist, and held many gracious meetings with his brethren almost all over the Conference. He spent several weeks with his devoted friend, the Rev. T. G. Wools, in the town of Goliad, preaching to large, interested congregations, and had an interesting time indeed. Here some liberal friends contributed generously to his support.

The reader will remember that old Goliad is of historic fame. There the lamented Fannin and his brave men fell under the rage of Mexican cruelty. It is now denizened with an intelligent, virtuous, and generous class of enterprising citizens, having large and prosperous churches, with one of the finest schools in the West, under the presidency of Professor Brooks, a teacher of unexcelled notoriety. The Methodist church there is the finest in the West, and it is one of the best stations in the Conference. It is honored with one of the very best stewards the writer has ever met. He is a lawyer and an efficient steward. All finances are kept to the front, not allowed to lag behind. M. M. Shive's name will find a record in the page of Goliad Methodism. Among this noble people Mr. Potter spent those several pleasant weeks, and after many long, prosperous journeys among his brethren that summer and fall, he repaired to the Mason and Brady Mission, and adjusted matters for the closing year, and then went up to the Conference at Gonzales with a good report from the mission and his evangelical tours at large.

It was now evident to the ruling spirits that the border-work was so extended that a new district was a necessity, and that the same necessity pointed to Mr. Potter as the man for the place. Accordingly, he received the appointment as presiding elder on the newly-formed Mason District. Immediately after the publication of the appointment his numerous friends hailed it with delight, and freely expressed a sense of gratitude to the Conference for conferring an honor so long deserved on their zealous pioneer minister, who had so often put his life at peril for their religious edification. Dr. Jacob West, of Boerne, a member of the Baptist Communion, no sectarian in an offensive sense, a neighbor and friend to Mr. Potter, for the sake of his merits, published in the *Union Land Register*, a weekly sheet printed in Boerne, his grateful emotions on learning of his promotion, at the same time touching some salient points of merit in the career of Mr. Potter, a copy of which we here furnish the reader:

Rev. H. A. Graves:—I herewith send you the *Union Land Register*, containing my article about the Rev. A. J. Potter, as you request. Please return it. Jacob West, M.D.
Boerne, May 9, 1881.

This communication is headed "Elder A. J. Potter." The prefix, "Elder," is the Baptist *cognomen* for their pastors.

ELDER A. J. POTTER.

Editor Union Land Register:—We are commanded in the Holy Scriptures to love God with all our heart, and our neighbor as ourselves. In accordance with this principle, we feel as much rejoiced at the success of our neighbor as if we had shared in his good fortune. The Rev. A. J. Potter held on Saturday and Sunday last his first quarterly-meeting and conference, with the Church in Boerne, since his promotion to the important position of presiding elder. He performed the duties of his new office in a manner that reflected credit to himself and gave general and pleasant satisfaction to all the parties concerned. Energy, and executive capacity, and financial ability, are three very important and requisite qualities possessed by our new elder in a remarkable degree. In proof of his energy and untiring zeal, we have but to refer to the difficulties, dangers, and tribulations over which he has come out more than conqueror, throughout his vast and rugged field of labor, on the frontier of civilization. In proof of his executive capacity, we need only point to the order and Christian harmony that he has brought up out of chaos and moral insubordination. The Churches and Sabbath-schools which have sprung up in his field of labor will stand as more lasting monuments of his efforts in the cause of moral reformation and pure Christianity than would piles of marble or monuments of brass. And as to his financial ability, we need only refer to the fact that, notwithstanding his duties have required that his entire time should be devoted to his work, and notwithstanding the small pittance in the way of pecuniary compensation, he has managed to keep his home, and raise a large family of children, and is giving them a pretty fair chance to acquire the rudiments of an English education. He can fully appreciate the advantages of a liberal education, because in his youth he did not enjoy that blessing. We have known the Elder for several years as a citizen, preacher, and neighbor, and take pleasure in stating that in every position in life his honesty and integrity have never been questioned. We were much rejoiced when we heard that a simple act of justice had been done; that his services had been appreciated, and the honors, responsibilities, and duties of the eldership were conferred upon him, not because of his great fluency of speech, nor for his powers of elocution and oratory, but because of his great individual merit, his personal worth, and his useful life. The time will come when the correct history of Methodism in the frontier counties of Western Texas will be written. Then the life and work of the humble and indefatigable pioneer of the cross will stand forth in bold relief—the trials, troubles, and dangers, the struggles with poverty at home, as well as the many narrow escapes from the wild beasts of the forest, and the more subtle and unrelenting foe, the savage Indian. His life so far has been full of thrilling incidents, worthy of collection and commemoration by the Methodist Church, in making the slow but sure steps that Christianity and civilization have made in those Western wilds, through sorrow and pain, through fire and blood. But under all circumstances A. J. Potter has kept aloft the banner of the cross—has preached Jesus Christ and him crucified to a lost and dying world. JACOB WEST.

That letter contains a hearty and deserved commendation of the life and character of Mr. Potter, which we have striven to render legible in these pages. Integrity, zeal, promptitude, valor, firmness, piety, cheerfulness, kindness, and hospitality, are all portrayed; but we place a higher estimate on his pulpit talent than that letter would seem to award him — usually above mediocrity, but often grand and lucidly brilliant, when an encouraging prospect promises good results. Dr. West is always closely worked in his medical profession, and does not often enjoy the privileges of the sanctuary, and seldom anywhere else has he heard Mr. Potter, except at Boerne, a German town, where Protestant congregations are small, and not many flattering hopes of a harvest of good results. To preach under such conditions is often like getting up precipitous cliffs, and rugged at that. Out at camp and quarterly-meetings, where anxious crowds gather about the preacher to hear his message, is like putting a new pair of wings to the soul of the preacher; then Mr. Potter is often powerfully grand in handling sacred truth. Mr. West truthfully states that his name shall occupy a prominent place in the history of Methodism on this frontier-zone of two hundred and fifty miles. His name must come first and last.

CHAPTER XLVI.

Mr. Potter visited a military post on the frontier. At these posts little towns spring up by citizens settling near them for trading purposes, and gambling men, who follow no other profession, gather there to gain a living by their skill in the use of dice or cards. These men sometimes number nearly a hundred about such towns, and when "pay-day" arrives with the soldiers these shrewd gamers have a harvest-time in winning the wages of the poor soldier. They constituted a large portion of the hearers when Mr. Potter would preach at such places, and for the most part were quiet, orderly men in society, in daylight. At this time and place one of their number had died, and just as they were about to start to the grave for interment they heard of the arrival of the preacher, who was a reformed gambler, and they sent a messenger after him to perform the burial service. Finding him, the messenger said, "One of our men has died, and we are ready to put him away under ground, but we don't like to bury him as a dog: can't you come and give him a kind of religious send-off?" The preacher accompanied him. It was early twilight when they reached the grave, and as it was a solemn hour, and a good time to impress moral truths on the minds of that singular crowd, after the usual ritualistic ceremonies he delivered a serious lecture to them over the grave of their fallen associate in the forbidden walks of life. He told them that "the life of every man may be compared to a river rising in obscurity, increasing by the accession of tributaries, and, after flowing through a longer or shorter distance, losing itself in some common receptacle. The lives of individuals also, like the courses of rivers, may be more or less extensive, but will all, sooner or later, vanish and disappear in the ocean of eternity. Whilst a stream continues within its banks it fertilizes, enriches, and improves, the regions through which it flows; but if it deserts its channel it becomes injurious and destructive, a sort of public nuisance; and by stagnating into pools, or lakes, or wet marshes, it diffuses pestilence and death all along its way. Some rivers glide away into obscurity, while others become celebrated, traverse continents, give names to countries, and set boundaries to empires; some are tranquil and gentle in their course, while others rush forward in torrents, dash over precipices, terminating in frightful cataracts, which pour down their foaming liquid into the hurrying stream below. But, however diversified their characters, or in whatever direction they may wind their tortuous channels, all their diversified waters eventually mix in the vast oceans.

"Men are born, and live, and die, in different countries. They follow various trades and occupations: some are beneficial, others are hurtful; some reach altitudes in fame, some remain in the degraded vale; but all meet in the common grave—

'dust to dust, earth to earth.' Here all meet—the great, the small—good and evil fall into the gloomy grave. It shall be well with the righteous, but ill with the wicked. Our dead bodies shall arise to live again. Time shall end, the last day shall come, and night shall be no more. The voice of Jehovah and the archangel's trump shall speak to the dead in their long sleep, and awake them to life. Then too shall this stranger rise up again, while all the ages shall deliver up their fallen millions, to meet the great Judge, who shall deal justice to men."

How grand and solemn the night-scene at the fresh grave! The cold, pale body encoffined there, is soon to be lowered to its last resting-place in the earth's silent mansion, and there hid in darkness till all the ages have passed. Night's dismal shades mantle the earth, while all the distant stars seem to stand far off in their deep blue homes and gaze steadily down on the gloomy crowd. There stands the preacher and the sad listeners, while a cloud of witnesses look down on the melancholy group from the battlements of the brighter heaven; but among that happy celestial throng can there be a kindred one viewing that dismal grave, and the crest-fallen band about it? Then might immortal friends weep over the ruin of dear ones here. But no; celestial saved ones may see the doom of related spirits, as Abraham saw the fate of Dives, but they have no tears to shed.

Here we are reminded that religion is the last hope of man. However far he may tread the path of sin, he desires the light of religious hope to shine on the end thereof. The mantle of her charity must spread over his grave, and the glory of her hopes must illumine the other shore. How wicked soever he may have been in life, and though no penitent tear may have moistened his dying eye, yet the minister of religion must plant the sprig of her cheering hopes at the head of the sinner's tomb. "Can't you," said his living companion in vice, "give him a *religious send-off?* we hate to bury him as a dog." Poor, sinful man! The minister may shroud him in Christianity's ritualistic robe, but he cannot clothe the sin-stained spirit with that garment made white only in "the blood of the Lamb."

Inconsistent, ungrateful reader, you spend your life in the service of an enemy to Jesus, then ask him to help you in the dying hour. You want a sinful life, but a religious death; and when your poor, dead body can no longer be the medium of evil, you want the minister of Jesus, in form, to coronate your soul with the pure in celestial climes.

Long years ago we read the Life of the great Arabian prophet, Mohammed. We remember that the author treated the prophet of Mecca as truly a great man, in evidence of which he referred to his power over the vast tribes of Arabian Desert wanderers; how he chained them, in innumerable crowds, sitting on the desert-sands for hours, listening to his forcible logic on the thesis of the being and the unity of God. He planted that faith deep in their rude natures, and led them, with the bloody sword, in its defense and propagation. When silent multitudes sat in deep meditation on the wonders of theism, he pointed them to the floating clouds under the great firmament, the storm-winds sweeping over the arid deserts, the lightning's fiery flash along the face of the skies, the thunder's deafening roar in its cloudy empire, and the great earth, with its mighty oceans, hung out in open space, as being the work of the God he preached to them, the All-powerful One who had called him to be his prophet.

Transcribing the simple story of our heroic preacher, standing at the head of the gambler's grave, telling that melancholy group of gamblers the doctrines of One greater than Mohammed, while night's dark mantle shrouded the earth and enveloped the tomb, we thought of his strange power over men—wicked, desperate, daring men—men of many languages, and of life-long evil habits, who would attend his ministry, and keep good order while he talked of sin and its final results, and told them of Him who was slain as their ransom from sin and its fearful issues; and when in solemn train they bear one of their number to his mausoleum, they want him to spread out a Christian mantle over the place of his dark repose. *Strange power! wonderful man!* In putrefaction, there the salt is needed most.

Many a lorn mother knoweth not where sleepeth the dust of her roving son—whether in the deep, or on the shore; whether on the mountain, or in the vale; whether with the dead, in battle slain, or in the desert-solitude; whether beside the pious saint, where celestial angels keep their vigils over the quiet dust, or with the fallen wicked, where ghastly demons hold domain. Earth's cold bosom is one vast charnel-house, and its surface-sands are mixed with the dust of dead life. Friends and enemies, acquaintances and strangers, the rich, the poor, the evil and the good, all return to our common mother.

It is a sad thought to be entombed under-ground, covered up deep in the cold earth. The thought produces a smothering sensation in the living mortal. But to be buried with a band of wicked strangers, where no tie but a common dust binds in sympathy the unconscious dead, is sad indeed; but ah! to be laid away in the dark vault dug in the ground, while the earth is all draped in night—emblem of despair—is more than sad.

The death and burial of Moses is full of the poetry of grief, the weeping sublime, though God and angels were there.

The bright, shining lights of religious ceremonials spread over the graves of the sinful do not dispel the night of eternal despair which hovers there. Life-throbbing hearts grow faint at the view of a lone grave, or one thronged by those that fall in sin, and sleep without hope. O let me not go where the godless dwell in haunts of vice, nor give me a place of rest among their dead! Bury me not in the wide, deep seas, nor shroud me in the tall, tangled weeds which in submarine forests grow, where the huge, unseen monsters of ocean roam; nor hide me in the shallow sand-bars, where the wild, dashing storm-waves may sweep over my cold head; nor cover me with the white shells on the lonely shore, where foot of man never treads, where naught but the untamed sea-bird and the foam of the mad wave may visit my grave. No, no! not on the distant mountain, piled into the skies, let me sleep, where tempest-driven clouds may mantle my grave, and the angry lightning's fiery fist may smite the face of my tomb; nor under the lone oak, in the prairie wilderness, make me a grave, where the timid wild deer may nip the green grass around the verge of my solitary home, where silent solitude reigns alone—silence so intense that the living can hear its oppressed breathings. Not there, not there, let me sleep alone; nor yet in the gloomy vale put me to rest, where night's deepest gloom robes the earth, and winter's bleak winds may sigh around my bed. But near the home of my childhood, beside those I love, let me repose, until the heavens be no more.

CHAPTER XLVII.

In order to give the reader an accurate idea of Mr. Potter's grade of ministerial talent and pulpit style, we copy a sermon from his own manuscript. While giving it a careful reading, remember that it is the production of a man who really learned to read and write his mother-tongue after marriage, and, we believe, after he joined the Church; and ponder in your mind the power of religion to elevate men, and the fertile adaptability of Mr. Potter's Church to develop character. Some of her ablest pulpit men were taken from humble spheres in life, and some from the lower haunts of vice. Mr. Potter's written sermon does not inherit much of his pulpit peculiarities, which render him at once unique, interesting, attractive, and successful almost everywhere. Potter's thoughts, in their self-mode of syntactical construction, are seen in the written sermon, but heart and visible manner are mostly absent. The living fire is not so sensibly felt burning the heart of the reader as the hearer listening to the same truths uttered by a tongue enlivened by a heart thrilling under the enkindling of celestial fires. Those heart-fires have touched the dry stubble of all this frontier mountain-world, leaving a clean surface for the uprising and rapid growth of a new crop of better things. Following is the sermon:

A PLEA FOR THE BIBLE.

"Thy word is truth." John xvii. 17.

Among the distinguishing features of the present age, which shall mark its history with imperishable glory, is the struggle at this moment pending, with no dubious prospects, between moral light and darkness. An immense mass of talent, of learning, and of hallowed benevolence, is on the march of conquest. The grand national institution, the American Bible Society, now hoary with the ceaseless work of an age against vice and the moral ignorance of the world, has expanded its field of operations with a degree of rapidity unknown to former generations. Moral enterprise has attained in our country a magnitude and a boldness which cannot be viewed by any inquiring and observing mind without the deepest interest. Nor can it be denied that the spring which has given this new impulse to the human heart is the Christian faith. The glorious gospel of the blessed God claims the exclusive honor of all the highest virtues and the purest happiness which have sprung up along the path of the benevolent works of the more modern ages. The history of the world affords no other instance of similar exertions to diffuse the influence of any other religion. That of the Arabian impostor was indeed widely spread, but with a zeal as fierce as its pretensions were groundless. Like a stream of melted lava, it marked its course with desolation. Its baleful influence on the highest interest of man, morally and politically, needs no other witness than the Mohammedan empire in Turkey, as it now exists. The religion of Jesus Christ bears no sword but the sword of the Spirit, the word of God; it carries no torch but the light of truth; its conquests correspond with its pretensions; its "fruits are love, joy, peace, long-suffering, gentleness, goodness, and faith." The efforts now in progress to ameliorate the character and the condition of our race are of the highest authority. They are in strict accordance with the apostolic precepts and examples. They are humble imitations of Him who, in the midst of all the discouragements that human depravity could oppose to his labors, went about doing good. It might be expected that in a system of benevolent operations grounded on the conviction of the divine authority and inspiration of the sacred volume, one distinguishing branch would be the circulation of the Bible itself; and it is so. Christians have derived from it a maxim, felt to be true by every regenerated human heart, that "Faith cometh by hearing, and hearing by the word of God;" and all experience proves that wherever men bid the heavenly messenger welcome, and give ear to its sacred announcements, there a great and effectual door is opened for the introduction of all that is ennobling to man.

It may be that the reader's mind may have remained until this hour void of any heart-felt interest in that book. Your neglect of it may be some secret sentiment which sinks its value in your eyes; yet you may possess candor and penetration. Permit me, therefore, to entreat your attention to a brief consideration of the claims of that volume. We propose, first, that it is an original production.

The antiquity of the Old Testament reaches upward to an age that yields no other authentic record of man's existence. Its language and all its allusions and references to the ancient world attest its origin to be as remote as the date which it bears; and it comes to us with this singular attestation of its genuineness, as well as of its great antiquity, that the very nation in whose language it was written still exists, and still cultivates and keeps up a knowledge of that same language. Can this be said of any other volume of great antiquity? On this ground, then, it argues a powerful claim, even upon the curiosity of every intelligent mind.

Secondly, the scope of the Bible is vast and unparalleled. It commences with the dawn of time and the birth of nature, and closes with the expiration of both. It colors all its representations with the light of eternity. Here we are invited to study a chart which marks out the whole plan of divine arrangement for our world. Precepts are given to regulate human action; promises, to invite obedience; terrors, to prevent transgression; and examples, to confirm all. It is true that these oracles are a dark and bewildering labyrinth to the eye that casts but hasty glances over their pages; and so are the starry heavens, where, nevertheless, to the eye of the astronomer, there shines a universe of wonders, holding their stations and tracing their silent courses with a harmony as marvelous as their great immensity. In like manner the word of God reveals its glories only to the ardent eye of faith. Nor do we exaggerate its richness or its depth in affirming its supreme efficiency as an instructor. It rewards the studious and upright mind with valuable knowledge more rapidly and richly than any other department of human research.

Thirdly, the Bible stands unrivaled as a work of *tastes.* In a work comprising so many detached and distinct compositions, written in far-distant ages, it were natural to expect variety; and, perhaps, the greater part of acute readers might look for some things below the level of a refined criticism. But this volume abides the most vigorous scrutiny, and stands unshaken amid the fiercest attacks of hostile genius and learning. A taste enlightened to discover its legitimate objects, able to divest itself of prejudice, and refined without perversion to fastidiousness, will find in this book its highest gratification. If genuine poetry has power to attract, and fix, and captivate the soul, we surely have it here. The fourteenth chapter of the Prophet Isaiah, Psalms xviii., lxviii., cxviii., and likewise the prophecies of Nahum, and the Lamentations of Jeremiah, may be given as vivid examples. If the sublime in description yields the highest of intellectual pleasures, it is found in the same sacred volume. On the first page we read, "God said, Let there be light, and there was light." Near its close it is said, "I saw a great white throne, and Him that sat upon it, from whose face the heavens and the earth fled away." As a few other instances, amidst a multitude of others I might mention, I point you to the fortieth chapter of Isaiah and the first chapter of the marvelous Apocalypse: of the moral and sublime we have examples here that utterly defy description — Joseph, Daniel, and the great lawgiver of Israel; the chief apostle, who, with every endowment desirable to man, gloried only in the cross—these and many others nobly suited to awaken emulation, as their moral dignity is worthy to raise our astonishment. In this connection we but name the "Author and Finisher of our faith." The discerning student of history observes numerous traits of excellence in that of the Bible. Moses, and Luke, and the penman of the Book of Joshua, perhaps, afford the fairest models; and no other narratives communicate truth with such simplicity and power as the Sacred Scriptures. Eloquence being the language of nature addressed to the heart, and adapted to the circumstances of man, history without it would lose half its charms. Passing, then, the flights of David and of Isaiah, let the man of genuine feeling and real candor compare the plea of Judah before Joseph, his brother, with the best-wrought specimens of classic antiquity, and he will pronounce the dying complaint of Dido, and the lamentations of Pantheia, cool and harsh in the comparison; or draw the parallel between masters of eloquence, and the result is the same—the Bible looms above all. While Cicero trembles before the armed enemies of Milo, and loses the cause of his client; while Demosthenes flies before the invader of Greece, Paul, arraigned and fettered as an outlaw at the feet of a wicked judge, shakes that judge on his throne, and almost persuades the proud, licentious Agrippa to be a Christian. Much more might be added on this topic, but we desist. It may

be thought that we owe an apology to the Church
of God for bringing the oracles of heaven at all to
the bar of human taste. Our design is to neutralize
a portion of the venom which ignorance and
infidel prejudice have cast into the sources of human
conviction. Beyond this limit we dare not go.

The excellency of the Holy Scriptures cannot be
fully appreciated by the rules of human criticism.
As well might we think of judging of the proportions
of the celestial arch, or the location of the
stars in the vast expanse, by the rules of architecture.
The word of God, like his works, is on a plan
too vast, too sublime, too profound, to be measured
by the feeble intellect of man.

Fourthly, the sacred volume approaches the conscience
with a dilemma of unspeakable interest on
its very front. The book before the reader must be
true or false. If true, it is what it claims to be—an
inspired revelation from the God of the universe;
and if so, its information and its dictates are of infinite
importance to the whole world of mankind.
It puts each individual upon his trial for eternity
by a divinely-prescribed mode of faith and consequent
course of action. But if not true, it leaves
man in a darkness more dismal than the grave. His
origin and his final destination are alike involved
in a cloud which man without the Bible has never
been able to dissipate. For peace amidst the evils
of this state he is driven to his own resources; for
hope he has no rational foundation left him; on
moral questions no appeal can be reasonably made
to the higher principles of human action, for no

tribunal is found to distribute accurate and adequate rewards and punishments, no judge is known who has power to carry retributions beyond the sphere of this life. With this question before him in an unsettled state, and with the strongest probabilities against him, can any man safely neglect to search the Holy Scriptures? Is it safe, is it agreeable to the common sense of mankind in earthly matters to treat a question of such fearful import with indifference? At the best, such a procedure is more unwise than the blind homage rendered by the heathen to the superstitions of their fathers.

Fifthly, the authenticity of the Bible is unquestionable at the bar of sound reason. Our limits confine us to a space unworthy of the argument. But our design being simply and affectionately to invite attention to the highest of all interests, we remark that the Christian religion, as contained in the New Testament and sanctioned by the Old, is strikingly fitted to the state of mankind. There is a feeling of guilt connatural to man. It has originated more than half of the idolatrous rites and customs of the heathen world. For this the gospel offers in the atonement of Jesus Christ an ample remedy—a balm which leaves no wound unhealed, no terror unsubdued. There is also a depravity in human nature which has ever defied all human restraints. Like a restless torrent that rushes over all the barriers thrown across its course, it has never been checked. Man's native depravity has descended from age to age, mocking every effort he has ever devised to arrest its progress. But for this vast evil the Bible offers a sure remedy in the hallowed effusions of the Holy Spirit; and if our world exhibits a scene of misery which has widened and darkened with the progress of its population, the religion of Christ furnishes a principle that dwells in the heart, and from thence puts forth an influence which deprives Misery of its keen edge, and Death himself of his poisoned sting. In addition to these peculiar virtues, the gospel possesses the unrivaled advantage of a perfect adaptation to all the gradations of human society. Far from disturbing the order of social life in any essential point, it defines the duties of each relation, commands denial of every disorganizing passion, and diffuses through the whole mass of human feeling a prevailing humanity. The external evidences of the truth of the Sacred Scriptures are as complete as the nature of the case requires. The miracles of Moses and of Christ were designed as credentials of a divine mission. For this end their fitness is seen in their admirable accordance with the character of God, merciful and just; as also in their immediate tendencies toward the benefit of man. This last quality marks every miracle recorded of the Son of God. All were directed either to the spiritual advantage, the mental comfort, or the bodily relief, of human beings. Not one is beneath the sacred character ever sustained by their divine Author. Those miracles were recorded by eye-witnesses, whose testimony has been preserved and corroborated by an unbroken chain of other competent evidence to the present hour. Prophecy is a species of proof which grows stronger with the lapse of ages. It challenges investigation. It presents its records to mankind along with the pages of history, upbraids their thoughtlessness and condemns their unbelief, while it fain would win them to conviction of its claims to truth.

The Christian Church could not so long have existed on a foundation of fable and fiction. Baptism and "the Supper of the Lord" both testify the verity of the gospel history as clearly as the London Monument points to the calamity it was erected to commemorate; and all the Jewish people are distinguished from all other nations by the very peculiarities described and predicted in both Testaments. They are found in the four quarters of the globe, yet have no political power in any one region. They bear with them through all dispersions the very Scriptures which condemn their unbelief, and the prejudices which hold them in spiritual blindness. A process of extermination the most terrible ever tried on any nation has been tried on them by the most potent empires of the world, and still they live and increase, and they still are Jews in spite of all efforts which have been employed to amalgamate them with other nations.

View the aspect of society wherever you may, where the religion of Jesus Christ prevails in its simplicity and power, in proportion to its prevalence you will find whatsoever things are true, and honest, and just, and pure, and lovely, and of good report, to prevail; and in the same ratio those vices which arise from corrupt appetites and passions, which lead with fatal certainty to misery and degradation, are unknown; there the virtues, the arts, and the sciences, which bless and adorn life, spring up and flourish. Man without ambition attains the maximum of earthly happiness, while every blessing is heightened and every sorrow is mitigated by the cheering prospect of eternity.

England's Christian Queen has said that the Bible is the secret of her kingdom's greatness. Bible Christianity has given the world its schools, colleges, and universities. Most of the great authors during eighteen centuries have reverenced the Bible. The libraries of the civilized world are burdened with the learned and useful works of Christian men. Only a few men of high talent have rejected the Bible. Their works fill but a small place in the world's book-case; their unread volumes lie in earth's great museums as the bones of the dead in the unvisited catacombs; while the vast catalogue of learned and able defenders of the Bible enumerate into the thousands. A long line of poets, philosophers, historians, linguists, statesmen, scientists, and other distinguished men, have left to us their exalted estimates of the imperishable value of the Bible.

There is a fact which involves both the truth and divinity of the Bible—a fact which is the more important as it combines all the external with the experimental evidence. No instance can be given where a real believer in Jesus Christ denied the faith in his last hours. At a period of our existence so solemn, so honest, and so awful, when the soul is very often found in all the vigor and clearness of self-possession, then, if ever, man displays the interior of his character. While there the ungodly have, in thousands of instances, honestly bewailed with their dying breath a life spent without having secured a saving interest in the Redeemer. Why must the Christian alone be suspected of insincerity when with his last breathings he triumphs in his Saviour's glorious grace? These facts, we boldly affirm, would be not only unaccountable, but impossible, if truth did not form the basis of the Christian's hopes. This argument acquires additional strength from those examples of sorrow and regret where dying Christian's deplore their unfaithfulness. They never bewail their past attachment to the faith, nor their firm obedience to the precepts of the gospel; nor do they exhibit fears that the realities of eternity shall detect falsehood at the foundation of their faith. They sorrow only for failures which have shortened their attainments in the divine life. If any fears disturb the peace of their last moments, they arise from thoughts of personal unfaithfulness.

But a book professedly delivered to man for the high purpose of regenerating his nature must possess some peculiar energy equal to the greatness of the design. This property must be something distinct from those qualities which meet the admiration of the scholar or the natural sympathies of the heart. It is certain that neither the venerable origin of the Bible, nor its boundless scope, nor its transcendent beauties, nor its overpowering evidence, nor all these combined, are alone sufficient to work a permanent change in the moral nature or structure of the heart. No pleasures of tastes, no amusements drawn from speculation, can in a spiritual sense enlighten the eyes or rejoice the heart, much less convert the soul. If such only were the sources of spiritual illumination, faith, and holiness, then indeed might the triumphs of grace be few, and the believer might weep over a world of unlettered and uncultivated souls placed under the ban of a hopeless rejection. But God has "magnified his word above all his name." His own image and superscription are impressed on the sacred page in characters of moral energy which nothing but experience can interpret or discern; and when seen, it penetrates and settles into a firm conviction of divine truth, which no attacks of sophistry, however plausible, no temptation, however strong, can overturn. With such evidences to the learned and the unlearned, the wise and the simple, the great change to a true faith and a new life is the usual result—great, truly, in many respects, but mostly in the manifest presence of divine power in its accomplishment. Men who had become bitter in their enmity to the whole subject of religion have sometimes been prevailed on to peruse the word they utterly disbelieved, and the experiment has been followed by a soul-transforming faith; a heart hard and sensual has been softened and refined; an imagination unbridled and gross has been purified; a will altogether enlisted on the side of sin has been renewed, and the creature in an important sense has been "delivered from the bondage of corruption into the glorious liberty of the children of God."

Such, dear friends, are the reasons, by the statement of which we hope to secure your attention to the holy book of God. Let it not offend that we have proceeded thus far upon the supposition that you have hitherto failed to give that book a close perusal. Please turn again to the fourth topic of this subject, and reconsider what is there said. If you have neglected the sacred volume, weigh that argument, and acknowledge the neglect as an infinite risk sustained for no possible good; then sit down to the work with a firm resolution to know by actual experience its whole amount of truth, of beauty, and its transforming power. Minds endued with penetration equal to yours, hearts of equal candor, have wandered as long as you have traveled in paths of trackless uncertainty, and have been persuaded to seek, and have at last found, the path of peace.

We shall now try the weight of a few of the principal objections which have been urged against the Holy Scriptures. One thing which may take on some force with some minds is the supposition that the whole matter of revelation is an unsettled point, and that as long as it is so every one is at liberty to await the issue. We answer that the truth of the Bible has long since been settled, and every objection deserving refutation has been refuted. The confident air with which groundless cavils have been reiterated proves nothing but the ignorance and the malevolence which gave them birth, and which still labor to revive them. But, admitting the case undecided in the minds of nine-tenths of the human race, even that, were it real, would involve a probability of the strongest kind in favor of a system which was able to hold so high a ground after eighteen hundred years of unremitted conflict with all that is corrupt in human nature; and such a probability would render wholly inexcusable the levity, the indifference, or the worldliness, which prevents inquiry into the subject. As, however, the state of the evidence really is, no language can utter the folly of that fatal presumption which can venture the hazard of the issues of eternity upon a ground so frail.

Were Bible truths only matters of opinion, or objects of vague speculation, then with some show of propriety they might be left to those who might be moved by taste or curiosity to examine them; but they hold at stake the whole existence of man—not of one, but of all; nor yet all collectively, but each severally; and "how shall we escape if we neglect so great salvation?"

It is urged that the Bible has been opposed from the first by men of great talents, while its advocates have generally been in the humbler and plainer classes. Both parts of the statement might be true without affecting the slightest breach in our faith. If genius has assailed our religion, it cannot be denied that genius has also defended it, and that triumphantly. If Porphyry, Celsus, and Julian, attacked the cause of truth, did not Justin, Origen, and others, maintain their ground? If armies of modern infidels have been headed by chiefs of preeminent talent, bad indeed must be the cause which is falling into ruin in their hands. If no Newton, Bacon, Boyle, Locke, Johnson, Watson, Butler, Scott, nor Chalmers, had ever appeared to breast the fury of the foe, the Bible, we doubt not, would have remained unsubdued and uninjured on the field. Compare the loose and profligate lives of Voltaire and his satellites, Paine, and the libertinism of Hume, with the morality of their opponents; extend the antithesis through all the ranks of the opposing forces, and how then will the controversy stand? Just where it has stood for more than a thousand years, with this exception, that the attacks of infidelity appear more and more in their real character. They are truly the rage of impotence against omnipotence, a struggling of depravity and vice to assume dominion over the universe.

The Bible is often reproached by its enemies as being a contrivance of an artful priesthood to serve their own interest at the expense of the rest of mankind. That reproach is as absurd as it is malignant. It supposes a conspiracy to have been carried on for three thousand and five hundred years. It imputes at the same time to these conspirators the greatest acuteness and the utmost stupidity. To frame such a scheme they must have infinitely surpassed all the world in talent, yet so blind to their darling object as to sentence themselves without reprieve to a life of hardships, opposition, and toil; for such is the general lot of the Christian ministry on the earth.

Again, it is given as a suspicious mark that the

doctrines of the Scriptures are so perpetually in the field of public controversy. We admit the fact, but we deny the conclusion. The matters in controversy among real Christians affect not the vital truths of the gospel. Divisions of this nature only prove that human judgments are fallible; that believers are not perfectly conformed to the spirit of their calling, and that the truth as they view it in the mirror of revelation—as being of divine origin—is the foundation of their faith, and the object of their fondest hopes. Meanwhile, the spirit of controversy contracts its sphere just in proportion as Christians advance in vital godliness. As their hearts approach Him who is the source of all illumination, they draw nearer to each other. Let the objector collect the sentiments and creeds of all the contending parties in the real Church of Christ, and compare them with the Holy Scriptures. He will find amidst all their diversities of opinions but one mind in regard to the grounds of the great Christian scheme. In their views of the corrupt and perishing state of man, the way of access to God by a Divine Mediator, the exclusive efficacy of his obedience unto death as the foundation of the sinner's pardon and acceptance, and the regeneration of the believer by the Holy Spirit—on these and many other cardinal points all true Christians are " of one heart and of one soul."

My brethren, preach the word. In it is your glorious commission to seek and to save the lost. Be filled, be fired with the enkindlings of the spirit of that great commission. May you, may the Church, may all of us who feel the force of that divine word, be more and more filled with the glorious object of the recovery of immortal spirits to the lost image of God, and guide the perishing to an almighty Saviour! May the Spirit be poured out from on high until the whole Church shall see and feel that these facts are now of chief importance! Man is lost, and the Son of God is seeking him to save him from his sins. He is lost, and the Church is commissioned to go forth in the might of faith and prayer to invite him to salvation. We often talk of it as children talk of the affairs of empires. We see through a glass darkly. Our conceptions are low and limited. "To save the lost!" tell, ye ruined spirits, what it means! tell us, Son of God, what it means! What stirred thy soul in godlike compassion to seek the lost? Tell us, ye ransomed and ye faithful spirits who never have sinned, tell us! O Father, tell the Church! tell thy ministers until every slumberer awakes, and every energy be aroused, and the way of life be pointed out to a perishing world! The Bible, God's book divine, points out that way. As some broad, fortress-guarded channel, it leads safely into the haven of eternal repose. As the grand old rock fortress of Gibraltar, where for twelve hundred years its cannon-crowned brow has been the object of international envy, around it, from the days of the Saracens, the thunders of battle have roared. Africans, Arabs, Castilians, Moors, and Englishmen, have been its masters. But around the Bible, the citadel of Christian faith, the noise of conflict has rung more loudly and for a longer period. Yet it stands to-day in the possession of its Christian defenses. Infested by foes wearing the uniform of hate and badge of opposition, the Bible has held its own garrison, unharmed, in the citadels of the reason and the hopes of mankind, and as some tall cliff its radiant head is elevated to-day above the region of clouds and shadows. Eternal sunshine is on its brow. Imperishable book! The Bible! It has stood too as impregnable amidst the hostilities and surrounding disasters as the fabled pillars of Seth. Crucial tests have not impaired a chapter or invalidated a verse. The tears of silver-haired patriarchs continue to bedew its pages. The widow amid her poverty still reads its precious promises to her fatherless children. The troubled heart and sorrow-bowed head finds its divine covenants softer than the pillows of down on which wearied kings have rested their aching foreheads. The sick yet touch their spirit-lips to the crystal "waters of its river of life." Its pledges of a coming resurrection keep the graves of loved ones green, and have made the cemetery magnetic to surviving friends. The dying turn their closing eyes to it as their only lamp "through the valley of the shadow of death," and clasp it as their last treasure, while their fingers stiffen in the last ordeal. Old Sun, twin-brother of Time, thou wilt cease to shine as god of the day. Thou Moon, thy form will disappear from the night-draped sky. Lamps of ether, ye will drop into the emptiness of destined darkness. Old Bible, thou wilt survive infidelity, outlive criticism, and stand as an imperishable rampart—immortal, indestructible! The mission of infidelity is to undermine the most valuable hopes of man. Its ambition is to force him out into the moral wilderness of dreary speculation and dark uncertainty. Its highest achievement is to drug his sense of responsibility to God, and blind his vision as to eternal things, and invest his mind with wretchedness in this life. The Bible is his only star of hope in death's dark night.

CHAPTER XLVIII.

There is a county newspaper styled *The Quill*, published in Castroville, Texas, by a noted, witty editor, who is a special friend to Mr. Potter. There appearing several communications of an outright infidel type, Mr. Potter undertook to refute them. Quite a number of barefaced infidel correspondents appeared in *The Quill*, attacking Mr. Potter's defense of Christianity. We herewith copy one article, written over the *nom de plume* of "Bruno," and then give Mr. Potter's reply, to give the reader an idea of his polemic tact. We copy infidel "Bruno's" article first, and then give Mr. Potter's reply. It is headed,

PARSON POTTER PUNCTURED.

Parson Potter in his last letter to R. P. says, "We are on the defensive." Is that so? Did not Elder Cox, on April 1, write to your paper the article headed "Christ *vs.* Ingersoll?" Was not this the first letter that appeared in your paper? He opened this real controversy, and we infidels are on the defensive. We stood the abuses of Solon, Pythagoras, Socrates, Plato, and others. After that we had to be called fools by David, and dare not wince when your correspondents tell us that our love of sin, our love of self, makes us what we are—*i. e.*, infidels. We dare not acknowledge God for fear of punishment—*i. e.*, hell-fire and brimstone.

We never took up for the old heathen philosophers, but ask, What is good in old David? Did not that man after God's own heart assassinate husbands to get their wives? Read his highway robberies in Gath—his mutilation of the dead bodies to make a disgusting necklace for his first wife. Plenty of atrocities, brutalities, and cruelties we can produce; and if such a "saint" calls us fools, we think it is a proud honor, and not a disgrace. We know it is a custom of the parsons to digress at once from the logic of the infidels to their private character, and point, as Dr. Thornberry did, as the legitimate fruit of skeptical teaching.

Another brother of Parson Potter's undertakes to correct his last letter when he tells him, "Union is strength, and a house divided against itself cannot stand." How nice and smooth could all the sects dwell together if they chose to do so! Are all the Christian sects such a brotherhood as the parson paints them? He admits we differ, but our aim and intent is to reach precisely the same results; in short, all the Christian denominations are one harmonious unit.

If the picture drawn by our worthy parson would be so in reality, our Christian part of the globe would indeed be a garden of Eden. But lo! that unrelenting witness, History, steps in, and with facts, figures, and dates, proves the parson's idea to be fallacious. This unimpeachable witness proves that every sectarian is an intolerant partisan in religion. No wonder that we read in Luke, "If any man comes to me, and hates not his father and mother," etc., etc. Hence, the Jews were hated by the Christians, the pagans were hated by the Christians, the Greek Catholics hate the Roman Catholics, and both hate the Protestants, and the Protestants hate both of them; and the Episcopalians hate the Presbyterians, and the Methodists hate the Baptists, and Campbellites are hated by all the others, and they—the Campbellites—reciprocate the affections of all the others. A very harmonious unit.

Further it is proved, beyond a possibility of a doubt, by the facts of history, that whenever any faction of faith, by hook or crook, became possessed of the temporal power, it invariably used the State's strong arm—its dungeons, and racks, and fires—to put down rival denominations. There is not a solitary exception. Hence, I say, how is it possible that a faith that teaches and practices such peculiar doctrines, such hate and intolerance, can be worth one grain of sand to the human family? We still take history as the witness, and prove that religious fanaticism is so blind that it will wrangle, fight, kill, exterminate, put to the sword men, women, and children, and quote text after text to justify their atrocities. What Moses and Joshua did we all know (we infidels get the Bible by heart); but look at the thirty years' war, the Inquisition, the Cromwell butcheries in Ireland, the Puritan outrages in this country, etc. A fine set of sectarians they were! To the last they demand of us infidels, upon pain of eternal damnation, that we believe that such a religion is the corner-stone of civilization, and its fabled creator the prince of peace.

O faith! fanatic faith! once wedded fast
To some dear falsehood, hugs to the last.

BRUNO.

Medina County, Sept. 15, 1880.

Such was the mess of slander Mr. "Bruno" published to the world as the legitimate fruits of a pure Christianity, and styles the immaculate Son of God a fabled character. To this tissue of false logic and sophistry Mr. Potter replies. The infidel editor heads his article as follows:

PARSON POTTER'S POLEMIC.

An Avalanche of Scripture from the Fighting Parson—Defense of Christians—A Scathing Reply to "Bruno"—The Parson pulls off his gloves and goes for the Unrighteous—Madame Roland and Liberty talked about—Sound Advice to Doubters.

EDITOR QUILL:—A writer over the signature of "Bruno" enlightens the readers of *The Quill*, in a late number, on the subject of Christianity. This writer is quite pretentious; knows, he says, the Bible by heart; and quotes, or rather misquotes, History too, as though he claimed to know it all by heart. How aptly he illustrates in himself the character described by the Apostle Paul in Romans, where he says that in professing wisdom they became fools!

His denunciations of the Christian system and its followers in all ages are general—no exceptions are made. The blessed gospel of peace is, in his view, a gospel of pure hate. The teachings which declare love to God and our fellow-men, and the Golden Rule of doing unto others as we would that they should do unto us—these, and such as are fundamental in Christianity, make no impression on his mind. In speaking of Christians everywhere, he declares that persecution is the rule, and tolerance not even an exception—that all denominations cordially hate each other.

To answer such a writer is simply to quote his tirade. Every man of candor or sense will condemn his palpable misrepresentations. Such a man as he cannot reason; his mind is all darkness; he is a fit representation of his father—the original, Simon-pure accuser of the brethren, as seen in Revelation, where it is said that the accuser of the brethren is to be cast down.

That individual Christians are faultless, no one pretends; that sects have sometimes been intolerant, no one denies; that crimes have been committed in the sacred name of religion, is admitted; and that David, and Solomon, and others named in the Scriptures, committed sins, the Bible itself reveals, and nobody conceals or justifies; but let me ask, What cause can guarantee the fidelity and purity of every man who espouses it? We all profess to love Liberty; it was our boast and our pride; we claim that we inherited the principle of constitutional liberty from our ancestors, and we hope to hand it down as a priceless legacy to our children; yet, have all the champions of freedom always been angels? Have not crimes been committed in the very name of that Constitution our fathers ordained? And is the sacred cause of Liberty to be abandoned because in Madame Roland's day, when blatant infidelity ruled the hour, she was constrained truthfully to exclaim, "O Liberty! what crimes are committed in thy name!"

Now, Mr. "Bruno," you are simply doing what many other sinners like you often do, permit me to say—that is, you simply deceive yourself; you know very little of the letter or history of Christianity; of its spirit you know nothing, and it is likely you never will. Of that immense army of devoted workers in our numerous literary and charitable institutions in our land—those monuments of Christian zeal and love—of truth, science, and enlightened progress—you take no notice; of the many churches in our great country; of the vast army of devoted toilers who go everywhere, teaching all men to do justly, love mercy, and walk humbly before God. See in Micah where it is said that that is what God requires of man.

Of these, and all of these, you know nothing, you see nothing. You perhaps see your models oftener in the saloon than in churches, and hence your power to criticise Christianity amounts simply to "find or forge a fault."

This is my answer to your tirade. I am not your enemy; I hate you not, but sincerely wish you well in this world and in the great "beyond." May you early learn that abuse is not argument or sense. Believe or disbelieve what you please, but you have no right to say to the world that Christians are, and always have been, bad men and women; nobody will believe it, nor do you believe it yourself. A. J. POTTER.

Mountain Home, Kendall County, Texas, Oct. 19, 1880.

Such a vile catalogue of false imputations against Christianity is not novel—it is hoary. The faults and mistaken zeal of ignorant zealots, and the crimes of false friends of religion, have been unjustly accredited to the pure doctrines and unsullied morals of the gospel of Jesus Christ; but, as the undimmed sparkle of the gems in the rough ore, they shine for themselves; they are pure, though all men be corrupt; they are true, if all men prove to be false; they commend themselves to the approving judgment and conscience of all minds where reason holds the scepter.

CHAPTER XLIX.

PROMINENT among the leading traits in the social character of Mr. Potter is his fondness for a witty joke among his brethren, at their great meetings on circuits, and districts, and at their annual convocations. He is fond of society; loves to talk; all the time merry and cheerful; never gloomy; not a trace of sadness in all his features. Time has not yet whitened his ebon locks, or corrugated a single feature in the plane of his ruddy, youth-like countenance. He enjoys a hearty good laugh at a good "take off," and a thrilling quiz. He is good at rejoinders and repartee. He has *many friends* and *few enemies.* Light and cheerful sunshine go where he goes, and he is always welcomed; and a shade of sadness gathers about the hall when he says "Good-by." At a late district-meeting, an æsthetic brother, in reading a report on the spiritual state of the Church, made an onslaught on the merry element in the Church, and arraigned the cheerful preacher for his share in the skinning tirade. Mr. Potter took it to himself, and shed tears over it. He was ever ready to own a fault when pointed out to him, and sometimes inclined to censure himself unduly in that line. If he was sometimes led near to the end of prudence in jesting, his brethren were also to be blamed therefor, as they would lead him into it by getting him to tell the funny events in his marvelous history, merely to have some interesting, innocent amusement at their infrequent comings-together. Dr. Walker, a member of the West Texas Conference, spent part of his younger life with the Cherokee and Choctaw Indian Nations, and is a dry humorist, and loves a good joke, and likes to see others laugh, though he does not laugh much himself. He is a great friend and admirer of Mr. Potter, and often spurs at him with his dry, sarcastic wit at the Annual Conference — the itinerant's jubilee—where and when, once in a year, he is allowed a few cheerful days of friendly greeting and merry joke-cracking with his brethren. The Nestor-doctor kept saying to Mr. Potter, at one annual session: "Potter, they say you are gifted in laughing. Potter, you must not laugh. Don't laugh, Potter. Come, now, try; be serious; put on dignity; be grave." Although it was said humorously, yet it was half in earnest. Mr. Potter tried to copy the staid counsel of his senior brother, but he made an awkward effort at "put-on." Unused to *affected* seriousness, his visage partook of the frightful, caricatured, woe-begone. Next morning was one of bright, Edenic loveliness, and the brethren were meeting and joyously greeting each other, when up walked Dr. Walker; and there sat Mr. Potter with his long puckered face, the comic almanac picture of grief. The Doctor caught sight of him, and said, "What is the matter with Potter?" Mr. Potter answered, "You said I must not laugh, and I am trying to pucker back against it." The veteran

Doctor saw that he was outwitted, and said, "Laugh, Potter — any thing but that frightful look." It is generally understood now that Mr. Potter was not born to walk under gloomy clouds, and the liberty of sunshine is allotted to him by mutual consent of saint and sinner. Weave no shading chaplet about the brow where beams of light love to glow.

Just here we give the reader a transcript of Mr. Potter's cheerful, humorous cast of mind. It is copied from the Texas *Christian Advocate*, giving an account of a visit to our great city of the West, San Antonio. It is there headed, "Potter's Peregrinations":

"I have for several years contemplated a visit to Galveston, but as I had never been in any thing like a large city, I had some misgivings about making the venture. I heard they were having some mighty big times in San Antonio, over railroad rackets and other new-fangled things, so I thought I would go down and take a few lessons in city doings. And one morning I hitched up my ponies and lit out for the city. I reached my destination at five o'clock P.M., and drove to a city hotel. I saw the word 'office' upon one door. I opened it, and a smiling-faced gentleman stepped out, took my baggage, and said, 'Come in, sir.' This courteous gentleman stepped around a counter and looked through a sort of window, over which was printed in large letters, 'Pay as you go.' And lying on a small desk, which seemed to turn on wheels, was a large book; with a quick motion he turned it, and handed me a pen. I stood for a moment, and said, 'Sir, the stage will not go up till to-morrow, and I will not write to my wife until morning.' 'Please register,' he said. But I told him I had registered about fifteen times since the war, and that the elections had all passed off without my vote being challenged, and I could not see any reason why I should register again. He said he only wanted me to write my name; so I wrote: 'To all whom it may concern: The undersigned is from Boerne, Kendall County, Texas. A. J. Potter.' This clever clerk seemed now to sympathize with me, and took me under his special care, and showed me everywhere I wanted to go. I passed the night quietly, arose early next morning, and found it was raining, which was a great drawback to my city explorations. Whilst sitting in the office waiting for breakfast, a boy came in with a bundle of papers under his arm, and handed me one, saying, 'Here is your morning *Express.*' I took the paper and began to read, the boy still standing there. I said, 'I will hand it back to you in a few minutes, sonny.' He said he sold them for five cents, and that he was waiting for the money. I told him that I would see the clerk. I was boarding at a dollar a day. I wonder if I have to pay extra for news? But as the gentleman was out at the time, I handed him the money. After breakfast I told the clever clerk that I had come to see the bigness of the city, and as it was raining I would have to get an excursion ticket on a street-car. He said I did not need a ticket—that one would be along directly, and he would point it out to me, and that I could just jump aboard, and it would be all right. So presently he said, 'Here it comes!' as he pointed to a great big wagon pulled by one little mule. So I boarded the thing, and found it pretty well crowded. 'Halloo,' said a well-known voice; 'here is old "Winchester" Potter.' I seated myself, and one of the passengers said, 'Mr. Potter, do you think the Jews, as a nation, will ever return to the balmy skies of their native Judea?' Slam, crash, went the thing off the track. Thinking I was gone, I cried out, 'Bill, tell my wife and children not to grieve.' I said, 'Halloo, driver, do you think there will be an explosion?' 'Explosion!' said he; 'did you ever know a mule to explode?' I soon found that I was more scared than hurt. 'Gentlemen,' said the driver, 'if you will all throw your dignity on the hind-part of this thing, we will soon be on the track again.' About this time several men walked up, who, so far as I knew, might have been the coroner and jury of inquest; but finding no corpse, they went to work, and soon we were moving again. The man said again, 'Mr. Potter, just as the car ran off I was asking about the return of the Jews.' I told him I did not think that they would ever get there if they had to go on street-cars. About that time a lank, thin-looking man, with a fine voice, said, 'Mr. Potter, do you think any of the heathen will get to heaven?' Slam, bang, went the thing off the track again. 'Bill,' said I, 'I guess I am gone this time; tell my wife she will find my horses and buggy at the Central, and bills paid; she will find my watch at Bell & Brother's, two dollars and twenty-five cents due.

Farewell!' I was soon conscious that I had not crossed the river Styx, by the vociferous swearing of one of the men, who seemed to have all the curse-words at his command. I approached the profane man, and said, 'Sir, you seem to be doing all the cursing for the crowd, and as I do n't swear here is twenty-five cents to pay my part.' He said he never charged preachers. I told him he had better not exhaust his stock of profanity, but to keep some on hand for the next occasion. He said he had a sufficient fund on hand to do for two more run-offs. One man swore he would take it on foot, and he stepped off with such a large amount of mud on his feet that our cursing-man said that 'every man in Texas was a land-holder.' So we got on the track once more, and got under headway. The gentleman said again, 'Mr. Potter, just as the last accident occurred, I asked if any of the heathen would go to heaven.' I told him I was not in a frame of mind to discuss the subject: the Almighty had not appointed me judge of the world; that if he ever got there he would find some of them there, or a good reason why they were not. By this time we had reached the main plaza, and the thing ran off again. I then made my escape, and reached the Central Hotel in time for dinner. So you see my first half-day's experience in the great city was full of mishaps.

"I took another voyage in the afternoon, and had only one run-off. So I hitched up Friday morning, and started for my mountain-home, a wiser if not a better man. I am convinced that a great city is not the place for me. Junction City and Ben Ficklin are large and grand enough for me. On reaching Boerne, I reported to Dr. Jacob S. West for examination, who said that the mule that pulled the great wagon was *non compos mentis*, and that the passengers were *non comatibus in swampo et railway*, or words to that effect: whilst my nervous system had been somewhat excited, he thought a seasonable tour, without the mule, city wagon, or the cursing-man, if made at once, would give me a fair chance to recover, and try my luck again. If so, you will be fully informed of the fact, by the unlucky writer, A. J. POTTER."

In social life he was ever ready for a good joke and pleasant humor, and his manner never gave offense, as in the case of the cursing-man. Yet he was grave in the pulpit, though eccentric in style. In him opposite extremes meet—that of cheerfulness and gravity, not those of sadness and joy. Sadness has not yet spread her veil over the even features of his placid face. Sorrow has not corrugated a single lineament there, nor Time whitened a hair. No clouds ever drape his smooth forehead; but in him meet the opposites of stern resolve and yielding pity. He can chastise the erring to the end of desert, and then heal the wounds his inflictions may have made. He can weep with you to-day in the darkness of your sorrows, but in the morning, if need be, he can, with as earnest a heart, correct you for your palpable wrongs.

In all departments of Nature there are points and

things at which, and in which, opposites meet and touch, and then begin to part, to widen the breach, and meet not again. Darkness and light meet in the twilights; winter and spring touch on each other's borders in the first budding morns; continents and liquid oceans have their lines of marginal unions; the prismatic colors meet just where one is and the other is not—where both are they part; the vegetable and the animal kingdoms meet at a given line, and then diverge to their opposite extremes, as rays of light leaving the central sun widen their separation as they penetrate into immensity's great profound. In the animal world, especially in man, opposite dispositions unite often in one person. Our divine Christianity infuses a new leaven into the souls of men which can weep with the sorrowing, and rejoice with the happy. It is glad at human joy, and grieved at mortal's woes.

CHAPTER L.

A LETTER from Mr. Potter from old "Camp San Saba," published in the Texas *Christian Advocate* of Jan. 8, 1881, will give the reader some idea of the work which has been done by that laborious, adventuring mission-apostle of the Great West. Camp San Saba is far out on the old Indian hunting-grounds, but now the military and frontier telegraph companies have extended their news-conveying wires from Austin along the vales and across the mountain-heights to that post. But years ago Potter and his "Winchester" were there, when Indian-bands dashed upon the unguarded wanderer along the wide belts stretching between the government camps. Here he erected the Church's Ebenezer alongside the government standard, though for want of a constant pastor, he tells us, the Church has declined; but he is there again, raising up its drooping standard.

Camp San Saba, Dec. 28, 1880.

As time rolls swiftly on the citizens of the frontier have discovered that Christmas comes on the twenty-fifth of December this year, and as the discovery is a new one, the majority concluded to celebrate the night of the twenty-fourth in a manner suited to the time and occasion. At the kind solicitations of the managers, I visited Voca, the most attractive and commanding point in the West, where the citizens had reared a Christmas-tree for the benefit of the children. It was a grand sight, worthy the admiration of all. The tree was most artistically decorated by the fair hands of the managers, and the numerous presents that were suspended from its boughs were well calculated to gladden the hearts of the merry children, and created a thrill of admiration and pleasure in the entire audience. It certainly reflected honor on the managers, more particularly the originator of the enterprise, Brother Hunter, a worthy and consistent member of our Church, and one of the greatest Sunday-school workers on the frontier, who had organized a Sunday-school at Voca, with a membership of sixty-five in attendance. He is also engaged at present in teaching a school, and meeting with merited success, which he richly deserves. Some three miles from Voca, on the night of the twenty-third, there was another tree-celebration, under the management of Professor Key, which I understand was largely attended, and gave general satisfaction.

I commenced a quarterly-meeting at Camp San Saba on Saturday last, had large and attentive audiences, and much good feeling was manifested. We intended to begin the meeting on Friday, but owing to previous arrangements of the citizens in celebrating the night of the twenty-fourth as did those of Voca, unfortunately we could not be present, but understood from experts that, for decorations and beauties, and the lavish display of costly presents, it has rarely, if ever, been excelled in the State. The affair passed off pleasantly, and all commended the lady managers in terms of praise. The able assistance of Professor Stephens did much in making it a success. He has charge of a large school in this place, and, judging from the rapid ratio of increase, his reputation has gone abroad. A reörganization of the Church in this place will be required. The prolonged drought of the past two years compelled many of the citizens to hunt better pastures for their stock, while others became disgusted, owing to the failures of crops, and left. As a consequence of there being no meetings the past year, because they had no pastor, many have backslidden, and it will require careful labors to restore the lost sheep to the fold. With the vigilant assistance of Brother Carpenter, we are in hopes the Church will be more highly represented within the next year than ever before. I am meeting with much encouragement. The citizens are kind, generous, and hospitable. Will commence a meeting at Paint Rock, in Concho County, on Friday next.

With kind adieus, A. J. POTTER.

Mr. Potter was in San Saba in midwinter, when

the Norther's cold breath had glazed the earth in sleet. More than one hundred miles from his own mountain-home, on Christmas-eve he attends a cheerful scene which would enchant an angel's heart—a beautiful Christmas-tree, all blooming with rich fruits of meritorious rewards to be given to hundreds of little, happy hearts, for Sabbath-school fidelity. Only a few years in the past the untutored Indian held his wild war-dance around the pole on which was tacked the white man's scalp. What a contrast!—scalps of "the pale-face" heightening the rude glee of a savage, wild dance; and an evergreen-tree draped in generous gifts, gladdening lily-dimpled cheeks! Schools, Sunday-schools, and Christmas-trees, are gospel products in that border-land, planted there by the unexampled zeal of our aggressive hero, the immortalized Potter. A Christmas-tree!—a fadeless emblem of the Tree of Life in the immortal land. "The righteous shall eat the *fruit* of their *doings*"—eat *there* the *fruit* of their *doings here.* All our good deeds in this life are hung on that Tree of Life, and we shall pluck and eat their fruit at the great, final gathering around that celestial Christmas-tree. Joyous throng! myriads of happy angels gaze down on the scene, and shall gladden all heaven with their rapturous shouts when the prizes shall be handed to each of earth's toiling children. Gentle reader, may your humble name be called out on that great day to receive a cake of life-bread from that immortal tree! If you sow, you shall reap, if you faint not.

This letter also reveals to the reader in other

lands the present civilized *status* of these frontier-regions. Heathens no longer tread the wild savannas, nor range the unfenced prairies; but farms, villages, schools, and churches, rise up to greet your coming, along this domain newly redeemed from savage rule. The great eagle and the cross unfurl their banners there, emblems of Liberty and Peace. The soldier planted the one, the preacher the other, and under their protective and elevating shields the arts of peace and the elements of religion begin to adorn the land so lately stained in blood. The present citizens lie down and sleep in the night-stillness of their own cabin-homes, while stars from tranquil skies look down upon their undisturbed repose—for none maketh them afraid. There is a peaceful, healthy home for you, dear reader, if you are one of earth's renting, delving millions. Be not afraid of the Indian's arrow now: peace reigns—the low of the wild ox is not disturbed by predatory hordes. Quiet Sabbath morn spreads its tranquil balm on dell and plain, and the dove's soft spring cooing is heard in the leafy woods, and here and there springs up the hardy stockman's cabin beside some placid pool, or sparkling stream, or rippling rill; and then you see the whited village—germ of growing town—looming up from the broad prairie's level bosom, disturbing the solitude of the long ages which have reigned in unbroken silence from earth's birth-morn till now, save when disturbed by the savage yell of the red man, and the tramp and howl of wild beasts in the dark night-gloom, or in the silence of lonely day. There too the storm-cannonading thunders may have rent asunder the bosom of the night-tempest, and maddened winds may have swiftly driven their cloudy chariots along the skies, and the fiery lightnings may have flashed their fitful lamps on the face of the prairie and the bosom of the muffled skies; but no civilized man was there to see the fearful majesty of the one, and hear the dread terror of the other. But now the voice of praise and the prayer of devotion are heard resounding along these ancient wilderness-wastes. Soon Sabbath church-bells shall send out their solemn peals upon the vast domain of mingled farms and cottage-homes of an industrious and peace-loving people.

The toiling hand of Mr. Potter planted the gospel "cuttings" there, and now are they rooting deeply and spreading their visible foliage in the open daylight. In a few more decades this late untrodden wilderness shall blossom as the rose. Homeless strangers, come over and join us in this new, sunny land; do not fear, for this is not a stormy, though it is a wintry, country. Texas seldom has gales or cyclones, except on her seaboard. Galveston, Matagorda, and Indianola, are subject to frequent gales and fearful cyclones at about a period of twenty years from their first occurrence, and sometimes their sight is more alarming than hurtful.

A night-storm at sea is the most terrific scene the eye of man ever looked upon. Far out on the ocean's agitated bosom one would think that the skies, and the ocean, and the winds, were at war in a life-and-death struggle. The wings of the tempest spread out their black shadows wide over the world of waters, shutting in the last ray of starlight from the scene, and night's inky mantle hovers close upon the deep. The wild, raging winds sweep along the towering waves, and howl along the naked decks of the dismantled ship, which topples like a cork, and dips and drives through the foaming seas. At one sight, when the lightning's sheen reveals the scene, you see a million of white-crested waves dashing their angry foam against the storm-clouds, while the lightning's fiery fist leaps down and smites the receding billows. But when the skies are blue, and the golden sun radiates the shore, and spreads its gilded calm on the sea, the scene is serenely sweet.

But in this mountain-world storms seldom come; the winds drive directly on, and do but little if any harm, but cool the heated cheek. The mountains do not peer deep enough into the skies to arrest the clouds or tangle the winds; and they drive their unmolested folds along their airy path.

Just here, for the information of strangers into whose hands this volume may chance to fall, we shall add a few remarks on "Texas Northers." They entirely control our winters. We have no winter only while they are blowing. At any time when the wind is not from the north, clerks and outdoor-laborers can leave off their coats. They usually begin to blow in the last part of September, and get cooler and cooler until night-frost nips vegetation — mostly about the middle of November. They cease to visit us early in May, when the spring and summer sea-breezes set in. In September, April, and May, they are more pleasant than otherwise, and sometimes so in March. Often they are mild as a gentle zephyr, but sometimes boisterous as the lion. Some of our hardest blows are under a blue sky; they are called "blue whistlers," and seem to gladden man and beast — they are healthy. But wet and sleeting Northers, which clothe the forest, and fields, and prairies, with ice, are trying on man and beast. They are of seldom recurrence. In twenty-three years we have seen perhaps not more than a half-dozen such. But when they come, a man or beast on open prairie, where the unopposed north wind may pour its ceaseless chill upon him, would freeze to death in a single hour. Persons *organically* diseased, or *very* delicate, ought to winter on the coast, or about El Paso, and retire to the mountains about the first of May, when the heat in other parts begins to be oppressive. All nights in these mountains are cool and refreshing during the summer heats.

CHAPTER LI.

Fort McKavett, Texas, April 12, 1881.

I REACHED Concho on the 5th, and remained five and a half days, preaching seven sermons—two at San Angelo, and five at Ben Ficklin—to large and attentive congregations. We always have good order on the frontier. Wicked men respect the gospel and the men who bear its message of mercy to this border-land. My Arkansas preacher, F. E. Townsend, is doing a fine work. Our bishops are doing noble service to this frontier by sending the best material at their command to supply it. Frontiersmen are not fools by a great deal. Many of them are well educated, and have listened to some of the ablest preachers in the older States. Our Church is gaining ground continually. I set out for this place, and traveled fifty miles that day, and "camped out" with the broad skies and shining stars the roof of my abiding-place. I reached here this morning, and have appointments to preach this afternoon and night. So you see I am pottering around on my "trail" at double-quick. By the way, there is something very poetical in camping out—at least, I found it so last night. After eating my supper, I wrapped my blanket around me, and lay down on the ground, with my head on a cornsack. I soon felt the poetical inspiration, but when I began to compose I found that my poetical pump was not in working order. I began thus:

Lonely and weary, I lay down to repose—

Just then I remembered that once while camping out a pole-cat bit me through the nose, and "nose" would rhyme with "repose;" but then that happened years ago, and that would not answer my purpose. So I began another:

When my life's work is done,
And my last setting sun
Will have sunk 'neath the hills of the west—

Here I stalled again. It would never do to reduce those towering mountains of the west to mere hills. So I made another effort:

> The rolling current beats with force,
> And often drives me from my course.

That may suit some places, but not this Western land just now. The drought has dried up all the streams, and instead of torrents we have to drive far and hard to get water for our ponies. I give it up. I don't think I am much poet anyhow. I wish some others who write for the papers would make a like discovery about themselves. I dropped out of my poetical failure into the deep sleep of a weary man, when I was aroused by the keen howling of coyotes around me. So I finished my verse:

> Lonely and weary, I lay down to repose,
> Where the coyote howls and the wild flower grows.

Poetry don't pay; it is hard to make, and often of no account when you have made it. The prairie-dogs added their yelps to the coyotes' howling, but I slept again, feeling that in the loneliest spot in this wide world a man may have a cheerful heart who bears within him a clear conscience, and is trying to do the work that God assigned him. — A. J. POTTER.

The foregoing is copied from the Texas *Christian Advocate*, to give additional instances of Mr. Potter's ever humorous and cheerful cast of mind, as well as his acuteness of mental perception. What a power he would have been in the Church had he been fully armed with all the helps of a thorough early education! But then he might not have so readily subjected himself to all the hardships of the awful border-toils. He is now the man for the place. Texas has only one Potter. See him alone among the wild beasts of the mountain, wrapped up in his blanket, and bedding on the hard earth, miles away from human habitation, while the coyote-wolf howls and the little prairie-pup yells around him. There he lies looking deep into the star-lit skies, and his merry, cheerful heart roams into the world of fancy, and he feels the humorous poesy of his solitude—

Nature's own sincere child, on an errand of mercy and love to the guilty and the lost. A cheerful heart is the companion of innocence. An accusing conscience is the voice of guilt. A great poet said, "Conscience makes cowards of us all." A guilty conscience does. But true moral heroism is the ally of guiltlessness. A good conscience is an unaccusing one, and it and the peace of God are ever inmates of the same temple; they are inseparably joined. No guilty clouds drape the soul upon which God smiles, and conscience approves. The shekinah of peace is in the inner temple of the soul.

> No changes of season or place
>   Would make any change in my mind;
> While blessed with a sense of his love,
>   A palace a toy would appear;
> And prisons would palaces prove,
>   If Jesus would dwell with me there.

At the late session of the West Texas Conference, at Luling, Mr. Potter made a missionary address, in which he mentioned the story of the pole-cat biting his nose, and said that he feared that little quadruped more than the biped Indian bands. Indian arrows had never pierced his flesh, but the little musk-sacked mammal had inflicted a wound on his nose, the only one ever made on his person by any antagonist. The truth is, that little skunk in Texas is a brave little fellow. He does not often retreat from the field before any foe. They abound from the Sabine to the Rio Grande, and from the gulf-beach to the mountains. The writer, traveling along a broad, beaten road, when thin, hurrying clouds veiled the moonlight, saw something moving in the road in front of him, but could not tell what it might be. His horse was not in favor of advancing too near to it. It paced along at an easy gait, with its rear plume erected to a perpendicular, ready for a discharge of its dewy-charged battery. Discovering at length the real character of our van-leader, we reined back our nag, refusing to venture a charge upon a foe so fearfully armed, and walked slowly along till the proud little hero gave us an open road.

Many years ago a raw Dutchman landed at Velasco, at the mouth of the Brazos, and the citizens got him out into a bear-hunt. He had never seen either a bear or a pole-cat. There were many of both along the lower Brazos at that early day. The uninitiated German was stationed at a certain place, in order to give him a good chance to kill a bear. No bear appeared, but one of the larger-sized skunks came along, with his large bushy tail erect and unfurled as a great striped plume, and the silly Dutchman made an onslaught upon it, thinking it a young bear, at the same time receiving a copious sprinkle. But he soon returned to Velasco, bearing the unmistabable odor of the late battle, when he was questioned about his bear-hunt, and he replied, "Me dish kill von leetle bar, but he vas so sthrong five hoondred mens coul'ent shmelt him."

Campers usually cook their meat by holding it near the fire on the point of a long green stick, and often use their fingers and teeth for forks and knives, and unless they are careful to cleanse their hands from grease, these brave little cats may make an attack on them in sleep. Mr. Potter must have left the temptation on his aquiline that fearful night. Most all the vast orders of the animal tribe inherit such a fear of man that they dare not venture on him, but the Texas musk-cat feels itself so securely guarded against all advances on its offensive odors that it seems not to fear any thing. Some of them are as large as great house-cats, and their musks are variegated in odor. Some of the older ones are sickeningly offensive. Their revolting scent will even turn the stomach of a dog. No wonder Mr. Potter feared them. He would not have truly known what had made the painful incisions in his nose in the dark night, when deep sleep was upon him, had not the aromatic intruder left some unmistakable perfumes about the camp. As the rosy-faced conk sings of the sea, the scent tells of the cat.

Perhaps the highest point of true greatness in the life of Mr. Potter is just where his privation and self-subjection to hardships meet. The highest display of divine love is seen in the humiliation and self-submission to suffering of our Lord Jesus Christ. Truly it is great to endure sufferings and toils for the good of others. We think too of a zealous apostle who passed through prisons and perils on land and sea for the Church when we read of the perilous life of our pioneer missionary. No feathery bed nor downy pillow gives sweet repose to his weary frame at night, but he lies on the cold earth, and a sack of corn or a stone pillows his weary head. No cheerful, friendly voices in merry halls delight his care-worn mind; no table of good things satiates the cravings of hunger; the howl of the night-wolf, the yelp of the wild dog, and the scream of the mountain vulture, regale his ears, and his lunch of bread, beef, and black coffee, make up his solitary meal. Here is an expression of real greatness that classes one above the order of the highest archangel. In their sphere of obedience there is no self-denial, no dangers encountered; but he who follows the greatest pattern of self-abnegation in the universe, and fills up a measure of similar sufferings for the Church, must not live in the flesh, but, denying its pleasurable enjoyments, must often travel a road sterile and bare of this world's easy comforts. His work in its grand issues of good to society and the Church is more than great. A single officer with a few timid soldiers subduing a great army, as Jephthah did, is valiant, but to establish the gospel kingdom in this wild land is greater than all.

Here we copy an account of Mr. Potter sleeping beside a lone grave of an unknown infant, on the mountains of West Texas. It is from the facile pen of Dr. Jacob S. West, of Boerne, Texas.

REV. H. A. GRAVES:—Inclosed please find the account which I have sketched of the little mountain grave beside which Mr. Potter passed a lonely night, which you requested of me, to be inserted in his Biography, which you are now writing. Respectfully,

JACOB S. WEST.

Boerne, Texas, May 5, 1881.

"The following lines were suggested to me by a circumstance related by my friend, the Rev. A. J. Potter. His ministerial duties led him to traverse nearly all of this vast Western wild, which is bounded on the south and west by the Rio Grande. On a recent trip night came upon him in the wild mountains far from any human habitation, and he passed its lonely hours in the untenanted mountain forest. After asking divine protection for the night, he lay down to rest, the blue canopy of heaven his covering, and the twinkling stars his lamps, and the greenswarded earth his humble bed. He awoke in the morning while the sun was flooding the world with his golden glories, the heavens flecked with fleecy clouds, and their shadows passing over the grand old hills and flowery vales, presenting a landscape view as those of a fairy-land. Examining his position, he found he had slept beside a fresh-cut log and another near to it, and between them he found a little grave — a humble mound of earth protected by those logs of wood. Unable to trace the history of that little grave, we suppose that some emigrant-train encamped there with a sick child, and there in the wild forest death ended its earthly career. After devotions appropriate to the presence of death, he gathered wild flowers, and decorated that little baby-grave, and bade it farewell. With this explanation, we give the reader the following verses about that infant's grave:

"He knelt beside that little grave,
And offered praise to God,
Who will the little stranger save
That sleeps beneath this sod.

"No mark to indicate the name
Of parent, nation, tongue,
The silent grave can but proclaim
The sleeper died while young.

"Bright stars above, grand hills around,
  Sweet flowers their vigils keep,
In silence solemn and profound,
  But mourners—none to weep.

"The winds may whisper as they fly,
  Or pause to drop a tear;
Or storms may rage, one Friend is nigh,
  Who conquers death and fear.

"Whose child sleeps in this flowery vale?
  Whose hearts appealed to God?
Who waked those wilds with mournful wail?
  Who sleeps beneath this sod?

"A long and dreary road they trod,
  And braved a fearful doom,
To give this babe away to God,
  And dig its quiet tomb.

"No bell to toll, no friend to call,
  No casket, shroud, nor box,
Its simple infant slip is all
  That screens it from the rocks.

"This unknown waif will sweetly rest,
  Though torn by wolves in twain;
Jesus will take it to his breast,
  And raise to life again.

"To regions bright, where angels dwell,
  This waif will wing its way;
No matter how or why it fell,
  'T will rise in endless day.

"By faith's pure light that region bright
  Our raptured eye can see,
Young children robed in spotless white,
  And heavenly harmony.

"Like visions from the land of rest,
  I see sweet cherubs fair,
Bright, glorious stars, that heaven has blest,
  Through thee, O Death! they're there.

> "Bright visions fade, dreams pass away,
>   Fast fleeting as our breath;
> Life cannot be freed from decay
>   Only through thee, O Death!"

Dr. West has just given the reader a touching account of the lone grave of an infant, and some pathetic verses on the same; but because of its exquisite beauty we here transcribe from the Texas *Christian Advocate* Mr. Potter's description of the scene. It is there headed,

A BABY'S GRAVE.

Mr. Editor:—Allow me to tell about the infant's lonely grave on the mountain in Gillespie County. On the great mountain "divide" there are broad miles of post-oak plains as level as a floor. Neat verdant post-oak trees shade the green grass carpet beneath them. No undergrowth, nothing but the unpastured grasses cover the smooth, woodland lawn, making up a scene on a calm and sunny day as lovely as sinless Eden. Well remembering the good grass there for my ponies, when on my late return from Fort Concho, I made a long day's drive to reach it, but did not get to the place I wanted to camp at till after nightfall. Being weary from hard travel, I hobbled out my ponies, took a cold lunch, laid down my sack of corn for a pillow, rolled my tired body in my blanket, and lay down to rest upon the cold bosom of "our common mother." When I awoke next morning, the sun's early beams were glistening the chilly night-dews on my head and blanket. On looking around, to my utter astonishment I had slept all night on the verge of the unsodded grave of an infant stranger! The thoughts and emotions which instantly thronged the mind a poet's pen cannot fully tell. Who could it be? How lone and silent its sleep! What loving hearts, perhaps far away, cluster round the baby's mountain-grave to weep! What mortal pangs ended its brief sojourn in these wild solitudes, and dug for it this little grave! Did not a thousand celestial angels escort its innocent spirit to a brighter Eden above? Ah, in my lone night-dreams I had slumbered with the early dead on the spot where glory-adorned angel sentinels tread around the young sleeper's grave! They were there, and "I knew it not." Till the last trump shall awake it from its long death-sleep, these immortal guardians shall love to meet at that little grave, and adorn the sacred scene with glory's mild hues more lovely than the moon's silvery beams.

> Let cold infidelity turn pale and die,
> For in this grave doth infant ashes lie.
> Say, is it saved, or is it lost?
> It died, for Adam sinned; it lives, for Christ hath died.

No doubt some emigrant stranger, passing over these mountain regions, buried their dear little baby there. It was done last summer. The little hillock is not yet grass-covered, and a post-oak tree cut down at the time had full-grown leaves. The log was cut in two pieces, and one piece laid on each side to protect it. Beside one of these logs we had lain all night. The wild forest around was clothed with many pretty mountain-flowers, and we strolled around and gathered many of them, and decorated the little grave with them. I took my knife and cut brush, and covered it over to protect its hallowed precincts from the wild beast of the unpeopled forest. Then I knelt down beside it, and gave myself and the infant sleeper to that kind Eye which sees the sparrow fall, and realized that God and angels were near; and feeling that if I should meet the sweet spirit in heaven, I should tell it that I had passed a night's lonely shade beside the grave of its dust in the mountain-wilds. May this story of the baby's grave enkindle some true poet's lute to sing of it in verse. I want to see it.

A. J. POTTER.

In this mountain-clime, where for hundreds of years uncivilized man has roamed over heights and vales in pursuit of game, and where for the past half-century the red and the white man have met and contested the ground in deadly combat, and too the untamed man has stealthily slain the father, mother, and their babes, and the heartless robber killed his unsuspecting fellow, we walk over their hidden graves, and tread unconsciously on their unburied dust; but for one to sleep beside the ungrassed hillock of a lone grave away on the summit of a wilderness mountain, far from the habitation of man, awakens in us a sense of sad loneliness akin to the dark solitude of the grave itself. Though we know that the grave is the end of man, the tomb his last earthly abode, yet we in life abhor its dust, and shrink away from its silent mansion; and though our dearly-loved ones are there, we desire not the fellowship of the grave, nor the company of the dead. Abraham bought the cave of Machpelah to hide his beautiful and beloved Sarah out of sight. We feel more at home at the graves of kindred than with those of strangers. But the grave makes all akin—it binds us in the bond of a common dust.

> The tall, the wise, the reverend head,
> Must lie as low as ours.

CHAPTER LII.

In the fall of 1879 the Conference was held at Gonzales. Bishop McTyeire presided, and Mr. Potter was appointed presiding elder of the Mason, or Mountain, District for the year 1880, and he soon set out for Ben Ficklin, the county-site of Tom Green County, on the extreme border of American dominion. Fort Concho, a military post, is near to it. In Ben Ficklin, the hotel-keeper is an old Californian. Having spent much of his life outside of the ranges of civilization, he is quite plain and a little rough in manners, a man of no put-on for patronage. He was one of the first settlers in Concho. His name is Robert Miller, but for brevity they call him "Bob." He was badly pock-marked, and does not present a handsome *physique*. When Mr. Potter drove up to his hotel, he stepped out, and Mr. Potter asked to spend the night at his hotel, to which he replied, "Yes; git out." While unharnessing the horse, Mr. Potter said to him, "I guess I might as well tell you who you have on your hands for the night. You have a Methodist preacher to entertain." Mr. Miller replied, "I guess you are at the right place. I am considered the hardest case in this town." After putting away the horse, he came in, lighted his cigarette, and said, "Preacher, I have not known any thing about religion since I was nine years old." "Well, sir, what did you know about it then?" "Well," said Mr. Miller, "my father had religion—preacher, he had it—there was no mistake about it. He could sing too. O how he used to stir up camp-meetings with his songs!" He then added, "I am a wicked man, but I am no hypocrite. All the infidels in the world could not make me believe that my father did not have religion." When bed-time came, he got down his large old Family Bible, and said, "Parson, you are the first preacher I ever entertained in my life, and here are some of my family grown who have never heard a prayer in their lives; you must pray with my family." After prayer, Mr. Miller began to hum over some remembered verses of his father's songs of long years ago—though not sonorous, yet of great earnestness. The long ago was as a shadowy dream to him; only a verse or two he could call up. At last he got started on the "Old Family Bible":

> How painfully pleasing the fond recollection
> Of youthful connections and innocent joy!

But here he stalled; he could go no farther, and he said, "Preacher, I have no hymn-book;" and then he turned to his wife, and said, "Lizzie, give me the Fourth Reader. It has the 'Iron-bound Bucket' in it, and it goes in that tune, and is a good substitute;" and he turned to it, and sung with great animation and pathos:

> The iron-bound bucket,
> The moss-covered bucket,
> That hung in the well.

Then addressing Mr. Potter, he said, "Now, preacher, when do you think you can preach for us?" Friday night was set as the time to begin to preach. Mr. Miller swept out the court-house, and lighted it up at night, and soon a large and interested audience was listening to the soul-renewing story of redeeming love under the border of the shades of heathenism. That is the way our frontier preacher plants the cross in the very shadows of barbarism, where the voice of the preacher and the wild Indian's war-whoop almost mingle their echoes along the border-line. In the case of Mr. Miller we are deeply impressed with the lasting impressions made on the young mind in early life by pious parents. Mr. Miller had no associations with the pious home-scenes after having passed his ninth year. Perhaps then his parents died, and he wandered over the world a strange orphan-boy, even in the domain of heathenism; but in all his strange pilgrimage among men, good or bad, he never lost the impression made on his boy-mind about the religion of his father. He saw its heavenly virtues as they shone in the face and life of his father. "By their fruits they shall be known." How encouraging to parents to be careful to set an example before their children that cannot be gainsaid! It is as seed sown in good ground—yielding its harvest in the future. O what an imperishable monument to his piety was that earnest compliment, "I know my father had religion!" No infidelity can disturb the foundation of that faith. Dear reader, are you an orphan in the world? Are your parents no more? Were they religious? And are you still in sin, and out of the Church?

Does memory often stray back to childhood's home, and call up the recollection of father, mother, brothers, and sisters, now no more among men, or far away in other climes? Then let her gentle memories make you a child again, and bring back your tender sense of Jesus and his love for you. Without religion you cannot reasonably hope to have a reunion in that land where home-affinities shall never be broken up, "where friends shall meet again who have loved, who have loved."

CHAPTER LIII.

Mr. Potter's labors as presiding elder have clearly evinced the wisdom of his appointment to that responsible place in the Church. He has met all its onerous duties with pleasing acceptability to the people and profit to the Church. He has made a good presiding officer in the Quarterly and in the District Conferences, managing the finances and church-building interest, and especially the great mission enterprises, at home and abroad; though his district is really a mission-field itself, yet it furnishes a quota for the home and the foreign fields.

The responsible duties of his office have enkindled a fresh flame in his zeal in the pulpit, and added to the abundance of his toils. His travels on wheels and horseback are almost incessant in the dreary winter's chill and the summer's scorching heats, and camping alone in the wilderness intervening between the settlements, when night's sable mantle robes the earth. He is at quarterly-meetings, camp-meetings, and extra-meetings, till the rolling year has stealthily glided away. Everywhere the Church is extending her borders and building up her temples of praise, and the land begins to echo with her songs of triumph and her shouts of joy.

To test a man's strength you must put the weight

upon him. Circumstances develop men's abilities. Great powers must have large spheres in which to operate. A great general does a small business while in the single command of a petty company, when he is endowed with skill to manipulate great armies. Mr. Potter sounds his trumpet with a double blast.

We have now passed over the salient incidents in the life of our hero, covering a chronological area of nearly fifty-two years, and we leave him in the hands of an unrevealed future, guided by that wise and gracious Providence which has safely conducted him through the dangerous vicissitudes of a half-century. We part with him in the realms of a vast field of ministerial toil, presiding elder of a mountainous belt stretching over a border-range of two hundred miles. In the quarterly discharge of the duties of his office he is detained in his extensive field from his home and family as long as two and three weeks at a time, being with them only a few weeks between the quarterly terms.

We shake hands with him in the narrow path of duty, along which divine light shineth unto the perfect day, with his back upon the past, and his eye fixed on the golden day-beams into which that path is soon to lead him. As he advances in age as the days and years roll by, so truly does he progress in the life of things sacred and divine. As a long train of connected cars, dropping off one or two at each station as it passes along the iron road, so he is leaving behind him peculiarities of nature and habit. Nearing the great celestial center of perfection, he is being more and more conformed to its transforming and hallowing forces. Though still in earthly spheres, he is becoming more allied to the citizenship of the celestial.

Such is even Nature's progressive methods: first is seen her tender blade, the verdant stalk, the ripening grain, and then the yellow harvest. It is truly so in spiritual life: we are first babes, then men, and then we are in the staidness of mature age in the life of things divine: as we near the future state we leave the earthly and take on the heavenly.

While in the body each man is a personal paradox: his "flesh lusteth against the Spirit, and the Spirit against the flesh." The earthly is first, but a Christian is to mortify the earthly, and give the dominion to the spiritual, the heavenly. Unique or eccentric natures, in which the paradoxical elements alternate, manifest prominent extremes; but with those temperaments where the antagonizing forces are of a more even balance, there is an exhibit of order and harmony. The universe seems to be constituted on the base of the opposite poles; its order is an equipoise between contrarieties, as the balance of the scales is the result of the precise equality of the opposite weights in each end thereof. But man in his fall inherited an evil force which gives preponderance to his animal, earthly nature; and those peculiar natures—as that of our eccentric hero—where the opposing elements of fallen humanity crop out so clearly, must ever, while unregenerate, display the usual superiority of the evil; but in the nature and life of our hero, in his worst days, his acts of social benefits to men are traceable to almost a parallel with the hurtful, and since the day of his regeneration to this writing he has gradually risen above the gravitating forces of the earthly. No longer is he the "Fighting Parson;" he now owns no "Winchester," carries no revolver; no belt of death-dealing cartridges encircles his waist—his sword lies rusting in its sheath. His Bible now has no fellowship with the sword; his armory is now of heavenly making. Belted around with the girdle of truth, clad with the panoply of God, and armed with the sword of the Spirit, to defend and build up that "kingdom which is not of this world," he traverses his mountain district in the name of that immaculate specimen of humanity who said to an eccentric Peter, "Put up thy sword." No longer do you see in him the preacher and the pugilist—in him the preacher is all, is alone. As the ancient zealots who wrought on the foundations of the temple and city walls with their carnal weapons in one hand and their good intentions in the other, so he has labored many years in laying the foundations of the outer courts of the true temple in this border-land; but now he moves amid the splendors of its inner glories.

In the parable of the rich man and Lazarus, our Saviour gives us the opposite extremes of wealth and poverty, showing that no depth of earthly want and misery can shut men out of heaven, and no elevations of riches and honors can prevent their deserved damnation. Man, from the highest possible attainments in earthly glories, like unto Capernaum of old, shall be cast down to hell according to his just desert, and from the lowest vale of disrepute, of poverty, and rags, shall be gladly borne by the joyous angels to the paradise of God, where the merits of grace shall unlock to him the portals of immortality.

But in the memorable instance of St. Paul, once the chief of sinners, we may shift the antithesis between him as the greatest sinner and the self-reliant moralist. The best specimens of natural men, the most upright and benevolent characters of self-made moralists, who feel not the need of a gracious Saviour, may not escape the final doom of the wicked; while the worst sinners who accept of that salvation which the gospel offers freely to all grades and classes of men, shall be saved and ranked with the "sons of God."

St. Paul and our remarkable hero are marked instances of the power of grace to save: one in the earliest ages of the Church, the other in modern times; the scenes of the glory of the one in ancient Judea and Asia Minor, and that of the other in the marginal borders of Western Texas; the first a learned, proud, bigoted, wicked Pharisee; the second an unlearned, impoverished, desperate son of the grog-house—both lifted on high by the all-powerful leverage of grace. The earthly fame of the first has sent its resounding echoes along the waves of time to our day, and his jubilant chants of victory swell the anthems of glory; while the merited honors of our living hero shall sound along the corridors of coming ages, till many unborn millions shall read of his zeal and talk of his triumphs in these savage wilds.

A physical force which might chain down the tides of the seas, or reverse the course of the Father of American Waters, and cause it to pour its vast liquid volumes into the Northern Ocean instead of the Southern Gulf, would not be a greater mechanical might than that wonderful power of grace which changed and reversed the life-course of such wicked men. As polished marble pillars on the path of life, they speak of the triumph of religion in the earth.

This little book traverses a vast field of facts and subjects directly or incidentally associated with the events of a most wonderful life of nearly fifty-two years. We have striven to be true and correct in all of our narrations, of both the evil and the good, and can safely vouch for their verity. If there is any inaccuracy, it may be in chronology and the names of places—possibly there may be some little incorrectness in those departments. Mr. Potter did not keep a journal or diary, and all the incidents of his early history have been copied from his memory, having been repeated to me verbally, or mailed to me in recent written manuscript.

But persons who have schooled their memories to retain facts and dates usually have strong and enlarged capacities of recollection. It is especially true with Mr. Potter. His mind is still like the paper which has just been pressed to the type—it retains all the impressions of the type. He seems not to have forgotten scarcely any thing which may have transpired between to-day and his childhood. Many of those remembered events do not appear in the pages of this volume. His mind is a library of facts, and contains a gazetteer of names and a volume of chronological *data*. So that we are of the opinion that if there are any errors at all in those things, they are insignificant. Hence we commit this little book to the reading public as deserving its confidence, in its strict conformity to truth.

If the reader cannot indorse all of our comments on some of the leading facts herein contained, we only ask of him to endeavor with all his might to avoid the evil and emulate the good, for the author's design is to do good in the world when his tongue and pen are silent.

CHAPTER LIV.

A CHAPTER in this biographical volume is due the wife of Mr. Potter. She was a native of Missouri. Her maiden name was Emily C. Guin. Her family moved to Texas many years ago, and were in the terrible wreck of the Independence off Pass Caballo. In that catastrophe they lost all but their lives. They settled in Bastrop County, where she was married to Mr. Potter, in 1853, as stated elsewhere. Her mother was a widow at the time of her marriage, and she remained with her till her death.

It was an evening of the dawning of a new morning to her life, when her husband came after her to go with him to that great religious revival on Craft's Prairie. When he informed her of his determination to reform his life, it must have been to her as the uprising of a new sun on a long night of darkness. For nearly three dreary years, with little hope, she had seen him go and come under the force of early-formed and long-continued habits of dissipation; his daily resort the grocery, the race-turf, or the gaming-table; his society the abandoned, the drunken, the blasphemous, and the reckless class of men — men armed with implements of blood and slaughter. She knew not when the saddening news might reach her that he had fallen in some bloody combat over the gaming-table, or brought home to her a bleeding cripple for life. In the long, long days of his absence fear must have spread a melancholy veil over her mind, and forebodings of evil must have caused those early years of wedded-life to drag their weary days slowly away. Three years of heart-cankering fears bordering on despair are enough to crush the most delicate thing the God of Nature ever made upon this earth—a *gentle woman's heart*. A lute broken, or a harp with all its chords unstrung, is the emblem of a disconsolate wife. Earth has no cement to mend a woman's broken heart. As the flower, when the little worm has eaten at its heart, wilts and fades, so remediless heart-griefs in silence wilt her charms and pale her for the tomb of her woes. When her almost hopeless husband said to her, "Emily, I have come after you to go with me to the meeting; I am going to do better and seek religion," she must have instantly felt the thrill of a new life for her earthly future. All the changed happy future must have loomed before her hope in a moment. A sober, industrious, home-loving husband, and all the peace and bliss of home-life glowed in her mind. Surely she was ready to go anywhere to see him changed into his right mind. More than a thousand seraphs of gladness may have danced in the sunlight of joy about her all along that ten-mile journey to the scene of that great revival, for there hope prophesied that her inebriate husband would be "born again"—begin life anew—be a new man—lead a better life. Sure enough, there he entered the path to a new era—began the first page in the novel book. At that great meeting she too professed religion, and joined the Church with her husband. That day to them was the first in their sacred year— a year to last to the end of life. One quarter of a century has now passed slowly by, and together still they advance, side by side, along that way where the light shineth to the perfect day. She was the woman to fill the station to which she was called— the wife of the great pioneer-evangelist of the quasi-savage border. Physically a robust, queenly-looking woman, of a strong constitution, and a picture of good health, and redolent with the charms of feminine beauty; endowed with decision of character, and a large share of practical sense in the department of the useful, she was well qualified to meet the duties of the onerous charge which should eventually fall to her lot, in the long-repeated absence of her husband, when on his lengthened tours along the Great West as a missionary pioneer. For many years he has been almost a stranger at home. Bishop Pierce significantly styled their mountain-home "his wife's house." There she is the all— head and manager in and out of doors; the house, the kitchen, the larder, the farm, and the stock, all come under her control. When he has a few spare days at home, and gets out to see after temporal concerns, he is likely to get hold of matters at the wrong end, and get them into a tangle, and have to call on her for light and aid to get things in order again. In the shifting events of twenty years she has managed mainly to raise the family, and collect and hold together the homestead, and a nice little stock of horses and cattle, the preacher's wages seldom reaching the scale of half, and sometimes not one-third, rations. She is a woman of great energy, industry, and zeal, in the duties of domestic life. She needs be of that class. God fitted her for the sphere, and fully indeed has she bravely met all its demands. She has this year given birth to her fifteenth child—twelve now living. Bearing all the cares of childhood, managing, governing, and training them in the multitude of infant and juvenile strifes and wrongs, with the addition of all the vexations arising from business affairs from the outdoor world, she ever had the heaviest end of life's burdens to bear; yet she has ever walked right on with all their toilsome duties upon her, as if their weight was unfelt. Not complaining or revolting, dutiful has she been to the calls of the Church to her husband. No matter where the path of duty led, she objected not a word. If it lay along the peopled plains, no matter; if away along the Rio Grande, no matter; if amid mountain-wilds, beset with brigands and savage hordes, all right with her, because her husband was the "called of God," "the anointed of the Lord," and over him hung the guiding, the protecting "cloudy pillar." Once upon a time the writer of this little sketch passed a night at her home, when she said to him that she had given her husband to the Church, and that she endeavored to take care of the family and their cottage-home. Noble woman! Soldier of the cross! Truly has she carried the most weighty end of that cross.

Her sense of obligation to God and his Church for the rescue of her husband from the dreadful vortex into which the path of sin had led him was as deep as life, and reaches unto the grave. As a brand snatched from the fire, he was the Lord's, and belonged to his Church. As a sinner, the grocery was his home; and now, as a wandering minister of Jesus, he is more at home, and a thousand times more pleasant; so withal she is the gainer. Had he continued in the transgressor's road, long ago he must have fallen a bloody victim to bar-room cruelty, or some catastrophe on the race-turf, or at the gaming-table. Had he fallen into the grave from the low haunts of vice, he would have left a dark example for their children to imitate, and hung a veil of sadness on her heart at the memory of his wrongs, and the terror of his future doom. But now she is more than willing to give him to the Church which arrested and saved him. He is her saved man. All duties in home-life are cheerfully discharged with one eye fixed on keeping him in the field of progress and triumph, and the other on her own, and the salvation of her home-charge. Surely, in the last great day she shall share with him in the laborer's rewards. The stars which may deck his crown may also shine as gems in her coronet of glory, for she has truly been his helpmeet here in the vineyard of Christ. God bless the noble, self-sacrificing woman, while toiling in her home-sphere!

CHAPTER LV.

Such is the interest involved in a minister's relation to female society in the Church and in the world, and the vital importance attaching to his timely and prudent marriage, we cannot willingly close this little volume until we shall have devoted a brief chapter to their consideration.

Forty years' experience has impressed us with the wisdom of Mr. Wesley's advisory admonition to ministers, "To converse prudently with women." That preceptive counsel of a grave divine the author has studiously and cautiously observed through his entire ministerial career. To him it has been a shield to ward off temptation. The manner of his early marriage was a rash act, and does not deserve a following.

Woman is the mortal angel—the queen of the earth. Helen's beauty caused the siege and cost the burning of ancient Troy. The charms of Egypt's queen, the lilied Cleopatra, captured Mark Antony of Rome. Woman's smile rules the world, and the dignity of the pulpit bows at the shrine of her bridal-altar. God has painted her face with the charms of fascinating beauty, so that her "witching smile will catch man's youthful fancy." He made her to be loved—wedded. Her smiles are thrilling, and her charms are dangerous. Ministerial celibacy is not in the creeds of Protestantism. Marriage is their right at a suitable time, and to a proper helpmeet. Many a promising minister of Jesus Christ has been enslaved and crippled through all his after-life by a hasty and unsuitable alliance. Virtuous female society is refining and ennobling to man, but young ministers who have not acquired knowledge and experience enough to justify their marriage had better not tarry long in the parlor where beauty flashes its mild fires from dove-like eyes—linger not till Cupid has pierced the heart and spread the magic charm of love about its affections. If you tarry there we cannot help you; you are captured—gone; and when you have won your Delilah, part of Samson's pulpit-locks are shorn. Do not linger there—to books and to prayers. Do not imagine that none ever were as she, and that none shall ever be equal unto her. Think not that no rose so pretty or so sweet ever bloomed on bush before, or that none so lovely shall appear again. While the ages last, the coming years shall reproduce those as rich in charms and as delicate in sweet odors. Since Eve, the primal mother, was driven from her flowery Eden, her daughters have been lovely and fair each revolving age, and shall still bloom, as the rose, along life's pathway, till time shall be no more. Do not fear that you shall nevermore look on one so amiable. As the wild prairies are clothed in variegated flowers in May's dewy morn, so the parlors of cities and rural shades shall be ever adorned with the charms of enrobed fair ones; and among the multitude of budding pinks and lilies there is one for you, if you shall prepare yourself to deserve one so like the nymphs which grace the halls in celestial spheres. Then be not hasty to fall in love with graceful smiles or jeweled fingers. Rash and hurried weddings often soon reveal the mistake the young lovers had made, but too late for a remedy. To be enamored with simple beauty is not wise, for it is a fading charm. It is Nature's gloss on the feature—a glistening ripple on the bosom of the tranquil bay. But there is a fadeless, peaceful hue that glows on the cheek and beams from the eye of virtuous merit, because it comes from the heart—an inward adorning of a meek and a gentle nature, which even in the sight of God is of great price. Rustling robes of costly silks, or glistening satins draped in tucks, bows, and ruffles, painted faces wreathed with factitious smiles, and heads attired, as Jezebel of olden fame, with queenly gems and flowers, do not make up the paragon of beauty a minister of the gospel ought to love. Beauties of Nature may be *loved*, but those of Art *admired*. Conjugal love, to endure when all forms of the visible tints have faded, must root in the imperishable virtues of the heart.

If you wait in toiling labors and patient study in the vast domain of theological research, until you have qualified yourself to fill the calls the Church may make for your services, and not burden her interest by the cost of a family, then may you love and wed a deserving one, who shall prove a help to you in the vineyard of the Lord. A preacher's wife, who is one indeed, is called of God to that sacred place; but if you get in a hurry, and take one to your side whom God has not chosen for you, she may turn out to be a thorn in your flesh, and a shade over your pulpit. An itinerant's wife has the heaviest end of life's cares on her shoulders, and her needs of grace and qualifications for her tasks are large. She must possess intelligence, industry, enterprise, economy, neatness, and a double portion of patience, and a full measure of devotedness to the cause for whose interests her husband is to give the toils of his life. All home affairs are in her hands—the smoke-house, kitchen, cradle, and parlor, demand her daily attentions. No novel-reading, nervous, sylvan nymph can meet their demands. A true Christian woman only can fill that important sphere—such a one as St. Paul depicts in his first letter to Timothy: "In like manner also, that women adorn themselves in modest apparel, with shamefacedness and sobriety; not with braided hair, or gold, or pearls, or costly array; but (which becometh women professing godliness) with good works." A fashionable attire on the person of a minister's wife is out of place, and, unlike the more valuable inner graces, intended to adorn the hidden person of the heart. And a costly catalogue of gemmed ornaments is the outcrop of a silly pride, totally antagonizing all the finer Christian graces of a meek and quiet spirit. Mrs. Potter never displayed any of those vain and silly desires after the outward glitter of fine or gay dressing. Her wardrobe has ever been of that modest hue so highly commended by the apostle as becoming women professing godliness. Indeed, such have been the incessant demands on her time and attention in her home domain, during the oft-repeated long absence of her husband, she had little opportunity of associating with the outside world. Display in society has had no place in the sum of her motives and duties. Her home has been to her a compact empire. It taxed all her abilities of mind and body to meet promptly all its ever-recurring requisitions. As a faithful sentinel, she is always at her place at the family-board of her mountain-home — ready to welcome her husband on his return, tired and worn from travel and toil; ready to bid him "Godspeed" when departing to renewed labors. Here she has served the Church in her sphere; there she shall be free to share the rewards.

CHAPTER LVI.

This chapter is devoted to young men and youthful ministers of the gospel. Too many young men pass their youth without any well-defined aim in life— no trade, no profession, no vocation, fixed upon. Every youth should have some settled object in his mind's eye, as his pursuit in all after-life, by the time he has reached his twenty-first year—if before that period the better. Life is short, and no time is to be lost in youth's valuable years. Each year spent idly is gone, never to be regained. A full day's work includes the gentle hours of the early morn as well as the quiet evening. The ninth and eleventh hours make up but a fraction of the day. Young manhood has no term of months or years to spend in "wild-oats sowing;" every hour is of priceless value; none to waste at the dance-hall, or the race-course, or at the gaming-saloon, or at the dram-shop. Life's demands of the young of this age are so numerous, so complicated, so high, that a preparation to meet them, and a full discharge of all their injunctions, cover the entire span from early boyhood to the tomb. Sport, fun, and frolic, have no chapter in youth's Book of Life in our day; *learning* and *doing* fill up the entire volume. Much is to be learned, and more to be done, in life's short day. Dear reader, you must not let the ball of progress take a backward turn in your day; you must roll it higher up the steeps of civilization than your fathers have carried it. The plane on which you begin your career reaches farther and extends wider than the one on which your predecessors have acted; your obligations are parallel with your sphere of operation; you must hand down the improved State and Church to the generation which is to succeed you, as your fathers have transferred, or will transfer, their valuable immunities to you. Do not let them be marred in your hands. Science, art, and religion, have gathered their vast treasures from the volumes of the ages, and they shall lay them, without price, at your feet. You begin where your fathers end life's career; you take hold on the destiny of the race where six thousand years laid it down—push it into zones of greater meridian splendors. The mysteries of science, the wonders of art, and the marvels of religion, still unexplored, lie in deeper spheres than the past has penetrated. The study, the discoveries of the dead have only tacked up the finger-board pointing out to you, young man, the road along whose margins truth is to be found: you must unearth it as far into its domain as your life may last, and dying, nail up the sign telling the directions of its leads to those who may follow you. With the aids which centuries have put into your hands, you can accomplish more in one decade than others have done in a life-time. A faithful use of the means at your disposal may accelerate the speed of the car of progress, and when you may hand it to the age beyond your day, the grand, golden age of the world's millennium-morn may begin to gild orient skies. All the mighty agencies of ignorance and vice demolished, the liquor traffic destroyed, all institutions of gaming put down with the things that were, the ball-rooms closed forever, and the theatric-stage buried with the past—schools, colleges, and universities, established in all districts of the civilized domain, and the press hallowed and dedicated alone to the interests of science, truth, morality, and religion, while the Church may pour into society's great heart its leavening virtues—then shall the dawning of virtue's triumph begin to appear—then shall man, redeemed and saved, approach near unto the precincts of his earthly glory.

But not until his youthful prime is utilized in the cause of knowledge and virtue; not until all intemperate habits are abandoned; not until all ostentation and vain pageant of costly mansions, furniture, and dressing, shall give way to benevolent deeds; when costly mausoleums for the dead are abandoned, and great-domed and steepled mansions and churches shall cease to grace the earth; when wars and luxuries shall be no more, and all the vast billions spent in these things shall, in one vast treasure-pile, be lavished on the improvement of the physical condition of the poor, and the mental and moral *status* of humanity—then shall the long-prayed for day begin to rise on the world. Hail, happy morn!

But, kind reader, are you a neophyte in the ministry of Jesus? or are you just intending to take upon you that office in some future time? If so, allow a word of advice from one who is now old, though once young as you. Delay not to begin your work. Time is passing, sinners are perishing. God has imposed the high duty upon you to warn them of their danger, and invite them to his mercy. The Church needs you to cultivate her untilled but open fields; China needs ten thousand preachers to-day to plant the gospel in her great empire; Japan, South America, and Mexico, call for hundreds more to occupy their pagan and semi-heathen temples. Do you feel the Spirit move you to enter as a laborer to cultivate Immanuel's lands? then tarry no longer in the precincts of Jericho. Do you need wisdom? then "Ask of God, who giveth to all men liberally, and upbraideth not." Are you deficient in the knowledge of books? and are you poor and unable to defray the costs of an education? then offer yourself to the Church. She has schools, and in them are theological chairs, where you can get all needed training for the Home or Foreign Fields. The Foreign Fields demand special qualifications for the work in their respective spheres; but the Church has all the preparatory helps. Lay your soul and body on her altars; give up the world—her wealth, her honors, her pleasures, her vain pomp and glory, for "the excellency of the knowledge of Christ Jesus." A full consecration is required. Now, while your young heart is untainted by the follies of the gay world, begin your life-long work. Have no experience in the silly pleasures of life, none in its tainting evils; immerse your youthful spirit in the love of Jesus, as young Paul or youthful Timothy. Let Christ's love *constrain you;* it is the holy anointing-oil, the unction from above; it gives the tongue of fire; it melts the indurated heart of sinners, and gives efficiency to your doctrines preached to the multitudes. Whatever else you may have—learning, oratory, or skill in the arts of style of address—yet, if you are wanting in that divine qualification, your ministry will be a tinkling sound, a bouquet of fading flowers, beautiful when taken from the parent stem, but faded and wilted in a day. Learning and natural gifts, hallowed by that divine anointing, carry both light and holy fire to the dark intellects and hard hearts of sinful men. The arts of logic and the tinsel of rhetoric win the applause of men for the orator, but the Spirit of God in the heart, and accompanying the words of the minister, leads sinners to think of Him who loved and died to save them. The first gains a following for the preacher, the second allies men to Christ Jesus.

Men are called into the ministry from almost all spheres and conditions in life, in order to suit each class of society to whom they are to minister. If you feel impressed to enter at once into the pulpit, and learn to "blow and strike at the same time," do not hesitate; but, at the same time, give diligent attention to reading and study; and there are no heights in a learned and divinely-hallowed ministry to which grace may not elevate you in the issues of a short life-time. A few things are requisite to make a truly great preacher: A divine call, native capacity, ceaseless application, and the aid of the Divine Spirit in the studio and in the pulpit. The last is assured to all men called of God to occupy the pulpit. But remember, dear reader, that you may idle away life's jeweled moments, and neglect the gift of God that is within you. Be ever stirring it up by unremitting efforts to do more and to get higher in the scale of usefulness. An advance is the inevitable result of well-aimed effort. Twenty years spent in devoted research, and a faithful practical experience in pulpit toils, may elevate to high plateaus of useful ministerial renown now not within the limited range of your most sanguine hopes. As you steadily ascend, the clouds above will vanish into pure air, and still greater altitudes will rise in increasing grandeur before you. Do not look back; keep your eye on the golden upward, till you reach that region where clouds float not, that peerless dome where celestial glories mingle their fadeless hues with the highest earthly.

But if you merely feel called to get ready to do a work yet to be more specially indicated—to school, to educate yourself for the Master's future demands of you—then wait not a day: lay down all earthly hopes and aims; apply your time and energies to *books*, to *study*. Georgetown, the great Vanderbilt, and other worthy institutions, are open to you. If you are poor, no matter: make your divine call, your intentions, known to the Church of your choice, and God will touch some heart to help you, as he did for Martin Luther, the poor, carol-singing boy of Eisenach; and light shall spring up along your way as the purposes of a gracious Providence may see fit to reveal to you the line of duty. Only trust the Lord, and discharge present, tangible obligations: the end, though now hidden from you, shall be sure, and radiant with glory. If God has called you to a scholarly ministry, the fields you are to enter are vast, and now are ready for the laborers. In that great empire there is a place for you, or God would not have called you to prepare for it. The demands of that place measure up to all you are now, and all you may be after having been endowed with all that man can impart, and all that God shall invest you with. Great acquisitions are needed, because a great work is to be performed. The temples of atheism are to be demolished; false science is to be uprooted and expunged from temples of a false philosophy, from books, journals, and creeds; a sound theism and a pure morality are to be deeply engraved on the human mind, and planted deep into its affections, refined by grace; the errors and superstitions made strong and sacred by the use of ages in pagan lands must be eradicated from the domain of heathen thought and affection, and the modern dogmas of the haters of God and the revilers of his Church must be buried in the *débris* of modern times by a learned and God-honored ministry. Therefore arm yourself now with all the implements of human wisdom and the whole panoply of God; then, like David, take your place in front of Israel's hosts.

With all the advantages into which you enter from the cradle, you begin life where the present veterans now leave it; hence much is expected of you. Like a youth walking on an empire of pretty, polished stones, the beautiful pebbles and larger stones of the million of facts of art, science, and religion, lie in vast profusion about you, and you only have to stoop and pick them up, and use them as occasion may require. The libraries of the world are open unto you, and the Bible—"book of books," God's book—is your text-book. Energy, zeal, faith, and the onward push, shall end your career deep into the golden victory awaiting the kingdom of our Lord Jesus Christ.

The Bible, my dear young brother, is not only your text-book for the pulpit, but it is your solace and guide in and out of the sacred desk; it is not to be substituted by any work of man on theology: commentaries, and biblical dictionaries, and books of sermons, are so many helps in your study of the Holy Scriptures; but you must read and study the holy page of God's own word; it will make you wise unto salvation, imbue your heart with the genius of its sentiments, and print all its literal phrases on the page of memory. Have all its doctrines, precepts, promises, exhortations, and holy maxims, at your command in the pulpit. Quote the Scriptures accurately, observe their nice distinctions, and use them appropriately. No word of man, however learned or great in popular fame, has equal force of authority on the human mind as the plain "thus saith the Lord." Divine statement is the end of all debate with men. God is true, if all men are in error. Wherever you can adduce the clear testimony of the Bible for your doctrines, men will receive them without dispute. A minister not familiar with the reading of the divine word is like unto the woodman having a dull ax, or no ax at all, in a great forest which is to be felled; or, to use another symbol, as a soldier antagonizing steel-clad warriors with a wooden sword, having only the teachings of men at his command. The Bible is the sword of the Divine Spirit, sharpened, and brightened, and precisely fitted for the work of the slaughter of sin. No blade of human invention can equal it. It lays open to the sinner the hidden secrets of his own heart, and reveals unto him the vileness of his motives and the vanity of his hopes. Your success as a minister of Jesus Christ, your victories achieved in his name, in the saving of men from atheism, infidelity, and the ruin of sin hereafter, must be the result of a dexterous use of the Spirit's sword—the word of God.

Beautiful, learned, and eloquent sermons, framed out of borrowed or original conceptions, and adorned with all the art and tinselry of refined rhetoric, uttered with the affectionate sweetness of an angel's tone and phrase to applauding thousands, may get your name into the books and journals of the day as a great preacher; the Church may honor you, and the world may hang on your lips with delight; but God doth know that it all is no more than the windy storm which rent the mountain-side, without the presence of any divine force—God's efficient voice was yet in the rear of the rending tempest. God's voice—his word—is the power that saves. Preach the word, is the injunction upon you, dear young man. The Spirit makes that word sharp to the sinner's conscience. Print all the facts of the holy word on your memory's page now while youth is with you, for when toils and age have piled their burdens upon you, Memory will not receive the impressions of things and events as now, when all her pages are smooth and white; soon she will blur them. Now fill her arsenals with a store of biblical truths, to be used in the future battles of life, or in its evening decline. A real *doctor* of *divinity*—one thoroughly versed and deeply skilled in the use of the divine record—is of priceless value.

Now please understand me, dear young reader: Schools, books, standards of all species of knowledge, are needful helps to students of all professions and trades, especially so to the learner in divinity. Like the busy bee, he must extract the sweet from all flowers. *Read, study,* every book, or journal, that is not foolish or vicious; cull out the good, and store it away; you may find a place for it a half-century hence. Read men, study Nature, revel among the stars, dive into the oceans, dig into the earth, inspect the arts of life, and acquaint yourself with the evils and virtues of the home-circle; but use all the facts you may learn therefrom to illustrate the spiritual genius of God's hallowed truth. Let one grand aim, as a silver thread, run through all your pulpit administrations—to instruct sinners, and lead them to turn from their evil ways, and come unto the blood-stained cross, where pardon and life are given.

Thus endowed with divine knowledge and an

abiding consciousness of your spiritual call, go forward with meek boldness, fearing nothing but sin. Though you may have been called, like Mr. Potter, from the hedge, or the ditch, care not for it. Let the past be buried, as if you are now raised up to a new life indeed. But be humble. Remember that the name of Jesus, written on your character, is a safe and welcome passport into the mansions of the celestial city, and also into the lowest and highest grades of society on the earth. The doors of the rich and the great swing open at the name of Jesus. He was born in a stable, and cradled in a manger, but now is worshiped in the grandest temples of the globe, and is honored in the halls of wealth and in the mansions of the great. You too, like your renowned Master, may have been rocked in poverty's cradle, but now his name seats you among earth's noblest and highest honored ones.

When Mr. Potter joined the Church, and took on himself the name of Jesus, fresh from the grog-shop, as the demoniac from the tombs, Mr. Holbert, a rich man in the State of Texas, said to him, "Now, Mr. Potter, you are welcome to my home; the latch-string is now outside for you; I could not invite you before — now you are welcome." The name of Jesus gives you a welcome into the private homes of the civilized world. Because he did no harm, but loved the sin-ruined race, you are expected to follow his harmless steps. O ye dear young men of the ministry of Jesus, betray him not, dishonor him not in the house of his friends, as many have done in this licentious age, and locked many an insulted hall against your approach! Innocence and heavenly-mindedness are expected to enter with you. Let not the slimy serpent leave his trail where you go. O think of the power of Jesus's name! It is embalmed in a magic charm; it comes as an angel visitant from a friendly isle, bringing good news of those we love.

I see you, youthful preacher, nearing a palatial home of strangers in a great city; you are making your first visit in a new charge; you are a stranger. You ascend the marble steps, and ring the door-bell: a young woman blushing in feminine modesty opens the paneled door, and seeing a stranger on the steps before her, in delicate modesty shrinks back a step or two; but when you announce yourself as a minister of Jesus Christ, her face instantly brightens up as she advances, extends her hand of welcome, and bids you walk in. What inspired that cautious young lady's heart with instant confidence and cheerful hospitality? Not you; no, not you, young man, but the hallowed charm of Jesus's name. That name imprisoned Paul and Silas, but to you it opens the door to the hospitalities of the small and the great. Mr. Potter, born in a humble cottage, is welcomed and esteemed in fashionable cities, and in the seats of rural pride, as also in the cottage home. O ye ennobled, ye honored ones in Christ's holy Church, see that you by a holy life honor Him who has called you to such distinguished privileges! A plateau of honor above all earthly fame is before you; arise and ascend unto it. Remember that your Master has a name that is above every name; that at the name of Jesus every knee shall bow, and you shall share in his glory if true to him here.

Before ending this chapter, please allow us to call your careful attention to some growing evils in the Church, which must be remedied in your day: The false estimate placed on the ritualistic pageant, and the emulating efforts at great things.—All nations have had their pet follies, and every age of the world's history reveals some special vanity. Egypt built her wonderful Pyramids, Greece erected her Parthenon, and originated her games and plays, and Rome built great palaces, supported by forests of colonnades, and constructed her amphitheater, and earnestly pursued gallantry and fame. Ours is an inventive age, and is bordering on the useful. That which is not of utility is passing away; the incoming generation may occupy the utilitarian epoch of modern times. Costly pageant in great buildings, in dress, in luxury for the sumptuous table, and all other outlays to gratify vanity and pride, must go by with the onward roll of the ages. Costly outward adornment, the varnished of the beautiful too, will pass away as men are enlightened and refined. Great steepled churches, costing vast sums, crowns and diamonds, with robes speckled with jewels—all must be dedicated to the useful. Countless millions now spent to gratify and adorn luxury and pride must be devoted to the elevating of the mind of the race. Mind is the thing to be adorned. Solomon's grand temple was a symbol of the mind; it was the *picture;* the mind, the *real.* The picture is no more;

the real remains. Ye are the temples of God—the living temples. The splendors of the divine shekinah glow in the mind. Neat and comfortable homes, clean and useful clothing, good and wholesome food, and commodious and substantial churches, school-rooms, and business-houses, are all that is needful; all the extra cost in these things must be devoted to education, the refining and instructing of mind—the mind of the race. Education is still in its cradle, or its swaddling-bands. It has not yet entered its First Reader. The human race is one family, and education is due each child; and when the many billions now wasted annually among the civilized nations on vanity, luxury, pleasure, and the useless, are all lavished on the redemption of mind from the fetters of ignorance, then shall mind begin to glow with the effulgence of the divine. The pulpit is in the van of the great educational domain. You must lift up your voice like a trumpet, and plead for the wasted millions of the children's educational fund, unrobe the Churches of their pageanted attire, and start them on a career of the useful in elevating mind. Simply take care of the body as the scaffolding of the mind. Many shall run to and fro, and knowledge shall increase; right knowledge shall cover the earth as the waters cover the bottom of the seas. When the pulpit, the press, and the school-room, see eye to eye, and unify their efforts to one great result of imparting the true, the good, to men, then shall the earth blossom as the Eden of olden fame. Imposing forms strike the imagination, but do not refine the heart. It is the power—the *divine baptism*—that purifies and ennobles humanity. It enlightens, quickens, and inspirits the mind with all the holy catalogue of the higher motives which Christianity gives to the world. The present redemption and final salvation of your race are to result from a faithful application of the gospel you are called to advocate. So preach it, that earth shall be the poorer when you are called up higher; but be sure that you leave no shadow draping the Church you may have served. Plant the germ of a stainless ministry deep in the age in which you may have lived. Print your virtues in indelible lines on its pages, that those who may come after you may read and profit thereby. All Nature strives to leave a blessing to the succeeding epochs. A love of life and a generous desire to transmit it is a living, benevolent trait in all her organized forms. The rapid and increasing speed of the car of future progress depends much upon the forces passed down to it from each preceding age. A learned and hallowed ministry should not only leave the impress of its knowledge and piety on its own age, but should in some form transmit them in some stable manner to coming generations. Books are of inestimable value; they contain the accumulated knowledge of the ages. The society of books is better than that of the living. They contain the good of the dead without their evils. The living have their faults and follies mingled with their virtues. Men put the best of themselves in books. Books, then, are your best companions; see to it that you make a timely use of them. Study *precision, condensation,* and *accurateness.* There is much knowledge in the world, yet it is poor in accurate, precise knowledge. *Indefiniteness* is the character of much of printed thought, as a vast pile of drift-wood floating on the bosom of a swollen stream without order—a mingling of odds and ends. Attention is needful to a nice distinction of facts and words. Ideas and language are the elements of pulpit greatness—let the first be clear, and the second pure. Let no vulgarisms or barbarisms enter the pulpit, or mingle in your daily speech. Close inspection into thoughts and phrases will guide you safely. Sir Walter Scott's descriptive greatness was the result of minute attention to all things he saw and heard. If he describes a tiny leaflet, he mirrors before the mind all its delicate peculiarities; the reader sees its finely-notched edges more nicely scalloped than the teeth of the fine tenon-saw; all its little veins and thread-like fibers magnify in his eye—he can even see its glistening, verdant hues. *Look* at all things proper to be seen, and *listen* to that which ought to be heard. Stamp them on memory's page.

All divines have not the same gifts or talents, either in kind or degree. Cultivate your *natural gifts*, whatever they may be. If discriminating logical powers, cultivate them to their highest possible attainments. Unveil the sophisms of error by the light of logical truth. If it is the pathetic, dive into the secret founts of pity and love; touch humanity's heart, and bedew your ministry with the baptism of holy tears, as did the weeping Jeremiah.

Be not ashamed of tears. "Jesus wept." This is a vale of tears. When truth calls up tears, it will bid your brother weep. When man loses his heart, he is abnormal—ceases to be man. If yours is the gift of poesy, indulge it, refine it, inform it, revel in all the true, the beautiful, and the good, in nature, art, and the Bible; paint it all in pathetic verse, but let the divine glow in the face of facts and fancies as beams of light on a golden world. Imagination has much to do in poetry and romance, and needs much curbing and refining. Romance is not poetry—it is wild. It is a reckless launch into the unreal, the strange, the marvelous. A romantic mind, of all others, in the sacred desk, needs the tightest rein. But let your heart-powers and mental machinery be driven by the romance of divinely-given love. The love of Christ *constraineth* us, said Paul, in his romantic life. Love-pointed beams warm and melt the heart. One dangerous error of this utilizing and fastidious age is the strong effort being made to unheart humanity, and lock up the tears of the pulpit—prepared iron-like castings in which to mold a heartless, stoical manhood. Man without a heart is a body soulless, a house without an inhabitant; a locomotive, but no steam to drive its wheels. Unfallen man possessed a heart. A God of love made him like unto himself. He planted in the corner of the eye the little lachrymal gland to secrete a tear of pity for the ruin of earth. Our Lord Jesus Christ is the Second, the unfallen Adam, the highest model of humanity that earth can ever have, because he is the Son of God. He is the pattern after which we must fashion our manhood. He had a divine heart of loving pity for an apostate race. Love incarnated him in a humble, frail mortal body. His entire life was one grand act of benevolent sympathy for human woe. He had tears to shed over the griefs of the sorrowful, and wept over the coming doom of devoted Jerusalem. The proud city of David, the beautiful home of Solomon, the city of the great king, with its magnificent temple, the admiration of angels and the wonder of the world, he dedicated its prospective ruin with the baptism of tears. Sin ironized man's original heart. His first-born son was a fratricidal murderer. God gave us a new seed, with a heart like unto himself, to begin a new race, called "the children of God," inheriting from Christ, by faith, his spirit, or heart of love. If any man have not the Spirit of Christ, he is none of his. Jesus put a new leaven of love in our earthen vessels—a feeling of loving-kindness to our race. All the institutions of charity and benevolence in the Church of to-day, and in the world at large, are the fruits of that regenerating germ Jesus planted in the world's great heart. But modern ritualism in the Church, and cold infidel philosophy in the world, strive to dry the fountain of tears and congeal man's pitying heart. A proud intellectual form of man is ashamed of the weakness of tears. Sorrow's tear seeks the closet, or the gloomy retreat, because there is a tacit admission of guilt in the causes of grief. Joy loves the light, for it is innocent; guilt draws the veil over its tearful eye. Jesus had no sense of guilt. His tears were pearly and unveiled as the morning dew-drop quivering to its fall on the bosom of the rose. The pulpit must have the heart of Jesus; its tears must be those of unfeigned innocence and pitying love. Be not ashamed, young preacher, of such tears; they are the visible baptism of an inward anointing. A tearless, heartless ministry is a fruitless one. A powerful, a successful ministry has its magazine forces stored in the heart. Tarry at Jerusalem, said Jesus, till endued with power from above—that was heart-power. Love drives your chariot wheels; love carries with it a bountiful supply of tears, and baptizes earth's graves and altars of sorrow with its pathetic dews. It is the weeping evangelist who is to return in the light of victorious joy, bringing his harvest sheaves with him. The learned, the great Apostle Paul ceased not to warn night and day with tears. If, dear neophyte brother, you have not a good supply of tears on hand, you had better not set out on your ministerial pilgrimage through earth's "vale of tears" without replenishing your stock, or you may need them, as the oilless five virgins, when no substitute can be had. If you commune with the dead in the perusal of books, you shall have many a call for unbidden tears over the recorded ruins of the ages gone—the perished glories of proud cities, the tragic downfall of pompous empires, the decay and dust of the noble erections of art, the demolition of the works of genius, and the blood-stained record of human woes. The voice of history is but the resounding wail of broken hearts. If you mingle with the living, in each town, city, hamlet, or rural home, in the events of each day, you shall have demands for tears. While you mingle with the gay and cheerful in the halls of merry delights, just over the street the noise of sorrow invites you there to weep. You may stand before angel woman in bridal-robes at Hymen's altar at eventide, and tell her she is one with him she adores, while all Nature's silent breathing whispers of peace and love; but, alas, in the morn you may read "dust to dust," and sprinkle tears on a newly-dug grave! Disappointments, misfortunes, bereavements, and sorrows, of your comrades in life, lay a large embargo on your tears; and the sins of men, together with the follies of the Church, require all you can unfeignedly spare in the pulpit. Tears are all-powerful. Who can resist the poetry, the magic charm of a tear? The world's iron heart can be melted only by the warm droppings of love's pitying tears. Suffering, love's wonderful charm, is to win guilty man back to God. The most powerful magnet in the universe to intellectual and moral natures is suffering love—love giving its life to save. A moral nature which cannot be attracted by its electric might is lost; it is as a planet which has passed beyond the sphere of the controlling forces of universal order. Suffering, dying love, all mingled in blood and tears, is your theme; with it you are to subdue sin and win your race to Him who has called you to tell of His dying love. Do not strive to illumine your intellect and congeal your heart, but let the radiant beams of divine truth glow in the mind, and pass down into the inner heart, till its stimulating fires shall enkindle all the soul's latent affections for the subjects of your divine message. While love fills and rules the preacher's heart he is safe. No hardships, no toils, too great a task for love. He who lives in dying love's radiant glow beneath the cross, must ever love the divinely-coroneted Sufferer hanging there. Let the poetic sentiment of the following stanzas ever dwell in the heart of the pulpit:

> In evil long I took delight,
>   Unawed by shame or fear;
> Till a new object struck my sight,
>   And stopped my wild career.
>
> I saw one hanging on a tree,
>   In agonies and blood,
> Who fixed his languid eyes on me,
>   As near his cross I stood.
>
> Sure, never to my latest breath
>   Can I forget that look;
> It seemed to charge me with his death,
>   Though not a word he spoke.
>
> My conscience felt, and owned the guilt,
>   And plunged me in despair;
> I saw my sins his blood had spilt,
>   And helped to nail him there.
>
> A second look he gave, which said,
>   "I freely all forgive;
> This blood is for thy ransom paid;
>   I die that thou may'st live."

Bring the listening thousands unto the Sufferer's cross, tell of his anguish-riven love till each one shall see him heave, and hear him groan, and feel his gushing blood. Fear not the result. The philosophy of suffering is in the agonies of that cross. A divine magic, as a celestial coronal, crowns the Sufferer's drooping head, and that occult power on which the universe leans is pledged to its ultimate triumph in the earth. Plant the standard cross on which your Saviour bleeds deep in the heart of your age. The jubilant shout of victory shall ring along the firmament of coming ages. You enter the battle after its severest struggles have passed away; you take hold on the cross after it has been erected far into the enemy's domain. The twilight of universal triumph is now gilding the victor's morn. Christianity has now passed its equinoctial zone— it is beyond the limits of a possible retrograde. Her collected arsenals of aggressive forces for eighteen centuries are now engaging the scattered ranks of the retreating enemy at every point of the populated continents and islands dotting the seas of the globe. The voices of the love-moved missionaries are now in hearing of each other in their voyage round the earth. The false religions—Mohammedanism and paganism—cease to be aggressive; they retire from the effulgent glories beaming out from the cross. Nations under the gloom of the ages are coming unto the light of its glory. The beautiful celestial cross has ascended to the mast-head of the world's commerce; it glides in mild triumphs on the waters of all seas, and visits and smiles on all shores where man has built his home. Surely the day cometh. The genius of the Decalogue and the Sermon on the Mount, like a silver cord, run through the Constitutions of States and the Governments of Kingdoms. Their hallowing spirit percolates the world's literature, and is diffusing its holy leaven into the press, the school-room, and the marts of trade; and in the home-circle it is beginning to consecrate the cradle and childhood unto Jesus. Songs from ruby infant lips begin to echo along the vaulted ceilings of his great temples in minareted cities and in shaded rural realms. In spring-time, in forest groves and new-clad, leafy dells, beside the placid bay, or the margin of the sparkling, flowing river, where modest flowers bloom, and merry birds in dewy morn trill their happy love-songs in the tender, verdant leaflet's shade, the Sabbath-school *cortege* of joyous little ones mingle their notes of praise to Him who said, Let them come unto me. I see their ensigns waving, and their banners unfurled. On one side is printed, "Unto the name of Jesus every knee shall bow;" and on the other is capitaled,

<blockquote>
And infant voices shall proclaim
Their early blessings on his name.
</blockquote>

It is a living army of infant millions coming up as fresh recruits from all islands swelling up on the ocean's bosom, from all regions and climes, from hill and dale, of the gospel-redeemed earth. O ye young men of God, lead surely on to certain victory this allied army of your conquering Jesus, till a regenerated earth shall reflect back the image of the celestial, as the calm blue ocean, veiled in night, mirrors back each glowing star in the concaved firmament, and as when all clouds have poured their showers upon the forest world, and have floated away to other climes, and the golden sunlight beams down on the dripping trees sparkling in praise!

THE END.

www.ingramcontent.com/pod-product-compliance
Lightning Source LLC
Chambersburg PA
CBHW022059300426
44117CB00007B/522